I0812731

IMAGES
*of America*

# POY SIPPI AND EASTERN WAUSHARA COUNTY

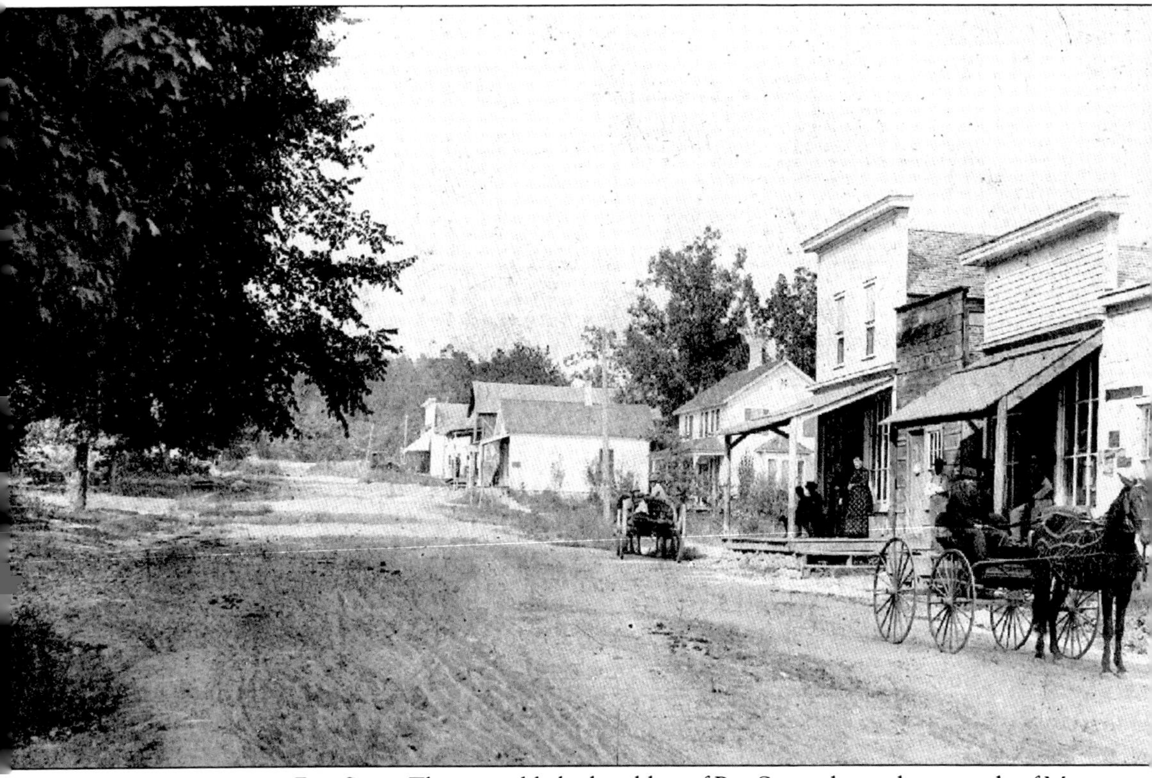

**OLDEST VIEW OF POY SIPPI.** This view, likely the oldest of Poy Sippi, shows the east side of Main Street. The farthest store is Riley P. Colt's general store. In the middle of Main Street, the house set back is at the corner of Liberty and Main Streets. Many of the buildings in the foreground have been replaced—some more than once. The man in the surrey in the foreground is Edwin Bowen, a veteran of the Civil War, serving in the 21st Wisconsin Infantry, Company D. He is buried in the Poy Sippi Cemetery. Judging by Bowen's age, this photograph was taken in the mid-to-late 1880s.

IMAGES
*of America*

# POY SIPPI AND EASTERN WAUSHARA COUNTY

Kim J. Heltemes

ARCADIA
PUBLISHING

ISBN 978-0-7385-4011-5

Published by Arcadia Publishing
Charleston, South Carolina

Printed in the United States of America

Library of Congress Catalog Card Number: 2005933808

For all general information contact Arcadia Publishing at:
Telephone 843-853-2070
Fax 843-853-0044
E-mail sales@arcadiapublishing.com
For customer service and orders:
Toll-Free 1-888-313-2665

Visit us on the internet at www.arcadiapublishing.com

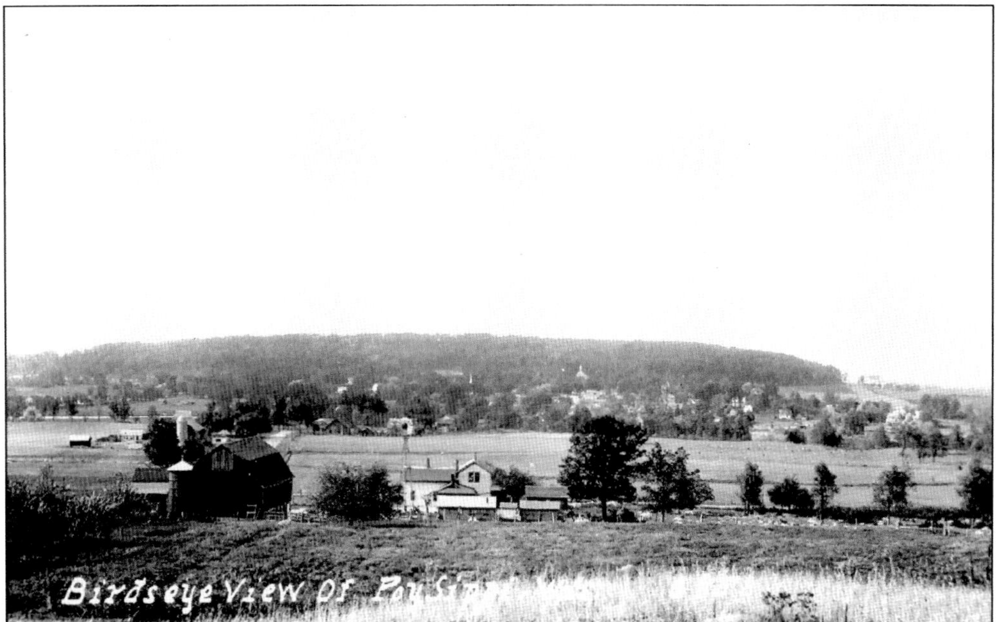


**BIRD'S-EYE VIEW FROM HILL.** Poy Sippi lies between two hills. This view was taken from the southern hill looking north. The German Lutheran Church can be seen on the hill in the background. It is surrounded by a farming community, as evidenced by the farm in the foreground.

# Contents

# ACKNOWLEDGMENTS

This work is dedicated to Marilyn Boyson Paulson, who has supported my efforts with much enthusiasm. This project could not have been completed without the use of her photograph collections of the Boyson and Blaisdell families. Since most of the images came from this group, included here are many of Marilyn's family photographs that also show life in those times. Her knowledge of the area also helped fill in the gaps that often appear when researching the past. Marilyn's dedication to the preservation of the area's history is something that should be commended.

In doing a book like this, one meets many people. I was fortunate in my travels to meet Jerry Much, who has become a new friend with similar interests. He offered his collection of postcards for this endeavor. Most of the Brushville photographs were provided by Lloyd and Genevieve Everson. Their family interest in Brushville goes back almost 60 years. Also, Jackie Hofflander deserves thanks. As chairperson for the history presentation at Poy Sippi's 150th celebration, Jackie was willing to share what was collected from the event. The contributions of Scott Cross of the Oshkosh Public Museum, Dave Carpenter, Joanne Brinkman, and Dale Hempel were important to the completion of the book. It is my hope that everyone involved is happy with his or her contribution to this work.

# INTRODUCTION

While the study of Wisconsin in the Civil War is what I do in my spare time, a person becomes involved with the history of the area as it is being researched. If a researcher digs into the history of the soldiers that came back from the war, he uncovers the postwar history as well. Many of these soldiers became instrumental in the development of small towns and villages. Soon, the histories of soldiers and of towns blend together for a history of early America. This past needs to be preserved along with the prewar occurrences.

During my Civil War research, the Poy Sippi Cemetery became a focus point. New to the area, having moved here six years prior, I still had much history to uncover. While conducting this research, I met Joanne Brinkman. Finding out that we both wanted to make the most of the research, she invited me to a planning meeting for the sesquicentennial of Poy Sippi in 2003. That started a relationship with the citizens of Poy Sippi, who voiced a desire for a book chronicling the history of Poy Sippi.

Most people do not know how or why the area they live in was settled. The people responsible for the early settlement of Wisconsin used the waterways as a means of transportation. The only roads were Native American horse trails. Green Bay settlers soon expanded south toward the Fox River Valley. Here, they ran into another system of water—and another roadway to expansion. Tustin was one area that was along the Lake Poygan shoreline, while Berlin was settled to the south along the Fox River. In between these two settlements, towns like Auroraville and Poy Sippi sprang up. If not for the foresight of these pioneers, towns and villages across the upper Midwest would never have been realized. The settlers looked for areas that could supply waterpower to run the mills. Without the mills, they could never have advanced past the log houses that were common before their time. And yes, log cabins were still being built for others by men like John McCue.

With all the marshes in central Wisconsin, travel was difficult as the wetlands were hard to cross in autumn. In the fall of 1849, Dr. James S. Ewing and a Mr. Eckley left Waukau, Wisconsin, to explore the Native American land north of Berlin. They crossed the Fox River at Strong's Landing (Berlin) and traveled northwest until they ran across a log cabin and sawmill at the location of present-day Wautoma. They went east when they had to cross the Willow Creek. According to Mrs. Ewing, the two "continued the search with much difficulty, being obliged to wade the marshes and ford the stream, they concluded to return" to Waukau. The next day, "they shouldered their guns and packs." When they needed to recross the Willow, they discovered it had swollen "to quite a stream." A Native American girl helped canoe them to the other side.

In early 1850, Ewing recruited George Hawley to return to the area north of his expedition of the previous fall. Hawley volunteered, and soon the rest decided to follow. They were Martin Becker and surveyor Vernon Evans.

Camping along the Pine River, the men wrote "claimed" on a partial shanty. They then returned home to get some lumber to build several such structures, including a 12- by 14-foot shanty that slept 20 people. The men stayed three weeks before bringing their families. In order to file a claim to deed the property, the men had to go to Menasha, Wisconsin, some 40 miles away. Some of the early settlers walked there. This was the start of Poy Sippi, with Dr. Ewing filing the first land claim.

George Hawley is often called the father of the town. He had the land plotted in 1856, and development began. Without a sawmill, residents had to travel to Stevens Point, some 40 miles to the north, to get enough lumber. Hawley then built a sawmill on the Pine River and began constructing homes. Poy Sippi was materializing.

When first asked of Menominee Indian Chief John what his tribe called the town, he replied, "Poy Sip," which meant Poygan from the lake's name and river from the Pine River's name. It was modified to Poy Sippi, and the name stuck.

Brushville and Tustin are tied together in some ways. Tustin did not have a cemetery but Brushville did. Some went to the churches in Poy Sippi. Several families were instrumental in helping the advancement of both towns. Brushville was started in 1853 with the sale of land to Herman Brush. His family settled on a stagecoach route and in an area where water was available for the mills. It is not clear if Brushville was named after Herman or Eliphalet. Herman sold his property in May 1864, but Eliphalet remained in Brushville until his death.

Tustin, an area first bought by Charles Freer, was called Fountain City because of a well dug by Freer. The well still exists today in the middle of the town. In 1867, Thomas Tustin bought the land. The town was then named Tustin in 1868 when it became a village. Since Tustin was on a major waterway, steamboats used that area as a delivery and pickup station.

These villages stayed relatively small, as there was too much area to settle outside of the villages. Expansion began, but with it came the dependency on lumber mills and gristmills. Farming was the most common method of income. Since ground grain sold for a higher price, the gristmills took care of the process.

Auroraville is another example of a town settled near a waterway. Eli Daniels bought the area now known as Auroraville in 1852. He, too, saw the need for a gristmill and sawmill as the land was settled. With many towns in the area springing up, there was an increased need for lumber. Soon, people like Nathaniel Cate, Moses Bowen, Chester Clark, and Joseph Mathews bought land. This spurred on the arrival of many more families, who, after the Civil War, had become the backbone of the community. Most settlers stayed in the region until their death. They had found a place to call home.

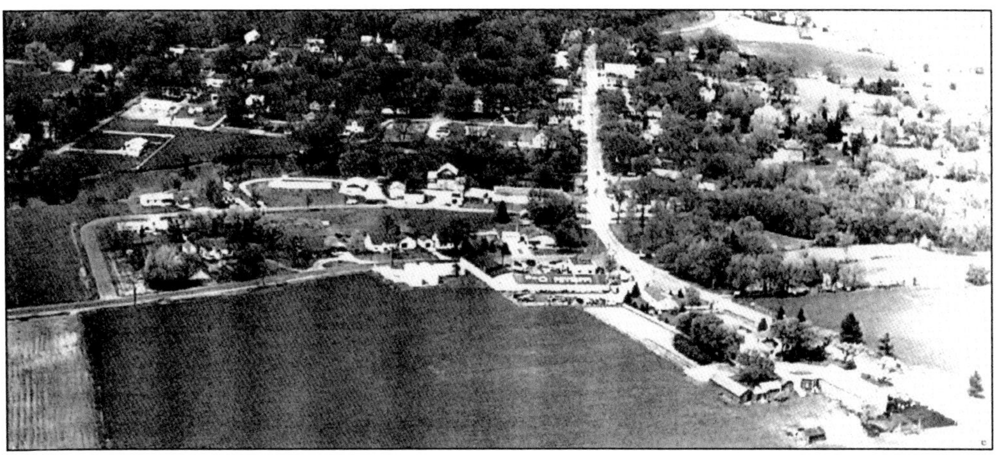

**BIRD'S-EYE VIEW.** Taken later than the image on page 4, this aerial photograph reveals more of Poy Sippi's development.

# *One*

# Poy Sippi in the Early Days

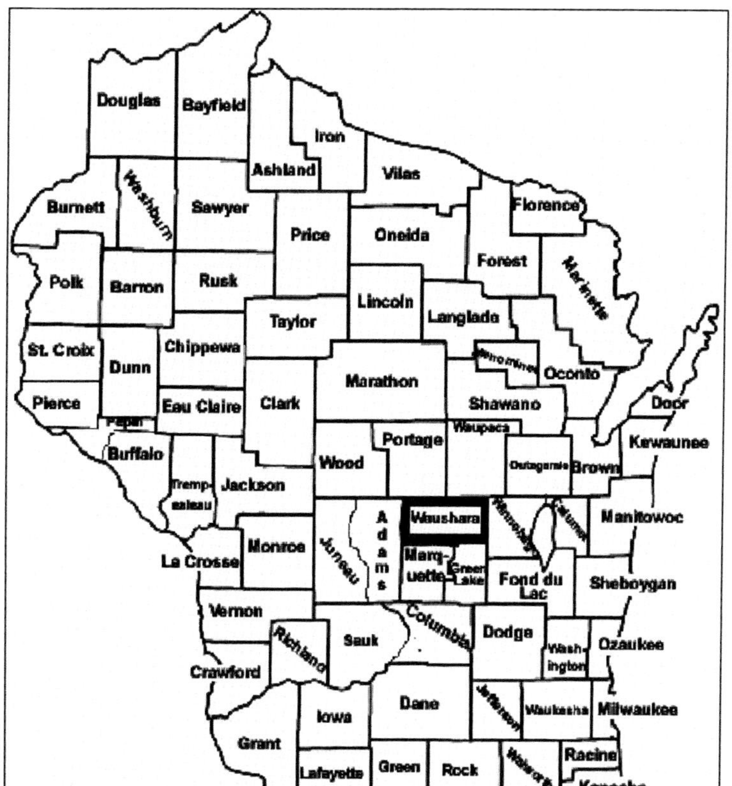


**State of Wisconsin.** Waushara County, highlighted here, is located in south-central Wisconsin. The towns of Poy Sippi, Tustin, Brushville, and Auroraville are in the eastern portion of the county.

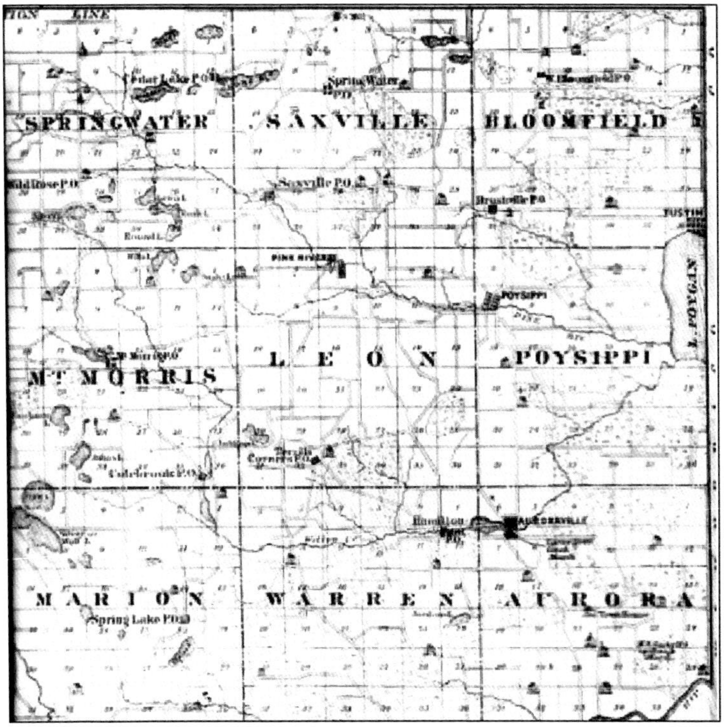


**EASTERN WAUSHARA COUNTY.** On this 1878 map, the towns are seen in the townships of Tustin, Bloomfield, Poy Sippi, and Aurora.

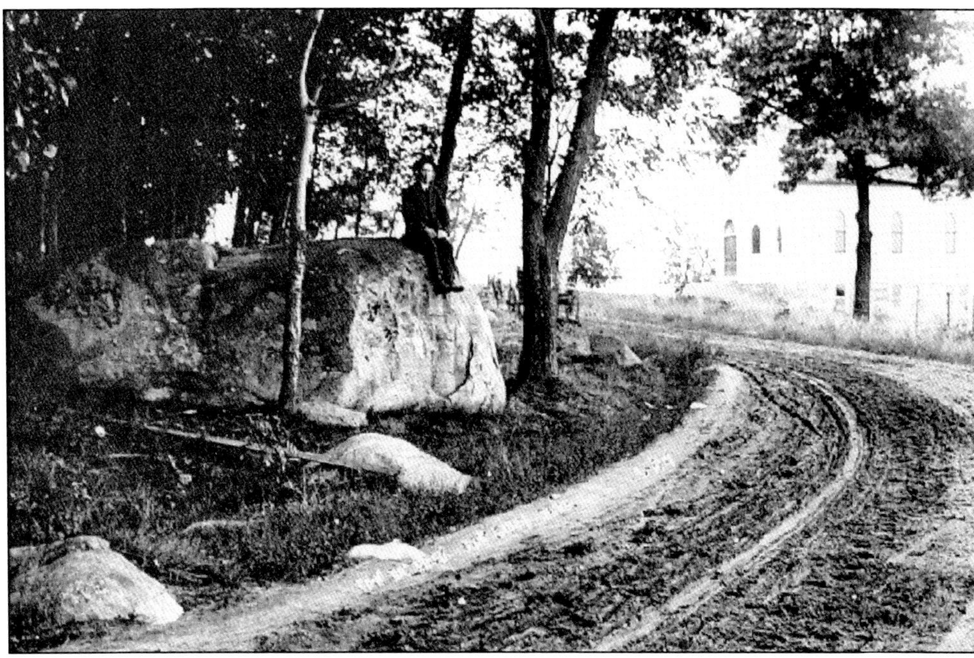

**THE BIG ROCK.** A boy sits on the big rock on the north side of town along Highway 49. This view shows the rock, called Rosie's Anchor, on the left side of the road. Used for picnics, the rock was later located on the right side when the road was reworked. The German Lutheran Church fills out the background. The church was later replaced.

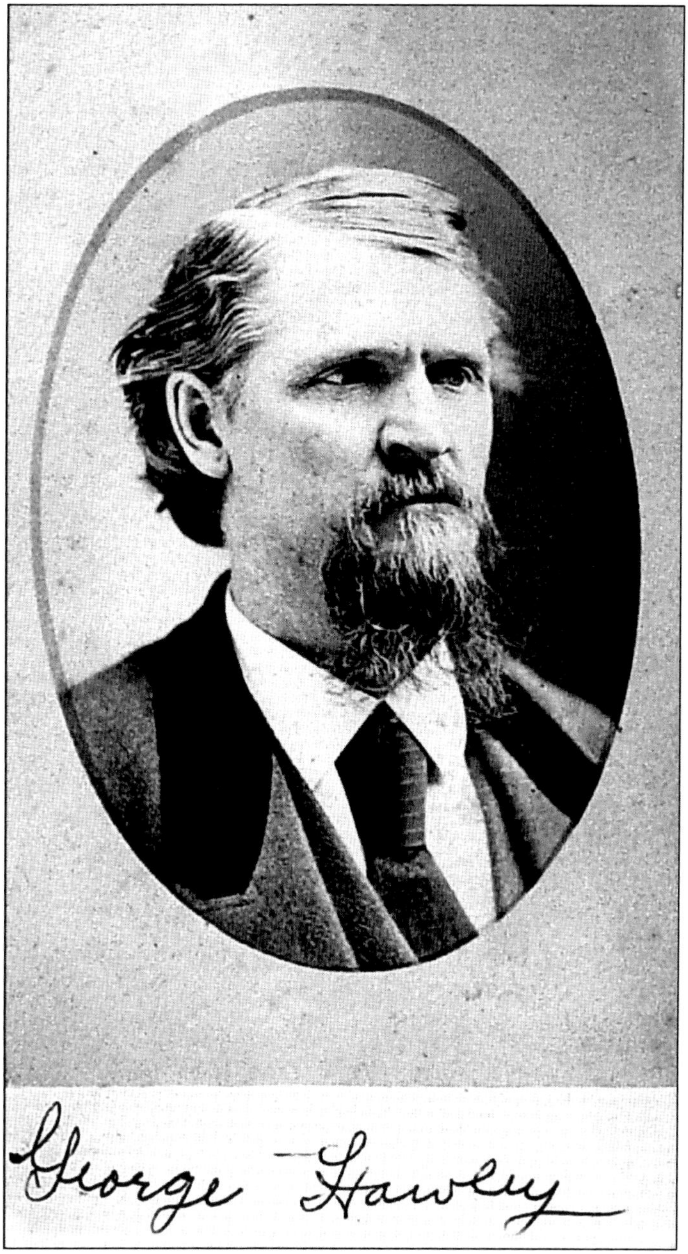


**George Hawley.** Considered the founder of Poy Sippi, Hawley and three others—Dr. James S. Ewing, Martin Becker, and Vernon Evans—traveled through Wautoma before settling down, in 1849, in the area of the future town. Becker became the first hotel owner in Poy Sippi, and Evans worked as a surveyor. It is not known whether Evans did the original survey of the town when it was plotted. Hawley is credited with the plotting of the town in 1856. In 1851, he became the first postmaster. Later, after establishing the first water-powered mill, Hawley made lumber wagons and sleighs. The first water-powered mill that Hawley built was the sawmill on the north side of the Pine River in 1852. Hawley later had a feed mill and gristmill made in 1870 on the south side of the river. The work was done with pegged mortise and tenon joints, a trade practiced by Hawley.

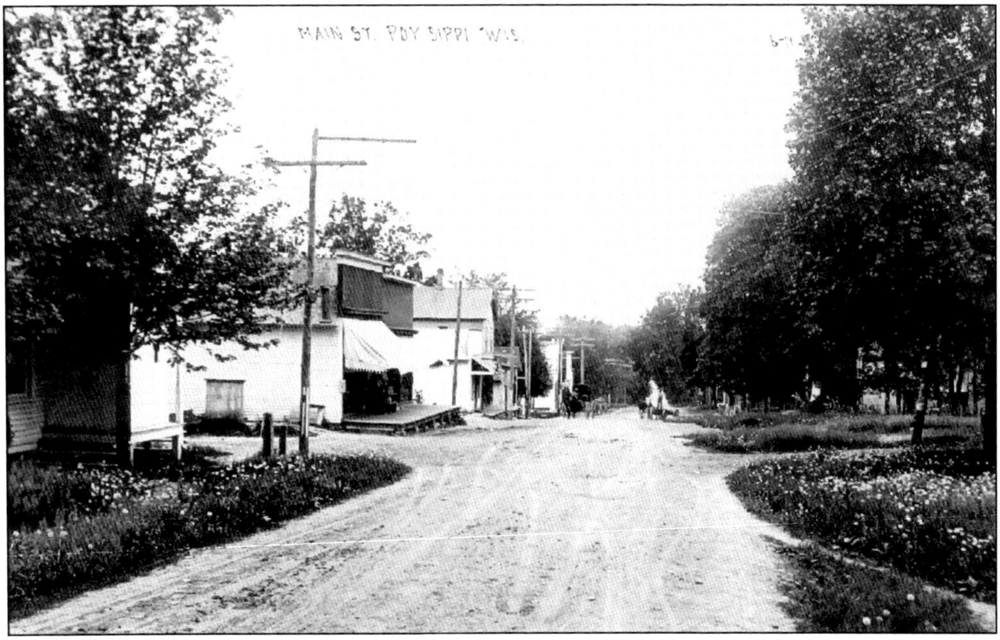


**SURREY TRAVEL ON DIRT ROADS.** When approached from the north on Main Street, Poy Sippi looked like this. Dr. Moffatt's office is the first building on the left and then the Prospect Street intersection and John E. Wendt's store.

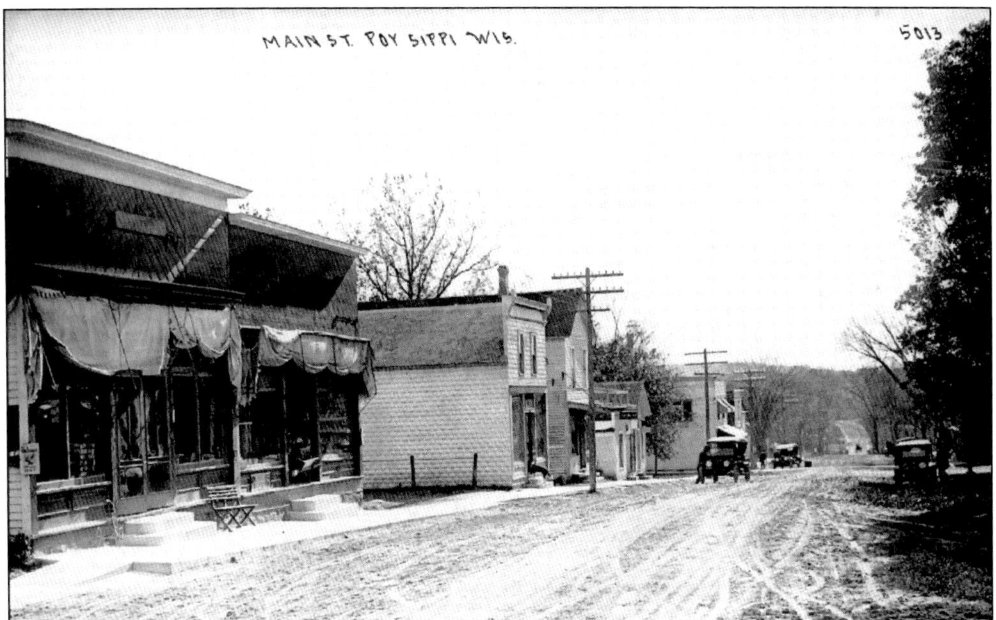


**SPRING IN POY SIPPI.** This spring view of Poy Sippi shows the J. E. Wendt Store, with its canvas awnings folded up, from a closer viewpoint. Notice vehicle travel replacing the surrey.

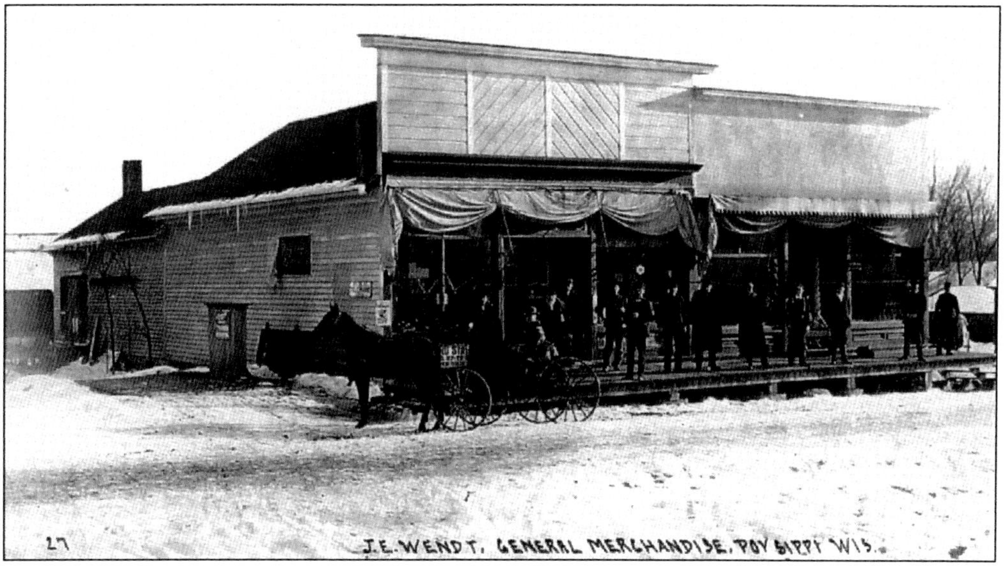


**WENDT STORE.** This building is sometimes labeled as the J. E. Wendt Store and sometimes as the Moffatt and Barr Store. It must have been taken during the switch in ownership. John E. Wendt, Nels Williamson, and Grant Boyson were some of the different owners of this store. It burned down in 1931 while Grant Boyson was proprietor.

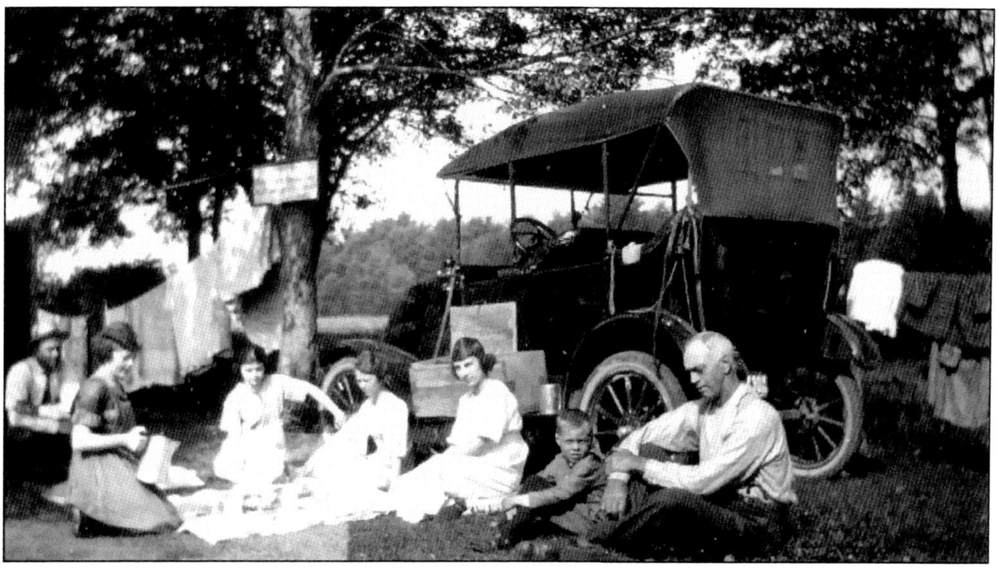

**BARR FAMILY PICNIC.** The J. E. Wendt Store was owned by Moffatt and Barr before being sold to Wendt. Here, Ben Barr picnics with his family. He was killed in a car crash at Highway 10 and County Trunk A in Waupaca.

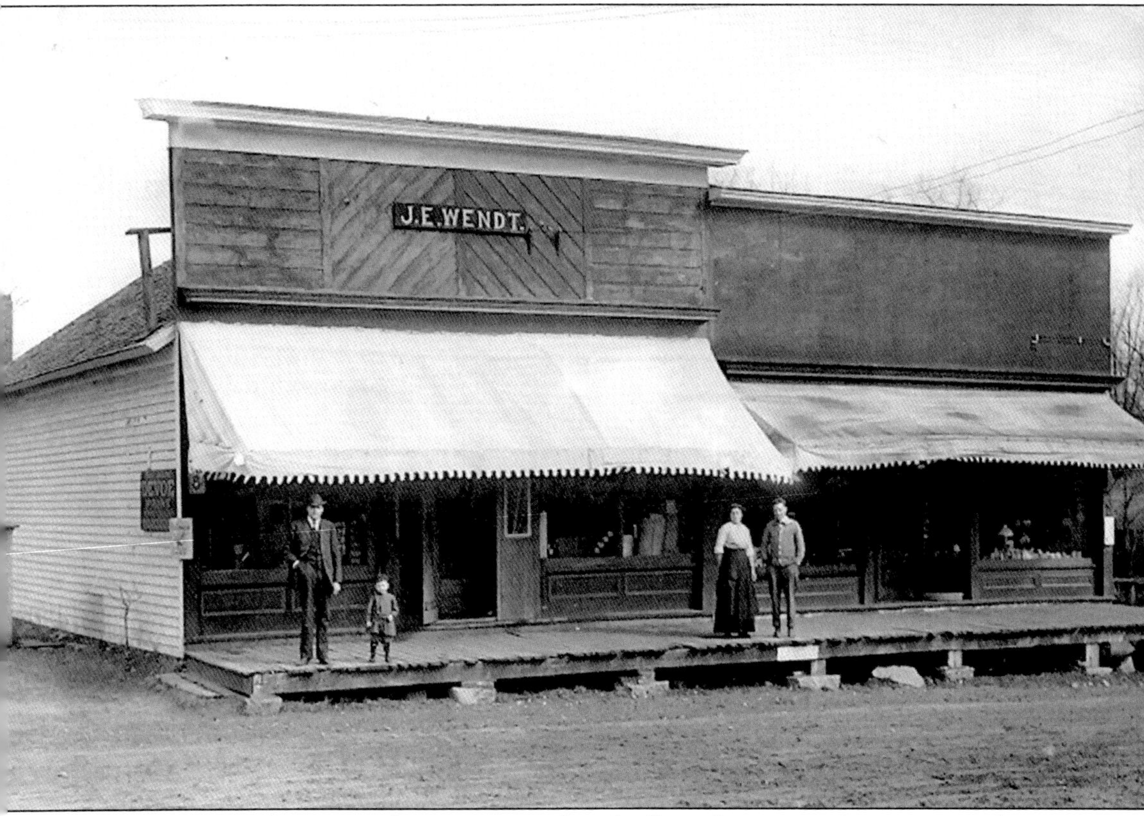


**J. E. Wendt Store.** With its attractive boardwalk and awnings, the store soon became a favorite for postcard images. It was also popular as the place for residents to get supplies.

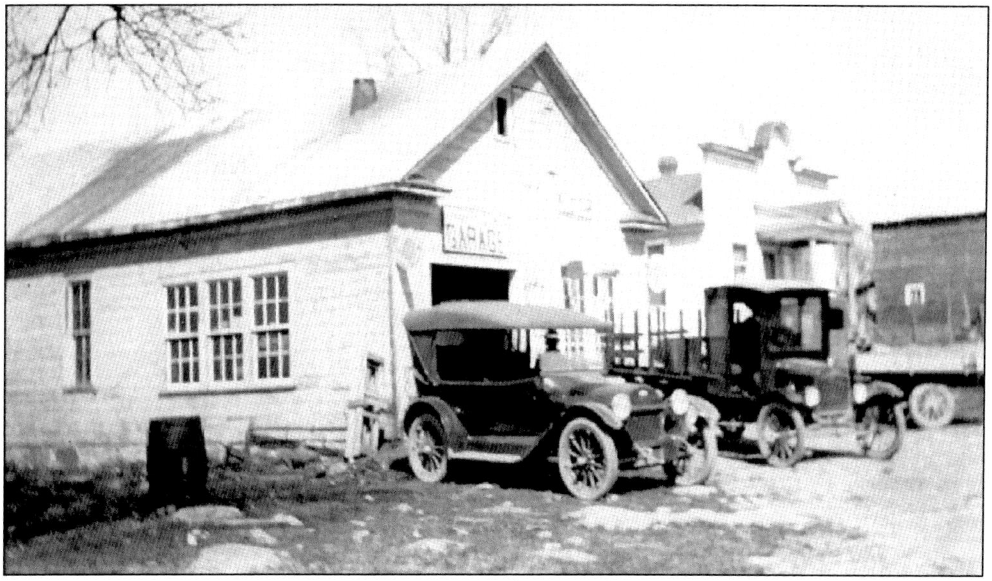

**IRA JOHNSON'S FIRST GARAGE.** Ira's Garage was located along Main Street. Dr. Moffatt's office is shown next door, behind the Model T truck.

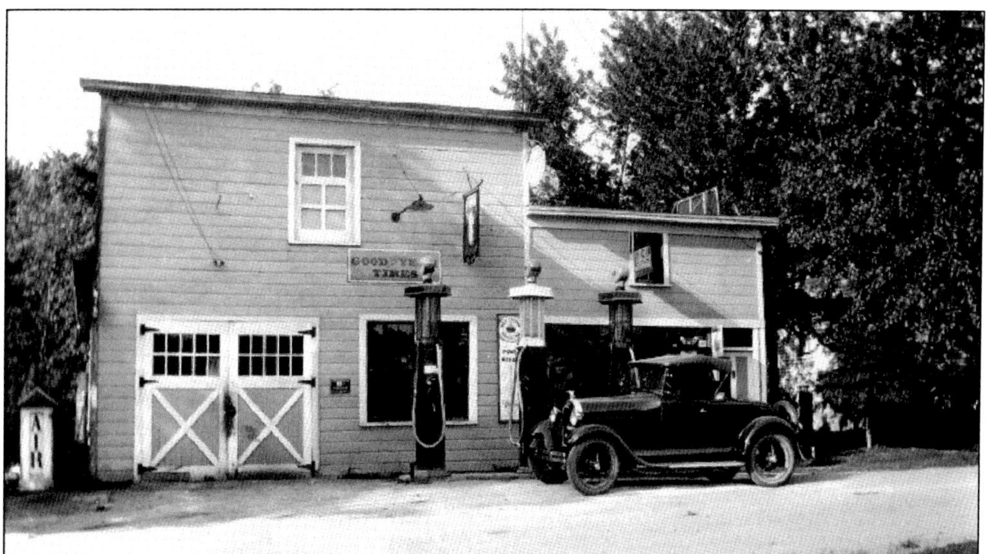


**IRA JOHNSON'S SECOND GARAGE.** Ira Johnson was a fix-it-all man who repaired anything from cars to washing machines. The 1929 Ford really stands out against the front of his second garage. This building, still standing on Prospect Street, has recently been renovated for living quarters.

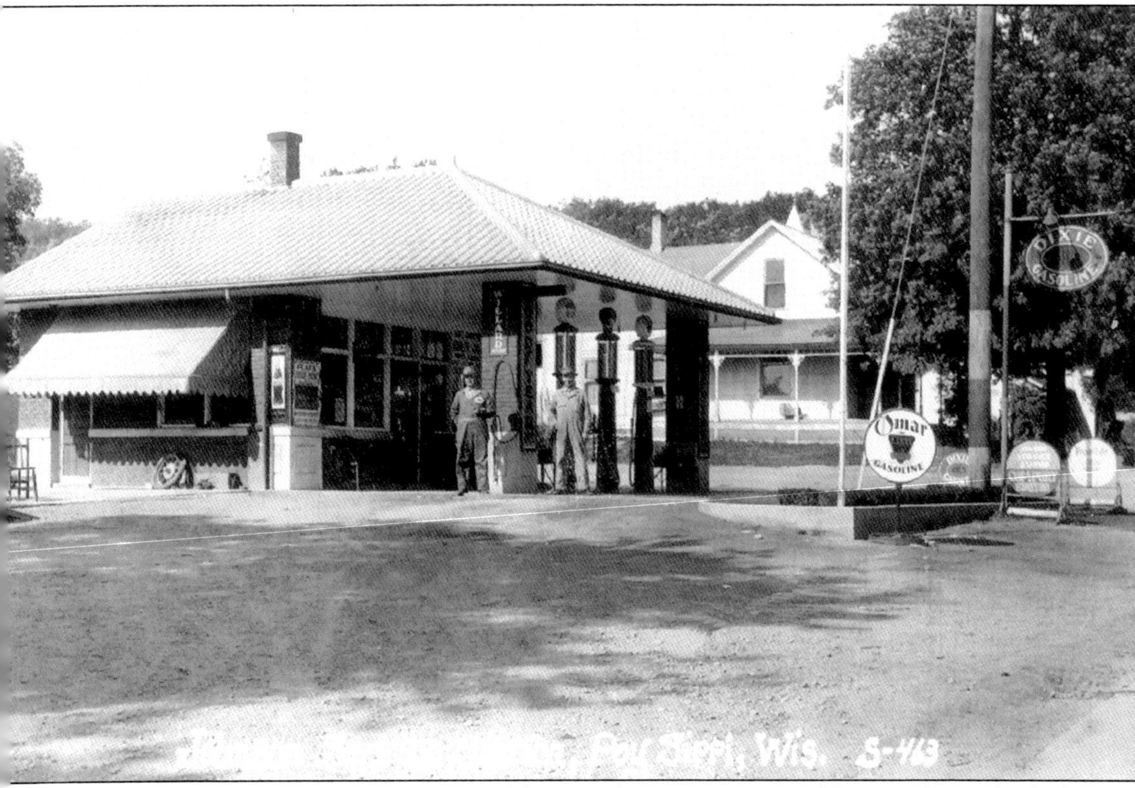


**IRA JOHNSON'S THIRD GARAGE.** Ira Johnson, also a carpenter, and Roy McGregor built this gas station in 1929—the same year the highway was paved. The land was purchased from Jessie Dodd. Initially manned by Ward Kissinger, the station had running water and a restroom and also served as a repair shop.

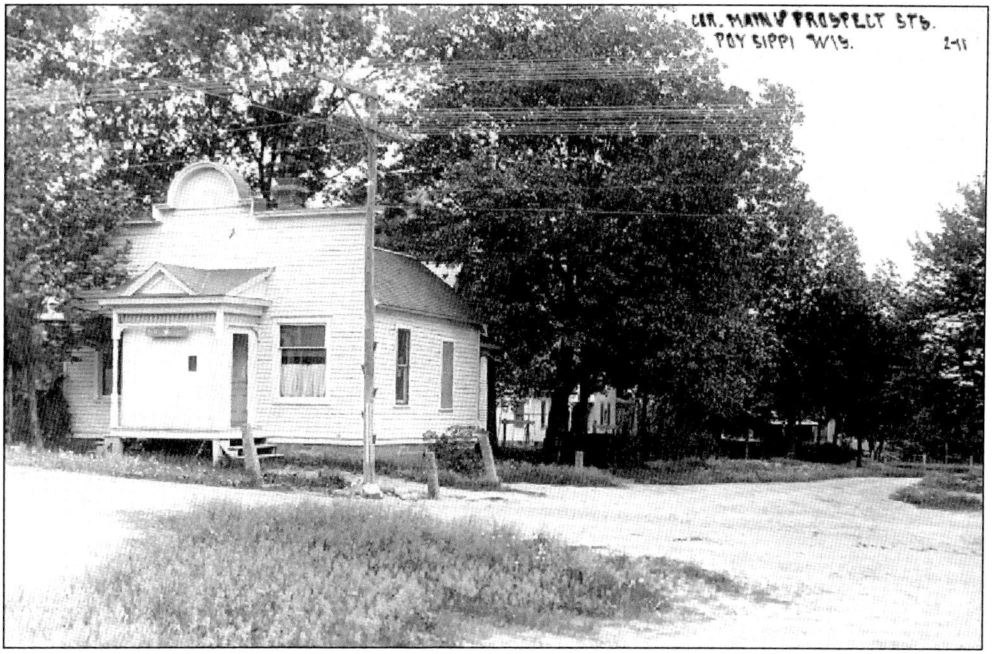


**CORNER OF MAIN AND PROSPECT STREETS.** As with many photographs of Poy Sippi, the granite posts made by Hans Henningsen are clearly visible. This northeastward view of the corner shows Dr. Moffatt's office.

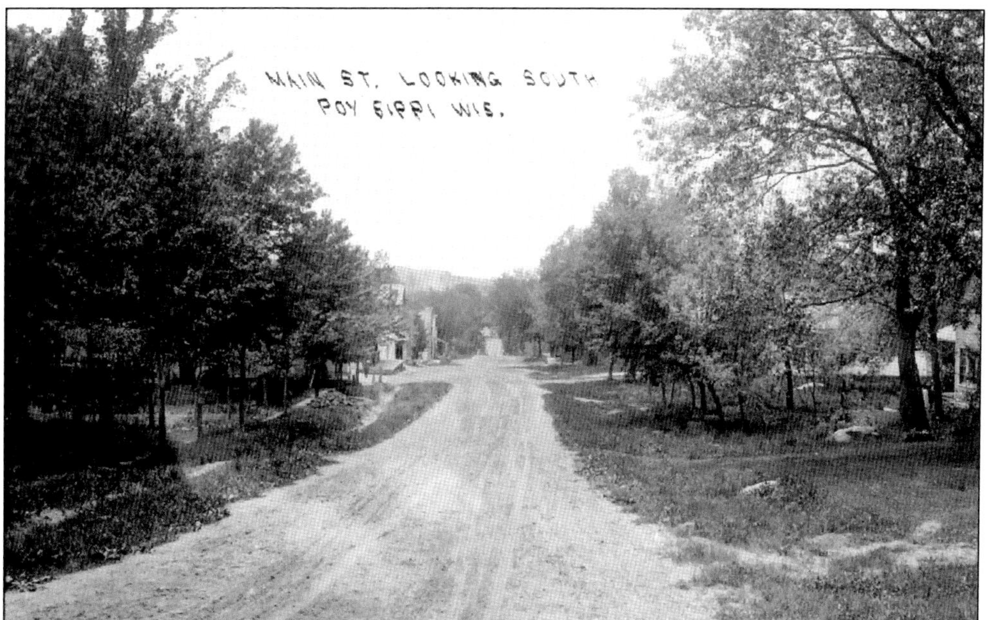


**MAIN STREET, LOOKING SOUTH.** This postcard view from the early 20th century was taken from the northern edge of Poy Sippi, looking south. The boardwalk of the Wendt store, situated on the left side of the street, can be seen in the center of the photograph.

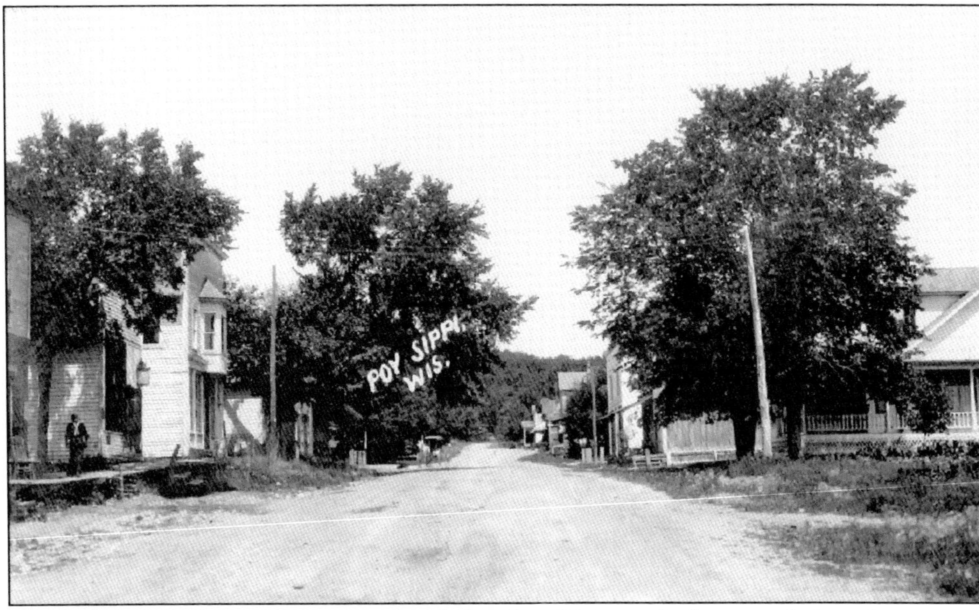


**Poy Sippi, Wisconsin.** The town is revealed in this 1914 view, looking north from Commercial and Main Streets. Horse-and-buggy transportation is demonstrated in the middle of the photograph, while a man strolls on the boardwalk by the drugstore.

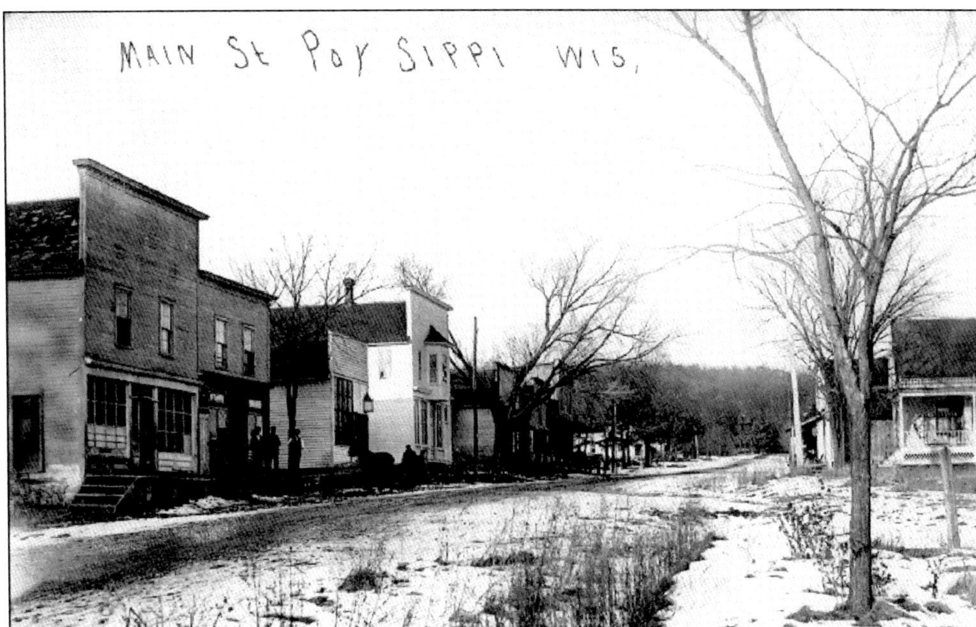


**Main Street with Snow.** This postcard of Poy Sippi in the early spring shows no change in Main Streets as the men stand on the boardwalk.

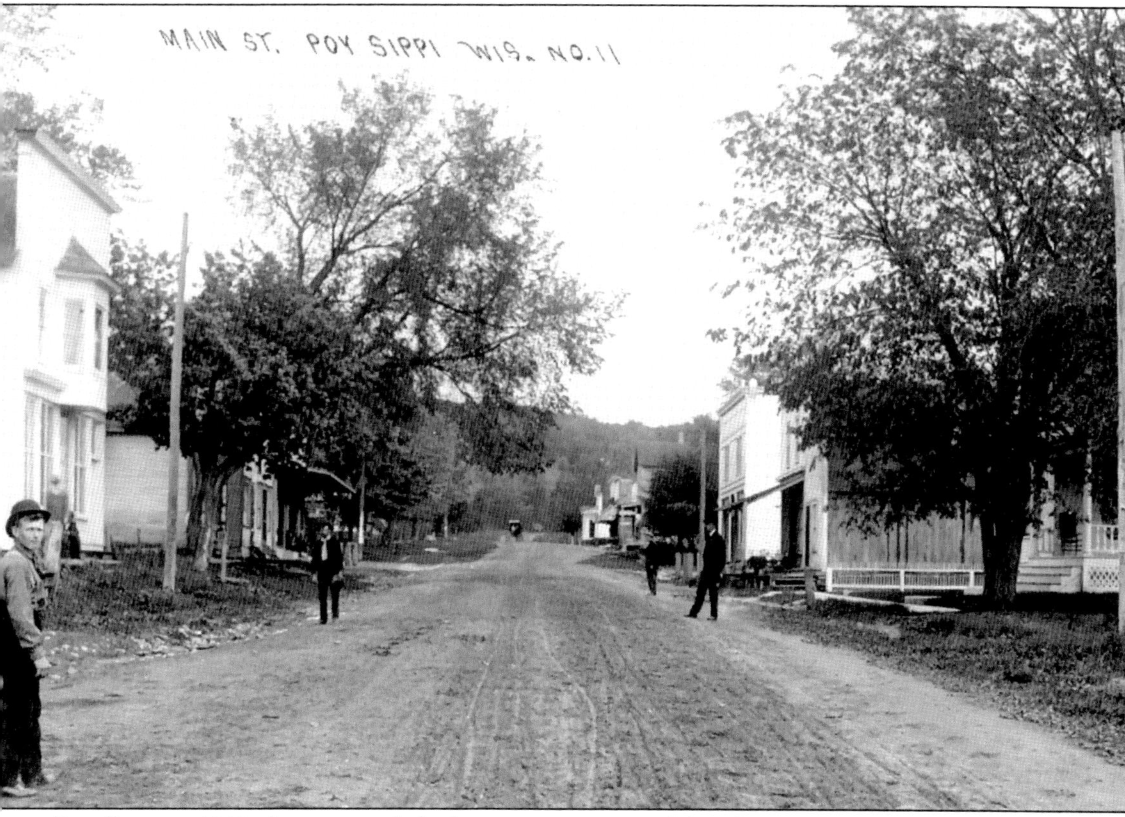


**POY SIPPI, C. 1910.** A man in a derby hat attempts to cross Main Street.

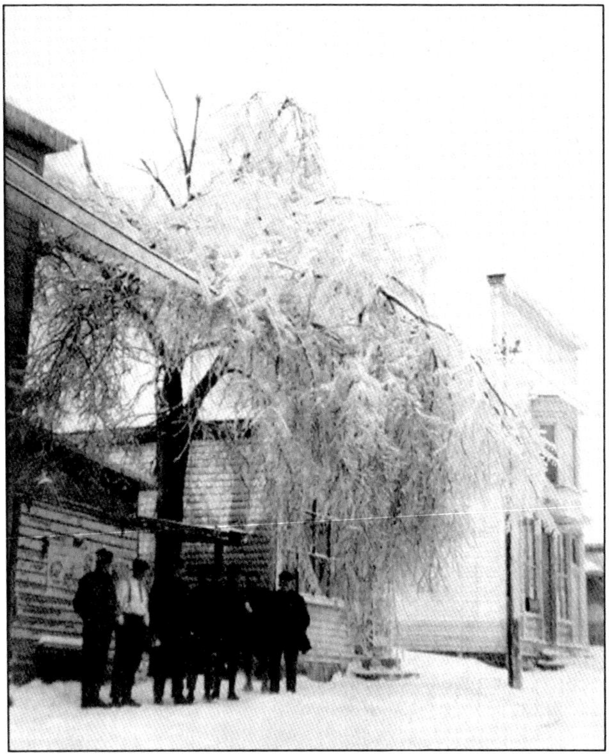

**ICE STORM OF 1922.** Many photographs were taken to document the ice storm that hit central Wisconsin during the winter of 1922. The drugstore in the right background was once a bank. The center building, behind the tree, was also once a drugstore.

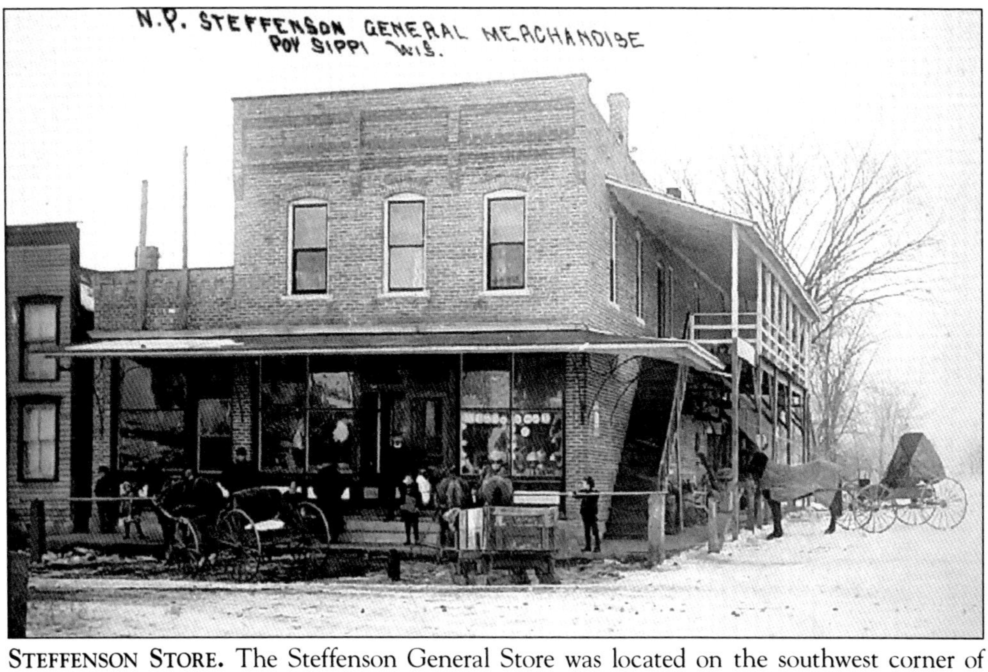


**STEFFENSON STORE.** The Steffenson General Store was located on the southwest corner of Liberty and Main Streets. Besides being a general store, the building also included upstairs apartments. In later years, a fire broke out, destroying the upstairs area. The lower area was saved. Afterward, the second floor was removed, and the building remains a single-story today. It now houses a grocery and meat delicatessen.

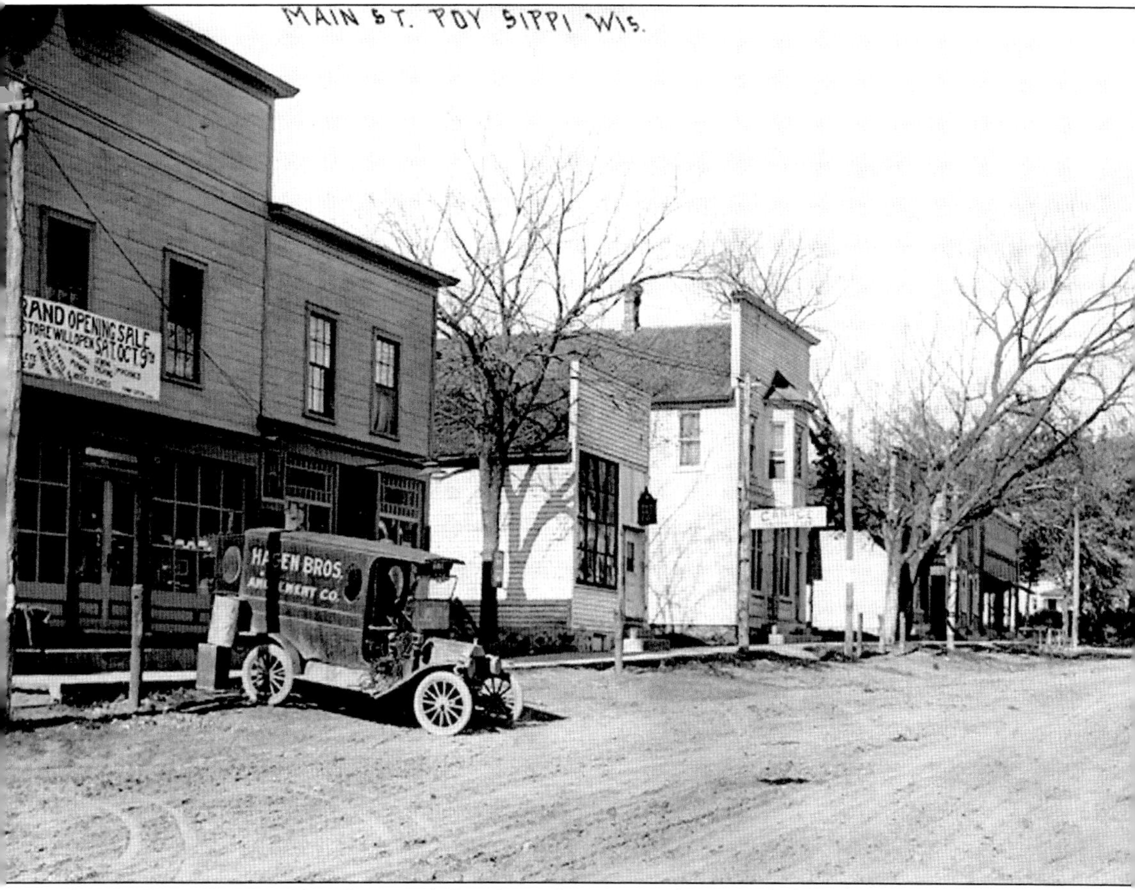


**Hagen Brothers in Poy Sippi.** Likely taken about 1915, this grand photograph reveals Main Street in Poy Sippi, along with the Hagen Brothers Amusement delivery truck on the northwest corner of Commercial and Main Streets. A couple of shops farther along is a sign for the Wilson Garage, located behind the stores.

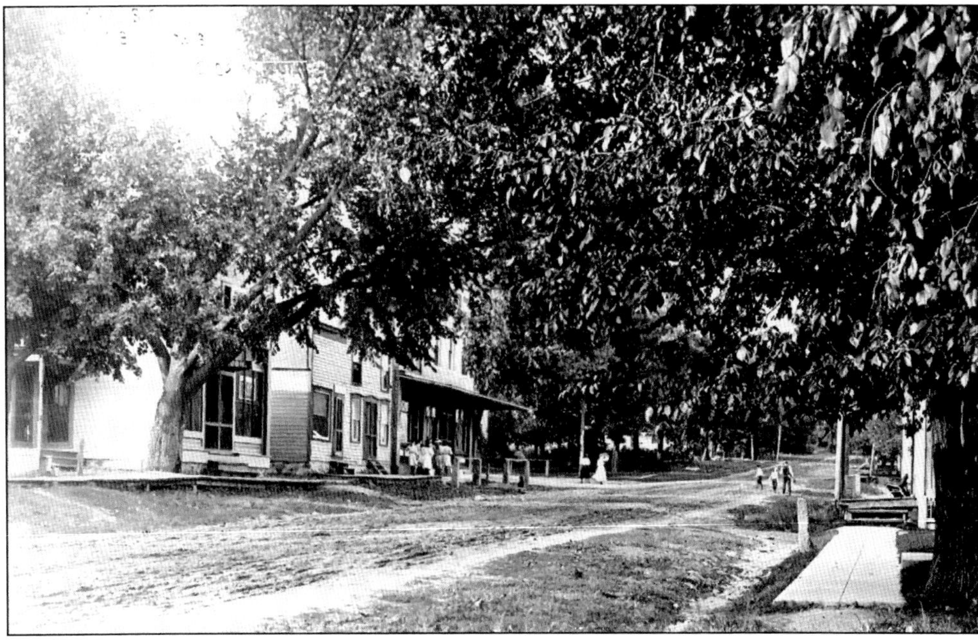

**A QUIET SUMMER DAY.** A little farther north than the previous postcard, girls stroll on the boardwalk on a nice summer day.

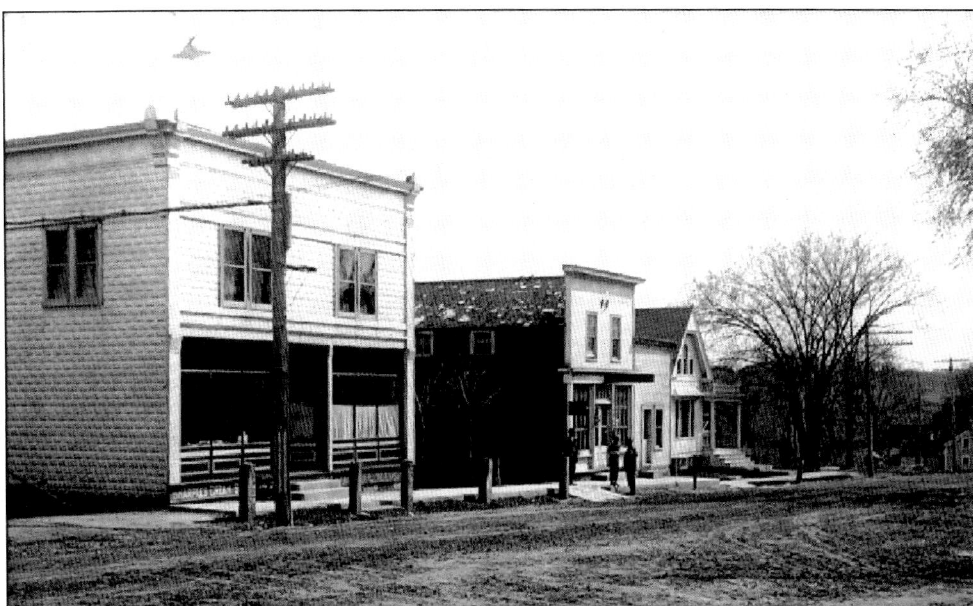


**SOUTHEAST CORNER OF LIBERTY AND MAIN STREETS.** The building on the far left is the second placed on that site. Divided in two, the structure was most noted as a hardware store, on the left, and the Grand Army of the Republic (GAR) Hall, on the right.

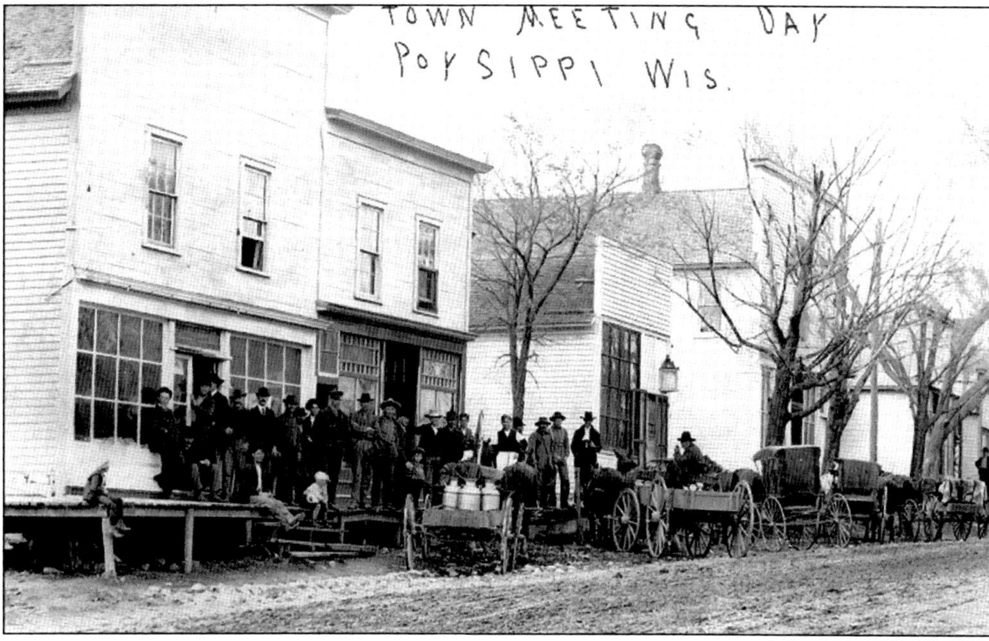


**TOWN HALL MEETING DAY.** Men of the town gather for a meeting in 1908. The streets are lined with buggies and wagons, one of which is filled with milk cans. Note the barber pole above the last wagon to the right and the boardwalk instead of concrete sidewalks.

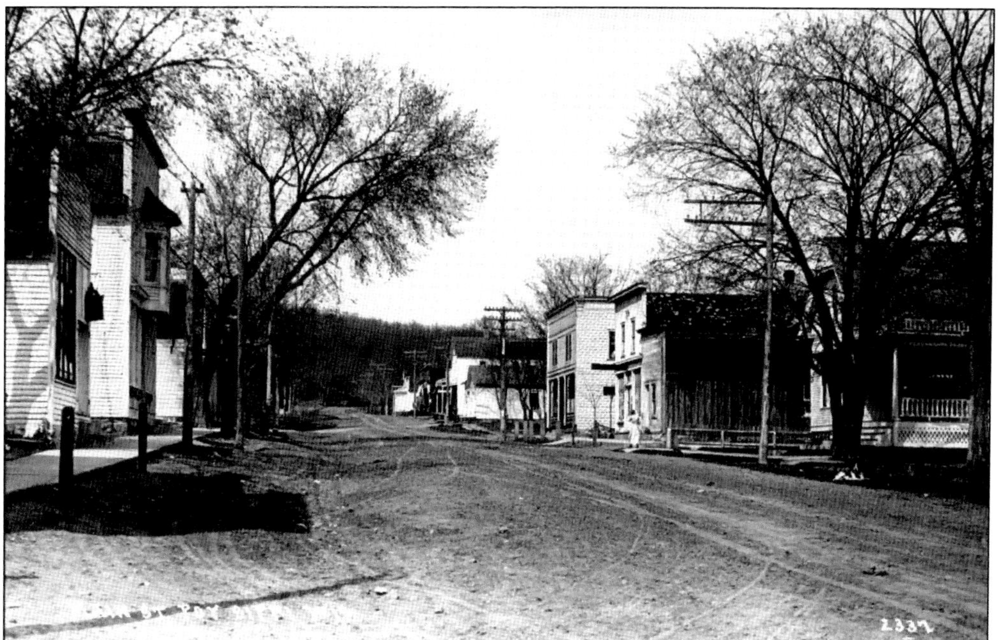

**EAST SIDE OF MAIN STREET.** The east side of the street is revealed in this view, looking north from the intersection with Commercial Street. The house on the far right and the next two buildings still remain.

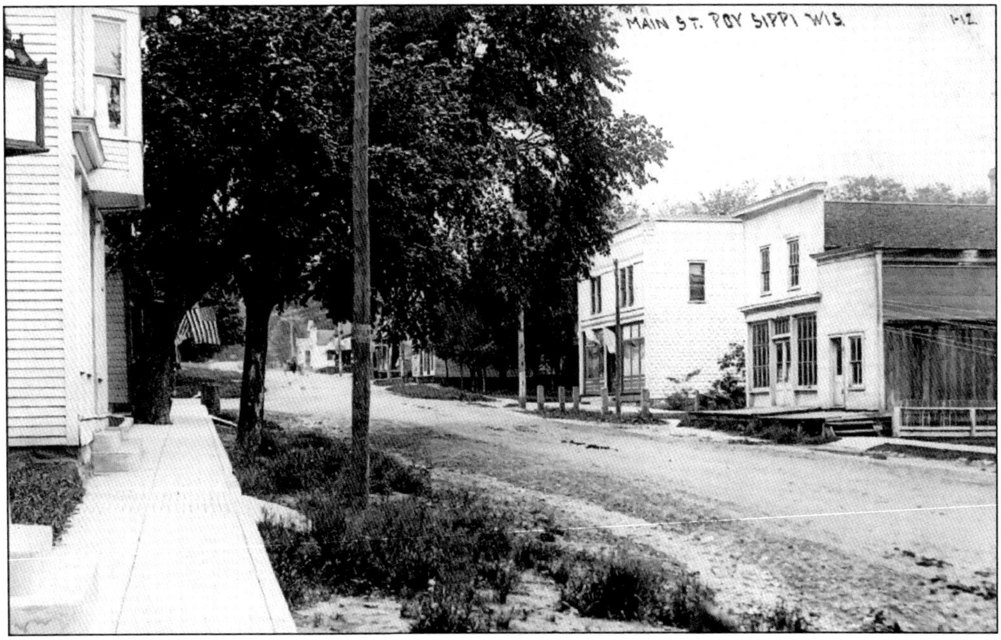


SIMILAR VIEW. This photograph was taken about 150 feet to the north of the previous viewpoint. It gives a better look at the buildings across the street. The far building on the right side of Main Street is Dr. Moffatt's office.

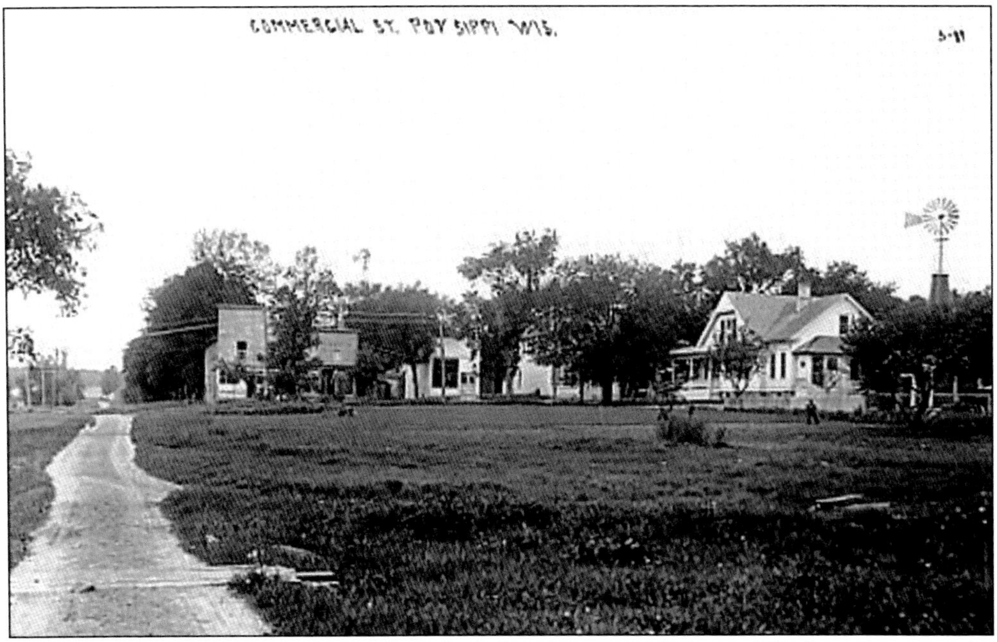


COMMERCIAL STREET. The dirt road on the left is Commercial Street. The large house to the right is the residence of Dr. Thewalt, whose front yard goes to the road. Note the windmill, which is no longer there. Sometime after Dr. Thewalt moved his practice to Berlin, Dr. Stimpson took over the house and the practice.

**Doctors of Poy Sippi.** Dr. Thewalt relaxes in the swivel chair in his office. This photograph was printed on the front side of a postcard, which was a popular style around 1917. Many doctors serving the town had been listed in other books but one that has never been listed is Joseph H. Turner. After receiving his diploma from Albany Medical College, New York, Turner came to Wisconsin and began practicing medicine in Poy Sippi in 1850. Since Ewing was already Poy Sippi's doctor, Turner moved to Berlin and quit his practice to sell real estate there. During the Civil War, he served in the 1st Wisconsin Cavalry as the assistant surgeon. He died on May 22, 1904, in Berlin and is buried in the Oakwood Cemetery.

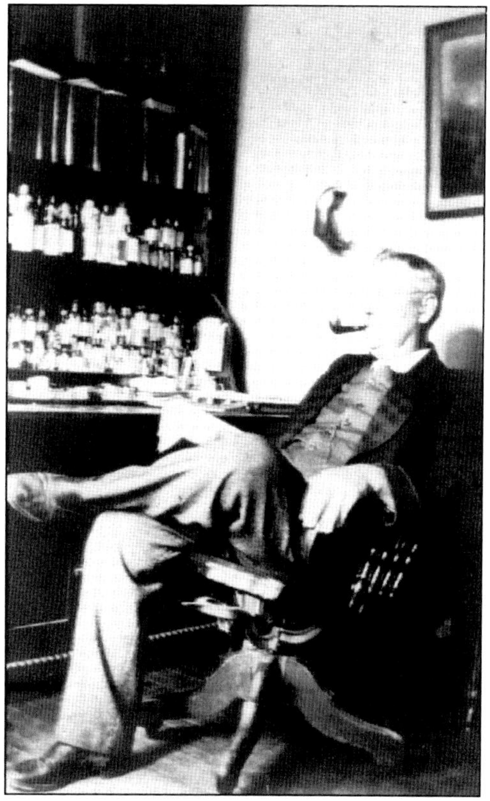

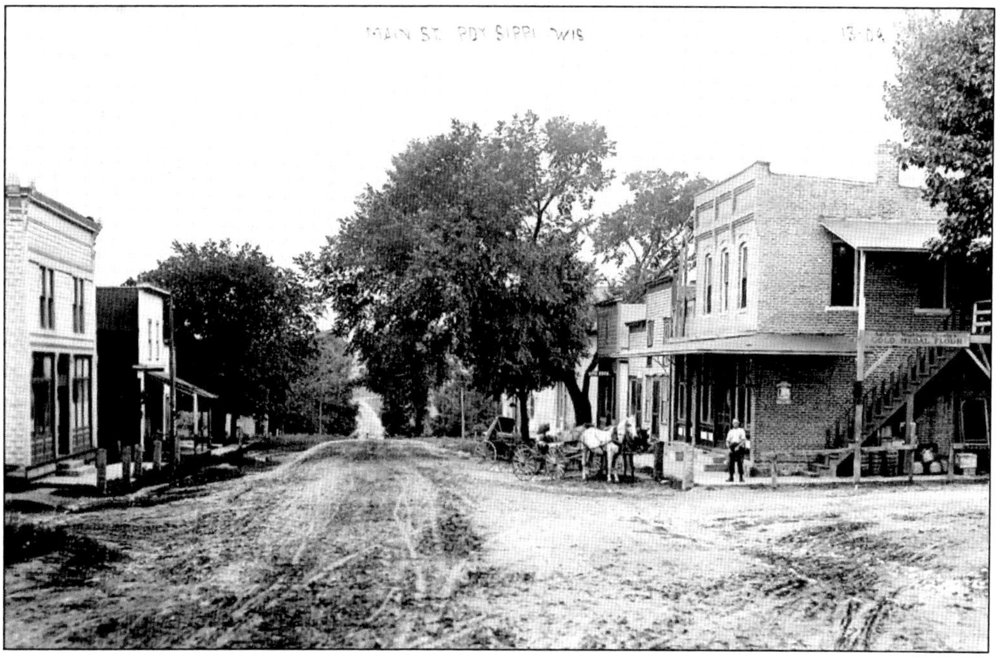


**Main Street South of Liberty Street.** The building in the right foreground was a general store with upstairs apartments.

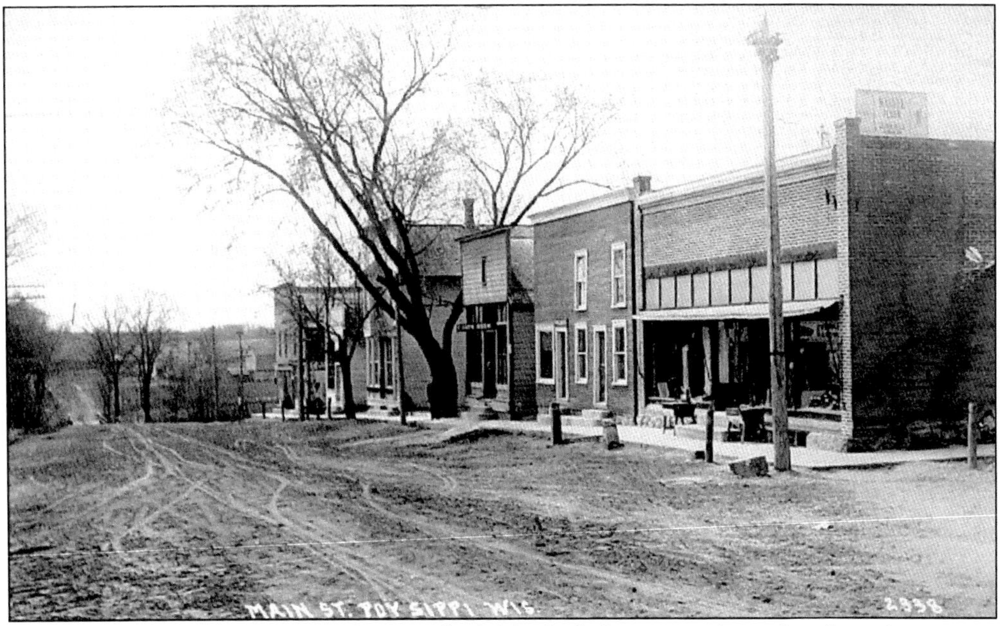


**STORE AFTER FIRE.** This is how the store (right) looked after it was cleaned up from the upstairs apartment fire. The upper floor was removed and the building renovated for business. The building with the big tree in front of it was the drugstore at the time.

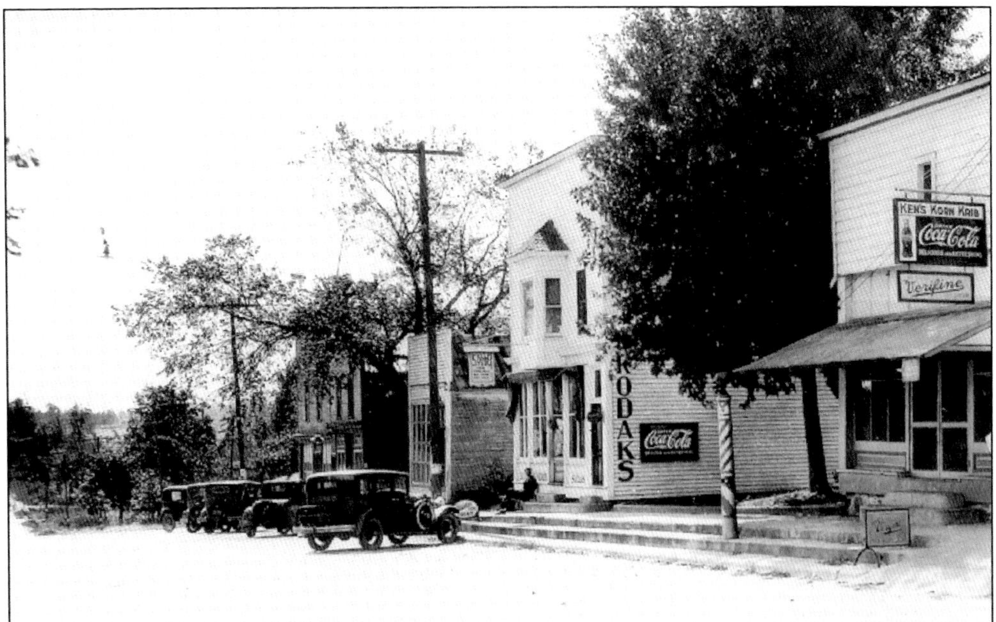


**KEN'S KORN KRIB.** Some of the business changes on Main Street are demonstrated in this image. The tall building in the center is no longer the bank but rather a drugstore. The barbershop signpost decorates Ken's Korn Krib (right).

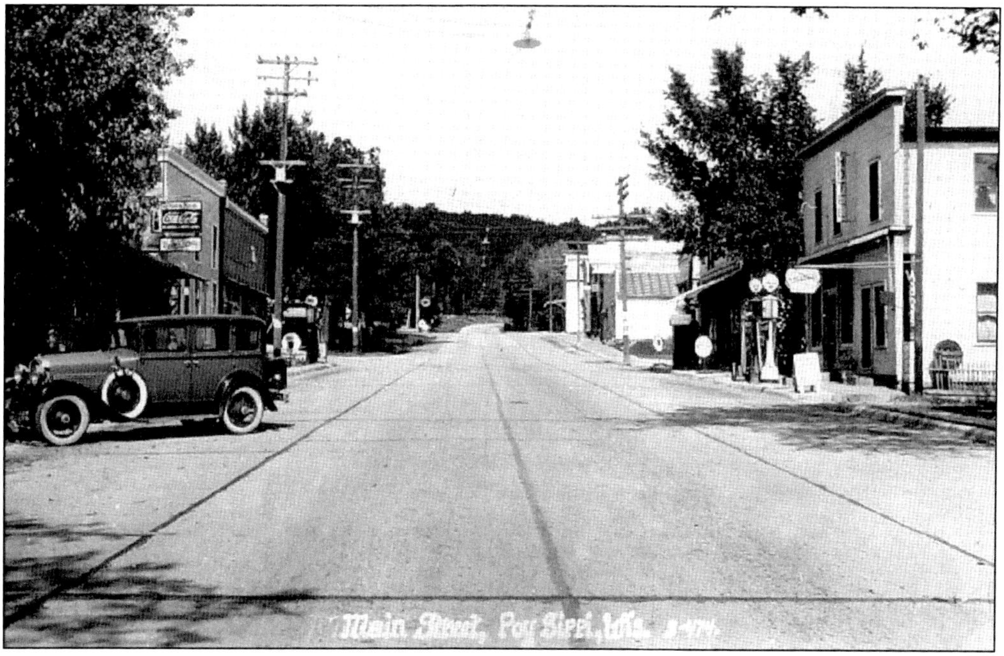


**Poy Sippi, 1940.** The building on the right also had gas pumps for a time, in addition to its nine upstairs hotel rooms and ice-cream parlor.

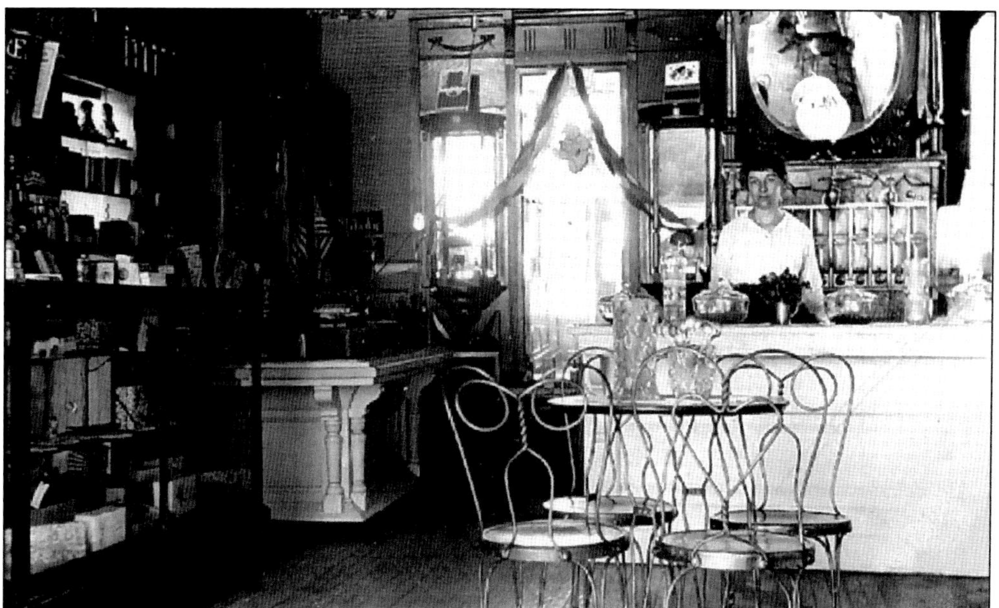

**Ice-Cream Parlor.** This ice-cream parlor, seen here in the late 1920s, was part of the Olsen Store and Hotel.

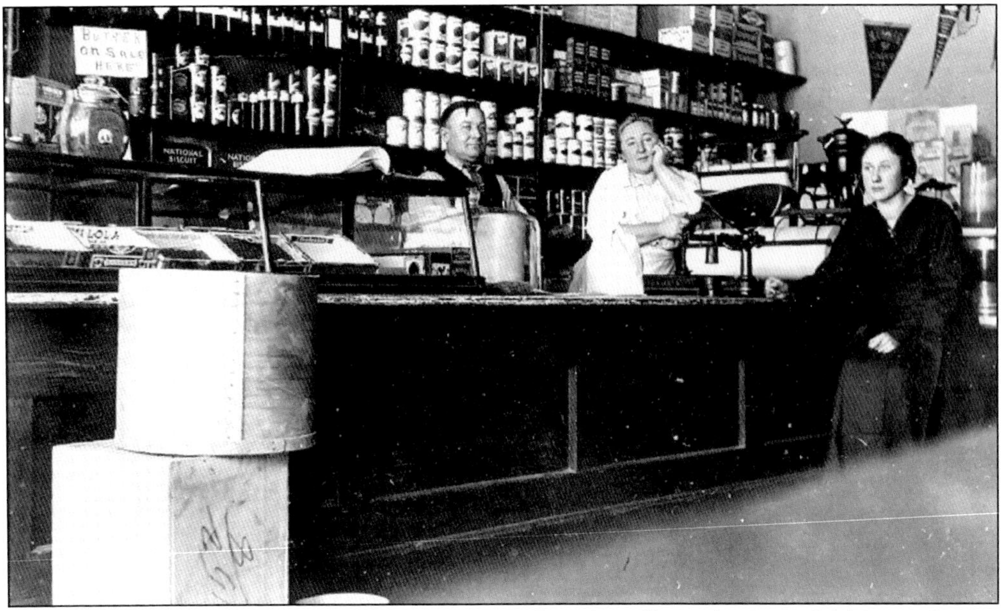


**CAMPFIELD STORE.** South of the hardware store and GAR Hall was the Campfield Store. George and Lil Campfield stand behind the counter, while their daughter Genevieve sits on a stool.

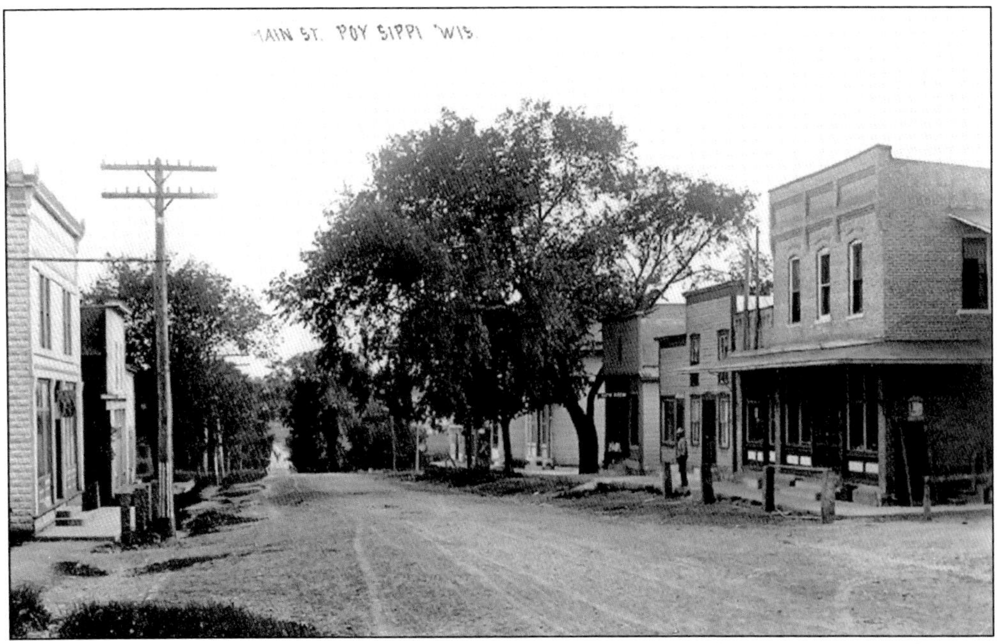


**SOUTH MAIN STREET, POY SIPPI.** The building on the right was the general store. The next building, to the left of the general store, was the 1920s and early 1930s residence of Lulu Bowen, the granddaughter of Edwin Bowen, pictured on the cover. Lulu was known for raising chickens on the upper floor.

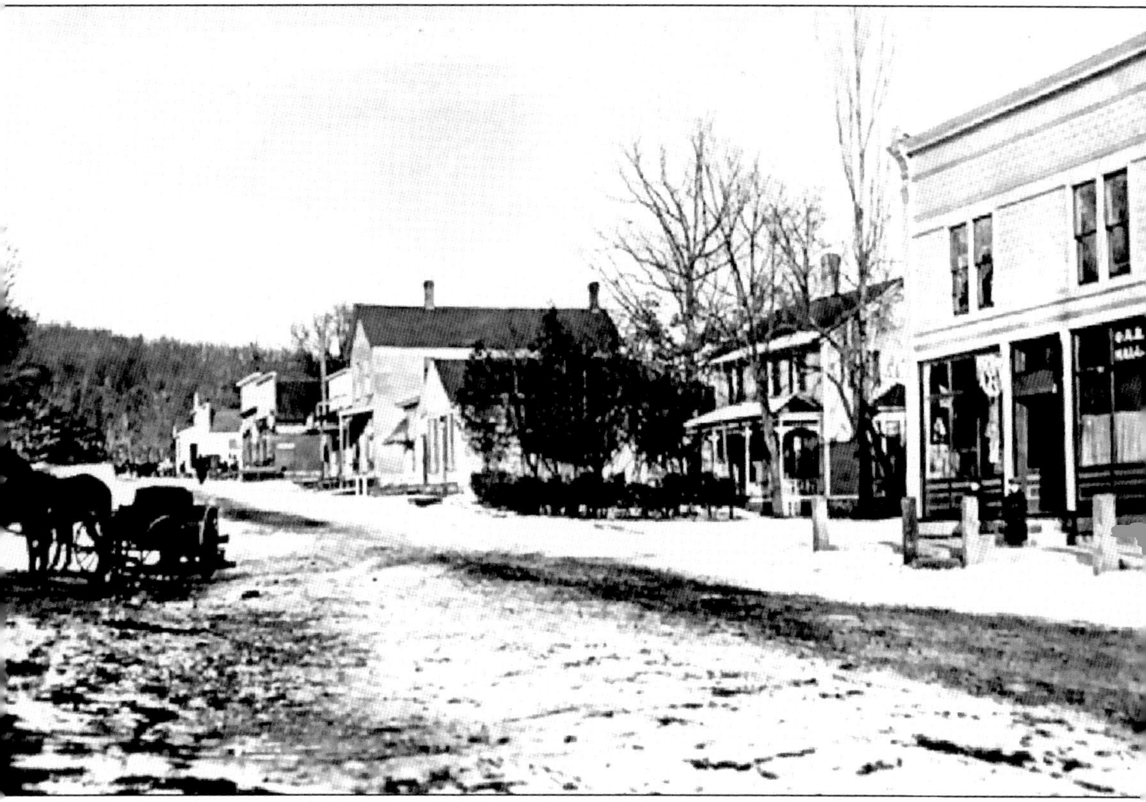

**ONLY VIEW AS THE GAR HALL.** Although this looks like just another day in Poy Sippi, this photograph is of historical significance. The GAR Hall building (right) was divided in two, with the hardware store on the left side and the GAR Post No. 231 on the right. Both the GAR and its auxiliary, the Women's Relief Corps, held meetings here. Many oyster suppers were eaten in the hall, as they were a favorite of the old soldiers. The oysters were shipped to Poy Sippi in barrels. As the soldiers died off, the organization started the Sons of Veterans of the Civil War, in 1881. The old soldiers and their sons held meetings in the same hall, though not always together. The Sons of Union Veterans of the Civil War, as the group was later called to avoid confusion with the Sons of Confederate Veterans, became the heir of the GAR. In 1927, the flags of their fathers were handed down to the sons and the GAR post ceased activity. Fred Hawley, the son of George, was the last member of the Civil War veterans of this GAR Post No. 231.

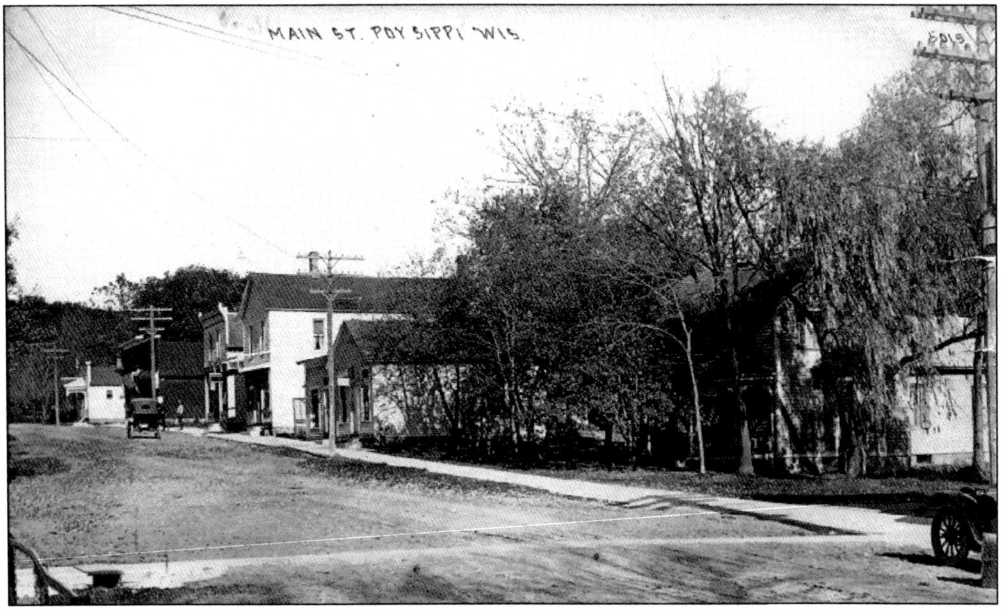


**MAIN STREET.** Taken about 1920, this photograph of the east side of town north of Commercial Street demonstrates that electricity has made its way to Poy Sippi. The large white building with the car in the front was the Christensen's General Store. After Christensen's the buildings are, from left to right, Dr. Dodd's office (with the screen door open), Dr. McWain's office, and the Sweat's home (behind the trees).

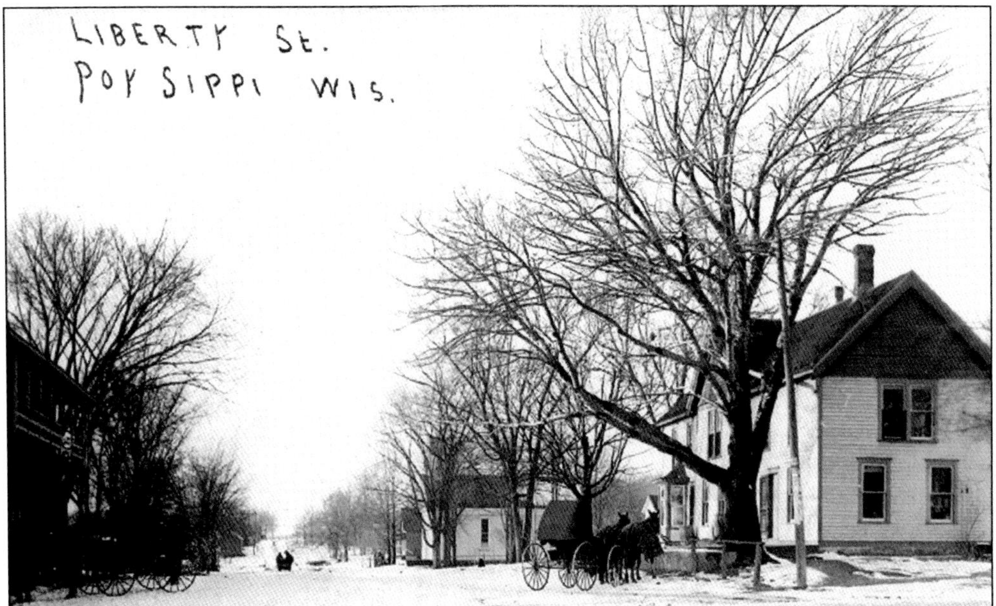


**HAWLEY HOUSE.** Fred Hawley had this house built by Fred Dewey on the northwest corner of Liberty and Main Streets. Later, Hawley ran the building as a lodging known as the Seven Mile Hotel for 60 years. His daughter Jessie then operated it until her health gave out. The building on the left was the Halleck Grocery Store, with second-floor apartments. The second floor later had a fire and was removed. The Catholic church appears in the background.

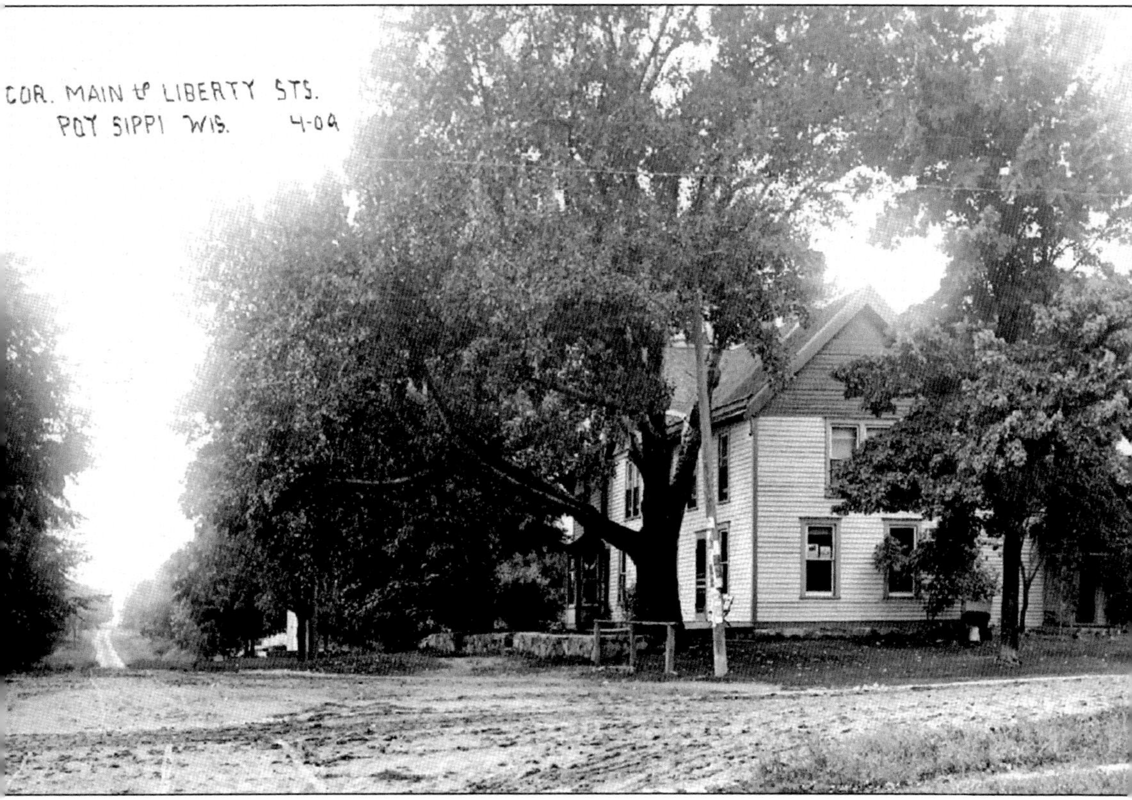


**HAWLEY HOUSE, 1911.** This postcard view was taken in the summertime, as the trees are filled out and blocking the background.

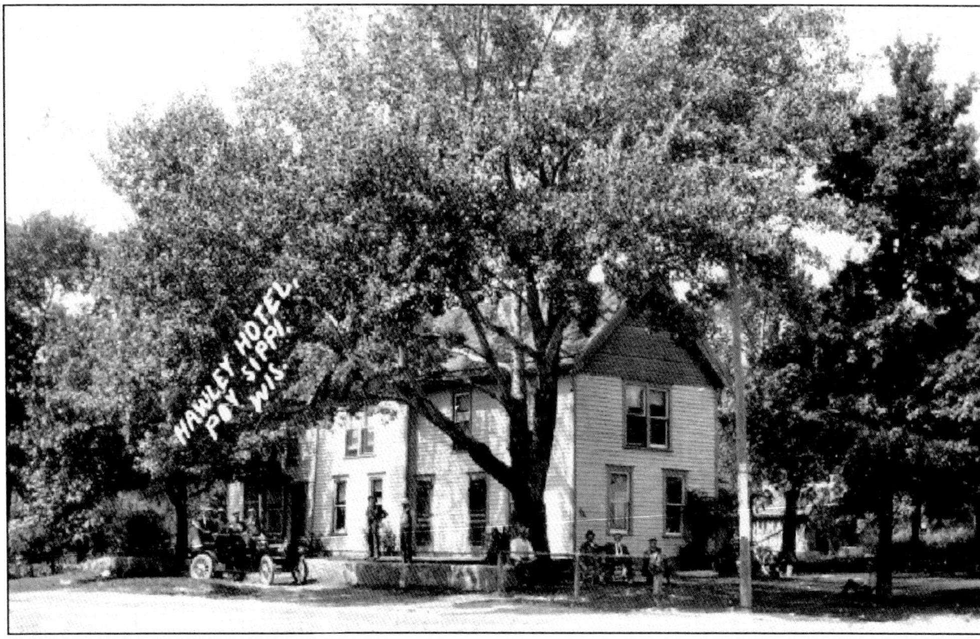


**HAWLEY HOTEL.** Located in the center of town, the Hawley House had private quarters on the northeast side. The house was later turned into a farm implement shop run by Clarence Zabel and Harold Madison. It was torn down, and the area where it stood is now a parking lot.

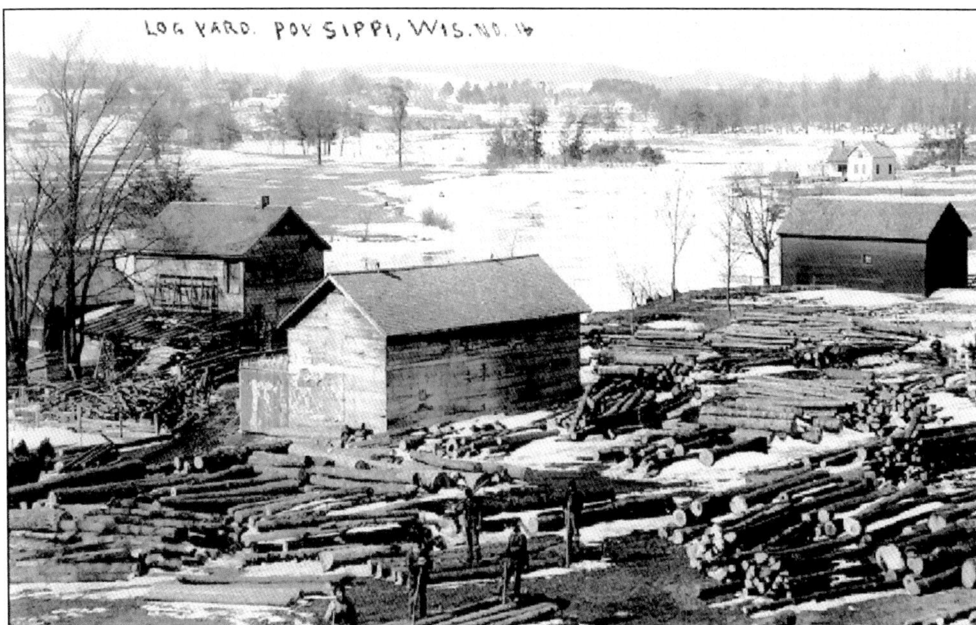


**PAULSON SAW- AND GRISTMILL.** This c. 1908 photograph shows the Paulson mill, situated on the north side of the river. The mill was the gathering place for logs that were floated down the streams that led into the Pine River. Appearing here are David Kimball (second from the left) and owner W. H. Paulson (fourth from the left). The mill was destroyed by fire on July 6, 1967.

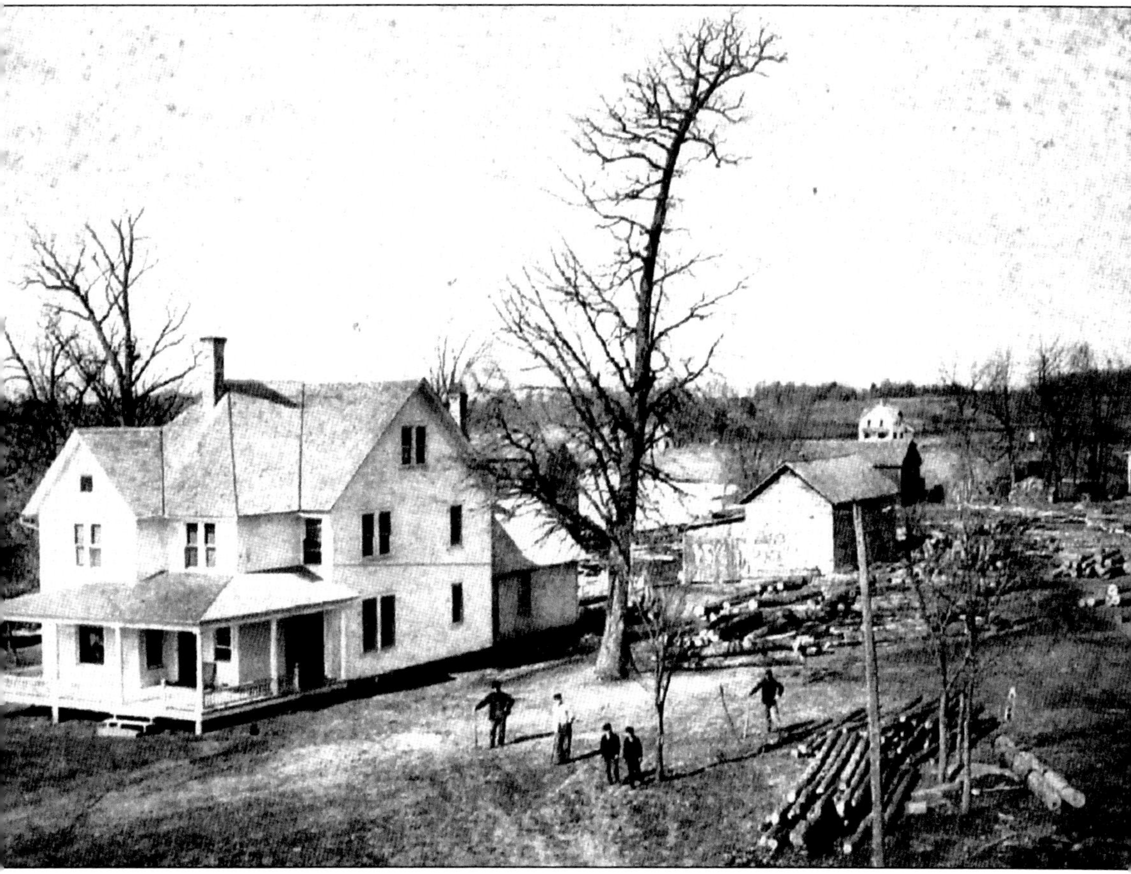

**PAULSON HOUSE.** The Paulson house, pictured about 1905, stood next to the feed mill and sawmill. This view covers up the mill, which was situated behind the house. The openness of the countryside is evident, and besides a few homes placed in the area behind the log yard, the modern view is not much different. The house is still there.

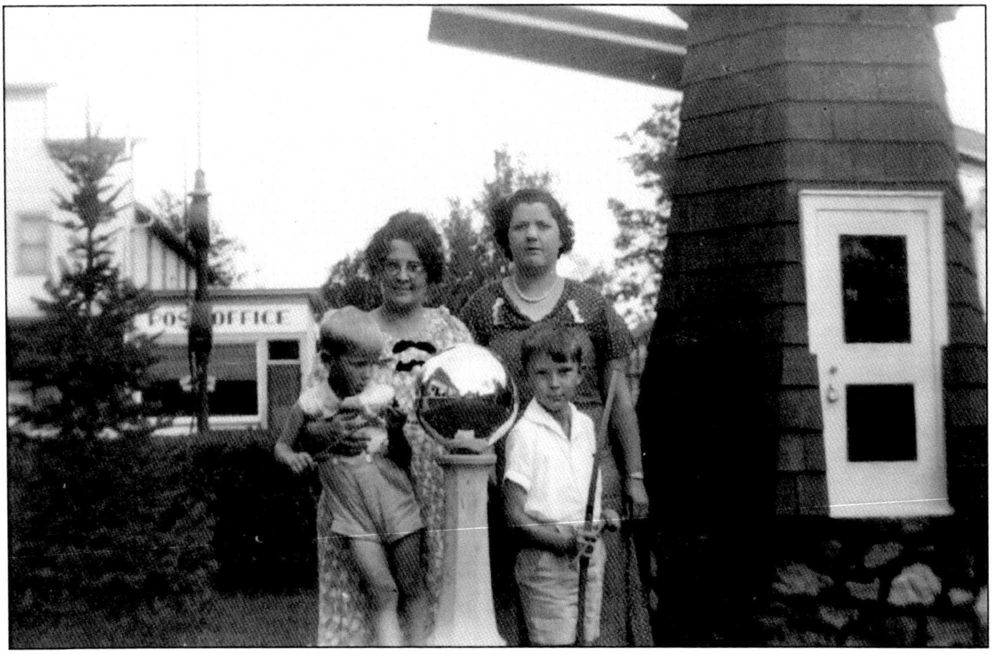


**POY SIPPI POST OFFICE.** Poy Sippi Post Office views are hard to come by. This photograph was taken from across the street, but the post office can be seen in the background. A newer facility has replaced this on the same property.

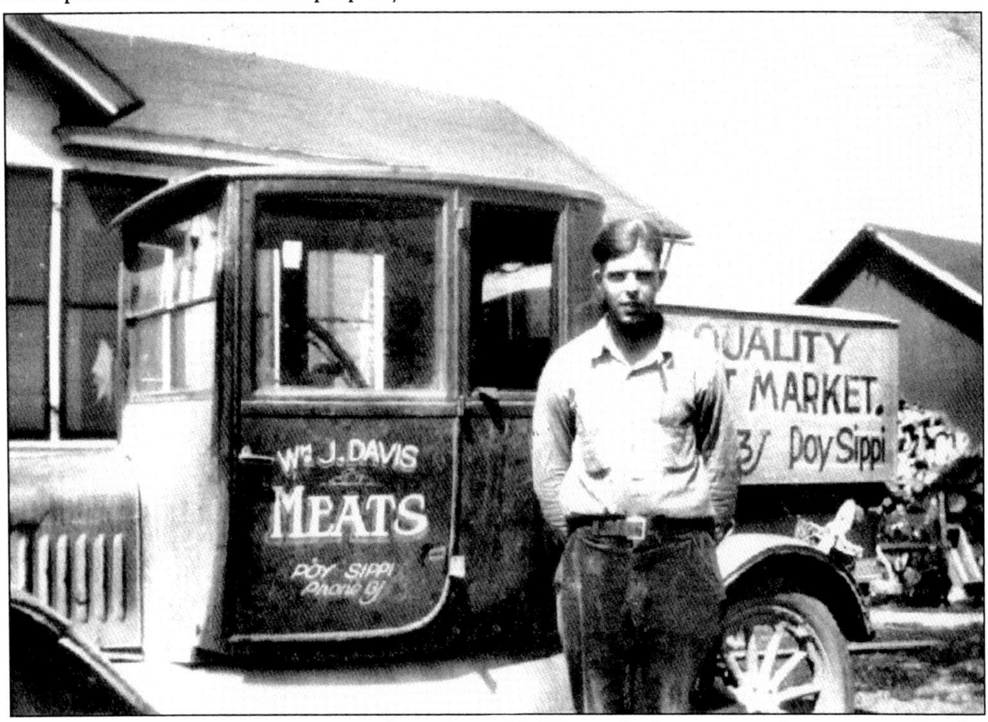


**W. J. DAVIS.** Once the postmaster of Poy Sippi, W. J. Davis had a meat market in town. Besides meat, Davis was remembered for rendering lard. Maybe that was why they called him "Waxey." He was also known for shoe repairing.

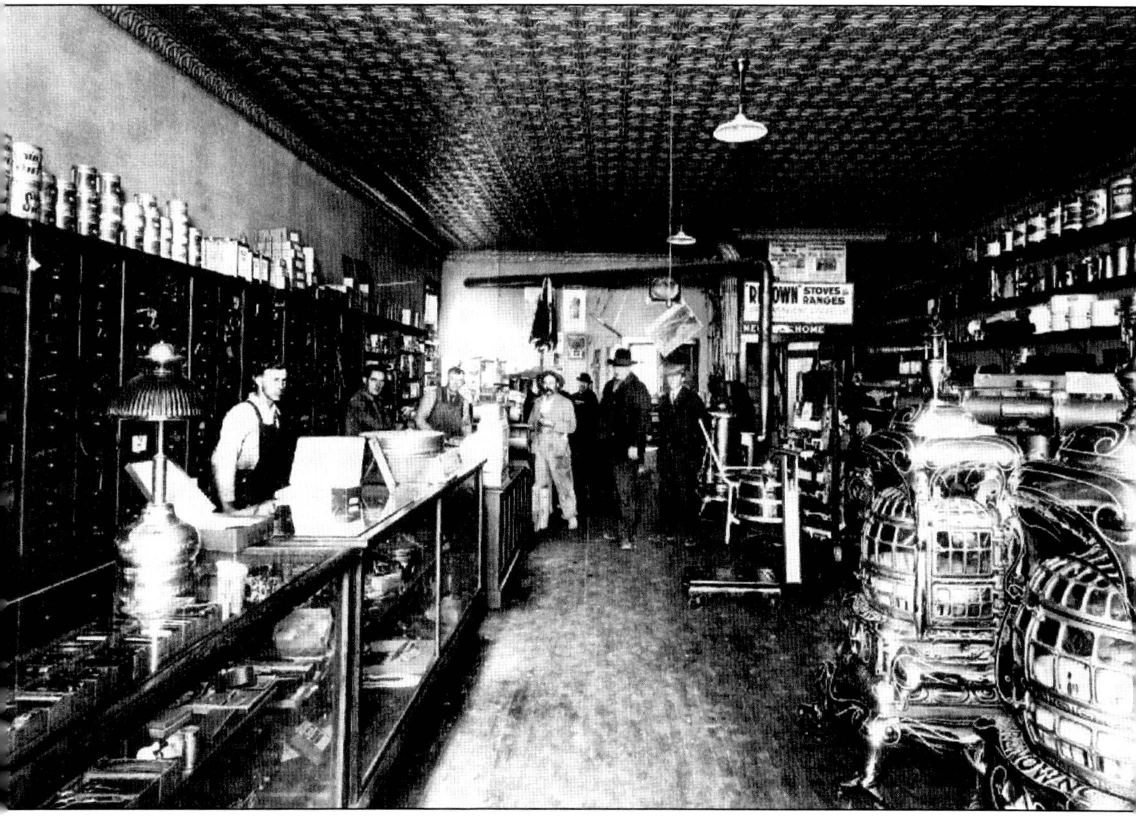

**HARDWARE STORE.** The hardware store occupied the north side of the building it shared with the GAR Hall on the east side of Main Street. This interior view shows that it was not a deep or wide store. Notice the great-looking wood stoves. The wall that once divided the building has since been removed.

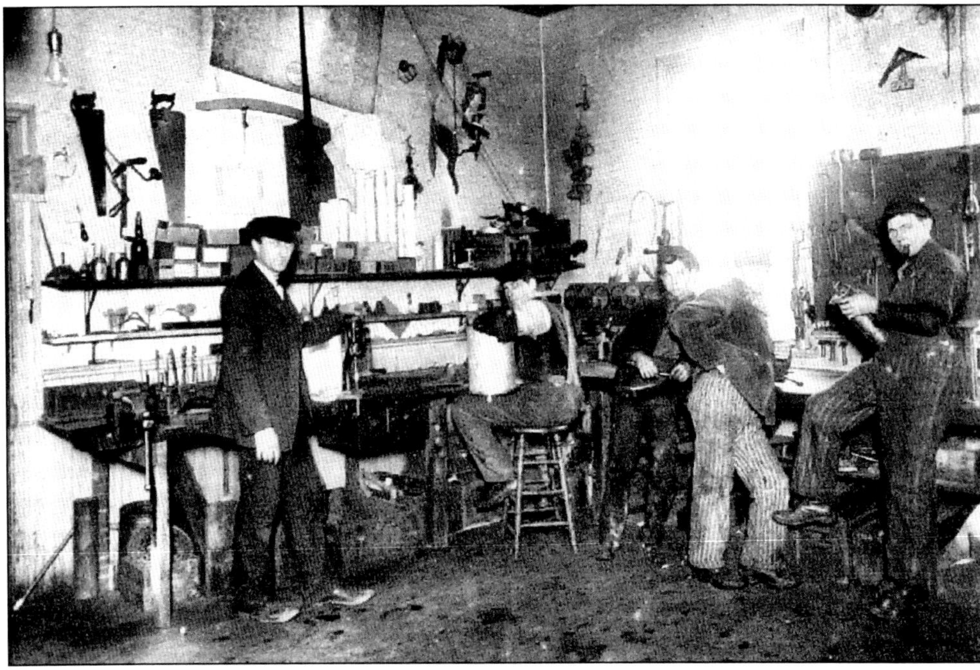

**BLACKSMITH SHOP.** The blacksmith shop was located behind the hardware store.

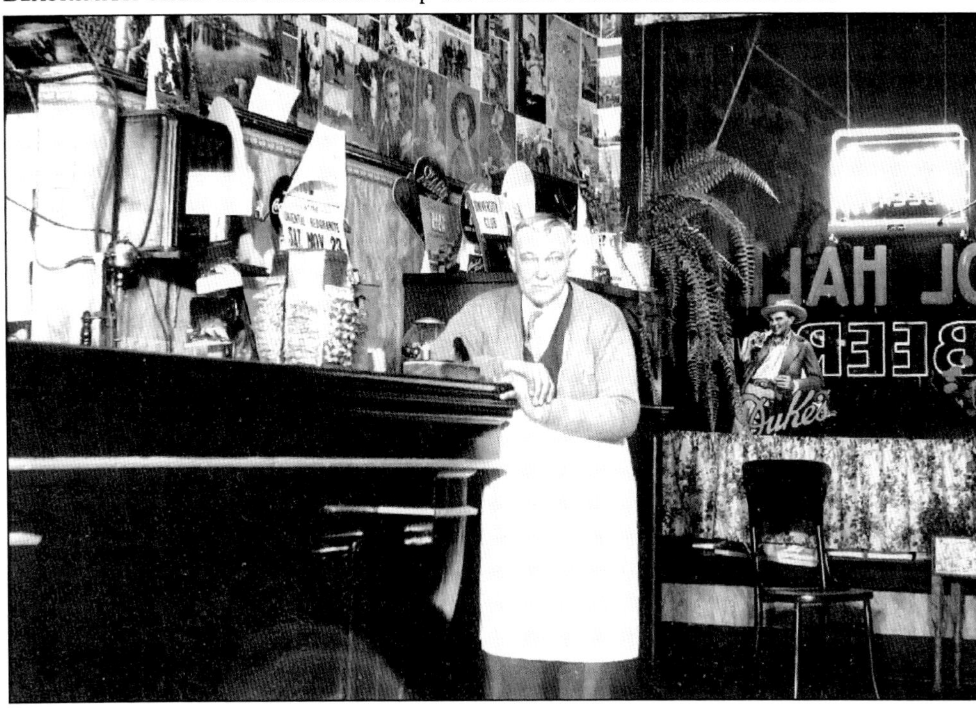


**GORDAN'S HALL.** Gordan's Hall, as it came to be known, was built in the early 1920s by Fred Gordan. When Gordan died his wife, Maggie Gordan, was left to run the saloon. She later married Ben Millertz, who owned the hardware store next to the GAR Hall. The couple then operated both businesses. The building eventually became a restaurant called the Hillside and, later, the Reflections.

# *Two*

# Poy Sippi on the Pine River

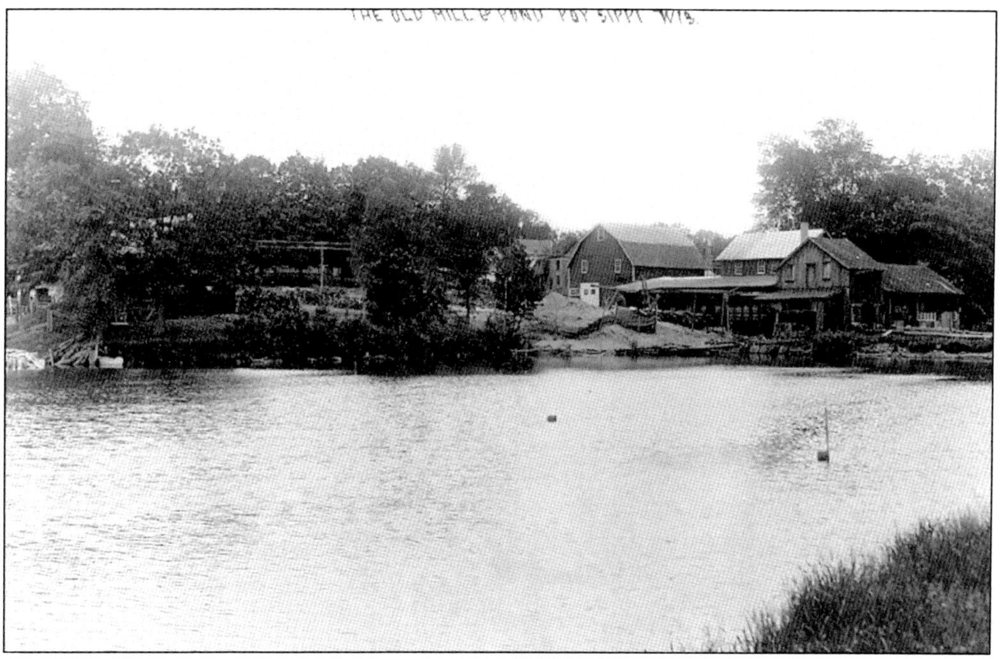

**Old Mill Pond and Mill.** The Pine River is held back by the dam on the right side of this 1911 postcard view. The old Paulson mill, as it had become known over the years, appears in the background. On July 9, 1967, the mill, originally built by George Hawley in the 1850s, burned down while owned by the Radkes.

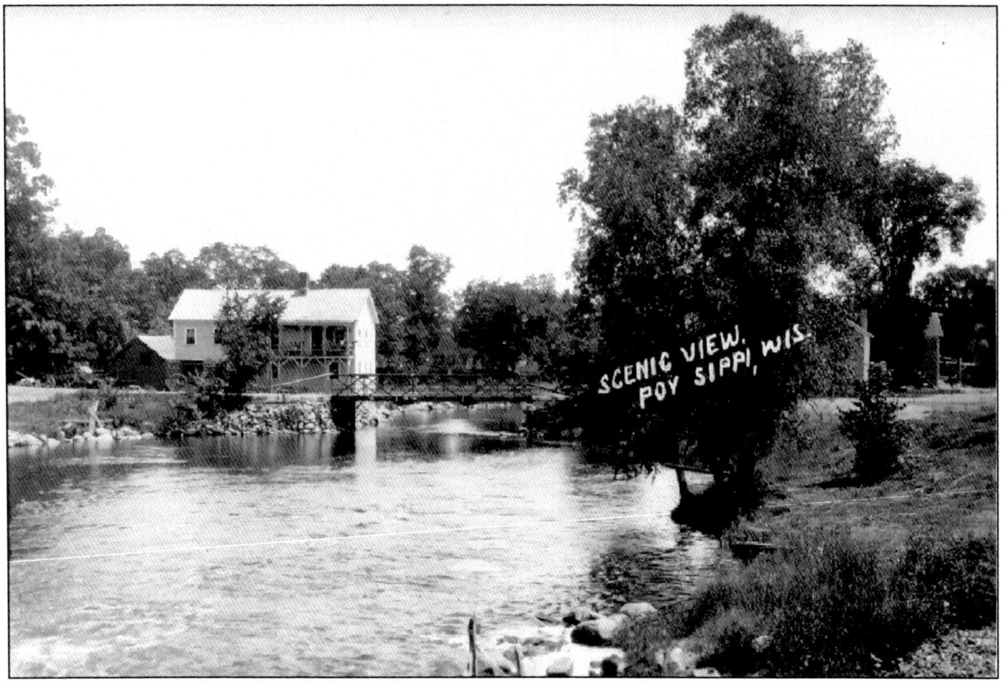


**SOUTHERN FORK OF PINE RIVER.** This postcard view of the river's southern fork, taken from Colt's mill, looks east toward Main Street. The building on the other side of the bridge was Nels Jensen's Garage in the 1920s and 1930s.

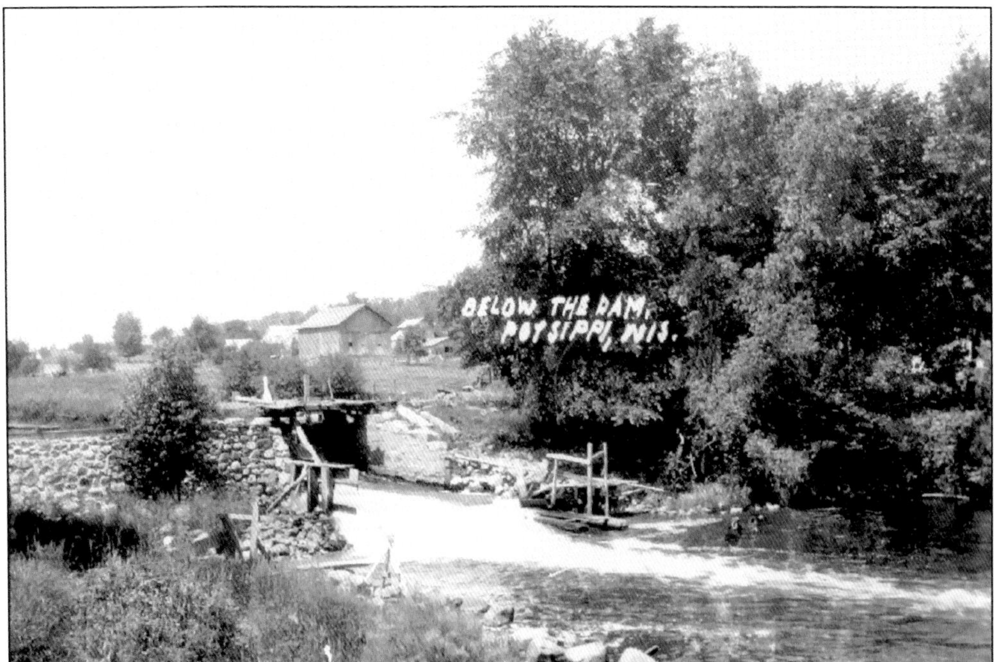


**NORTHERN FORK OF PINE RIVER.** The river's southern fork is shown in this view, taken from the bridge and looking back toward the dam. Hidden behind the trees is the Radke mill. The countryside west of Poy Sippi appears in the background.

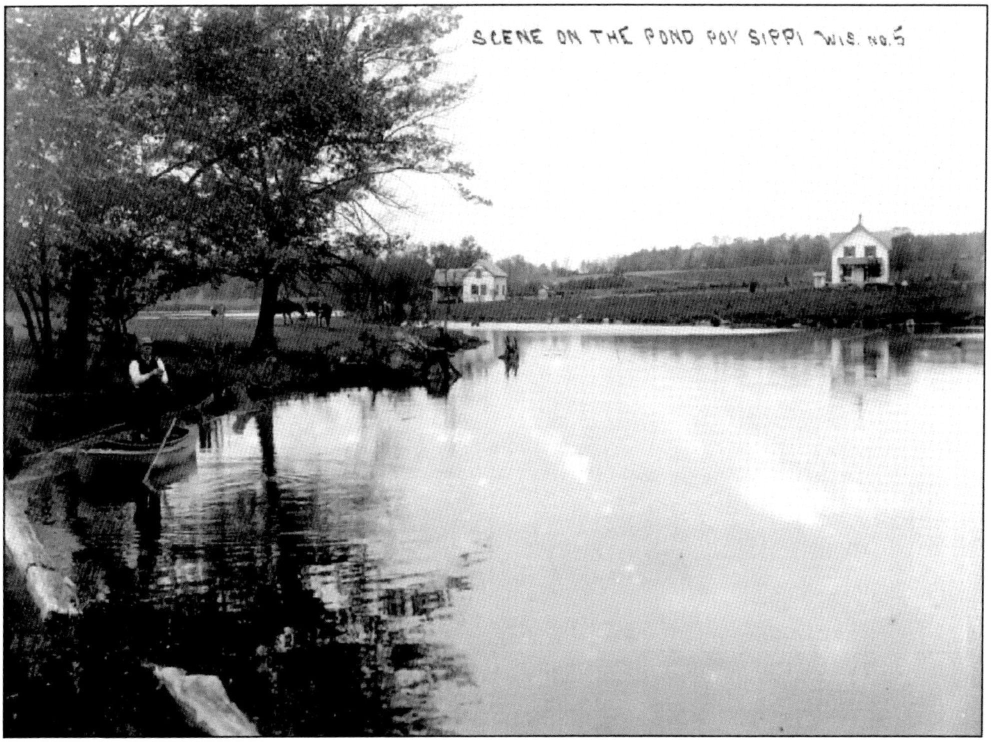


**SCENE ON THE POND.** Here, a man fishing from a canoe tries his luck on the pond of the Pine River, just west of the dams. While fishing in the pond area has not been as popular recently, there have been some nice-sized fish caught in this part of the river.

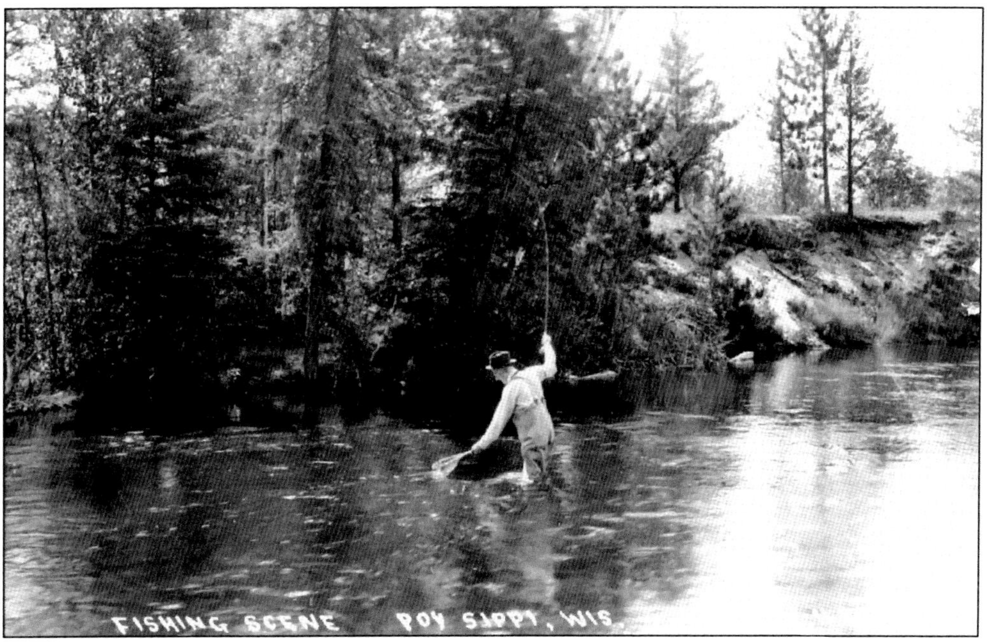


**FLY-FISHING IN PINE RIVER.** Since the banks in the postcard are higher than the banks of the river in Poy Sippi, this photograph must have been taken just west of town.

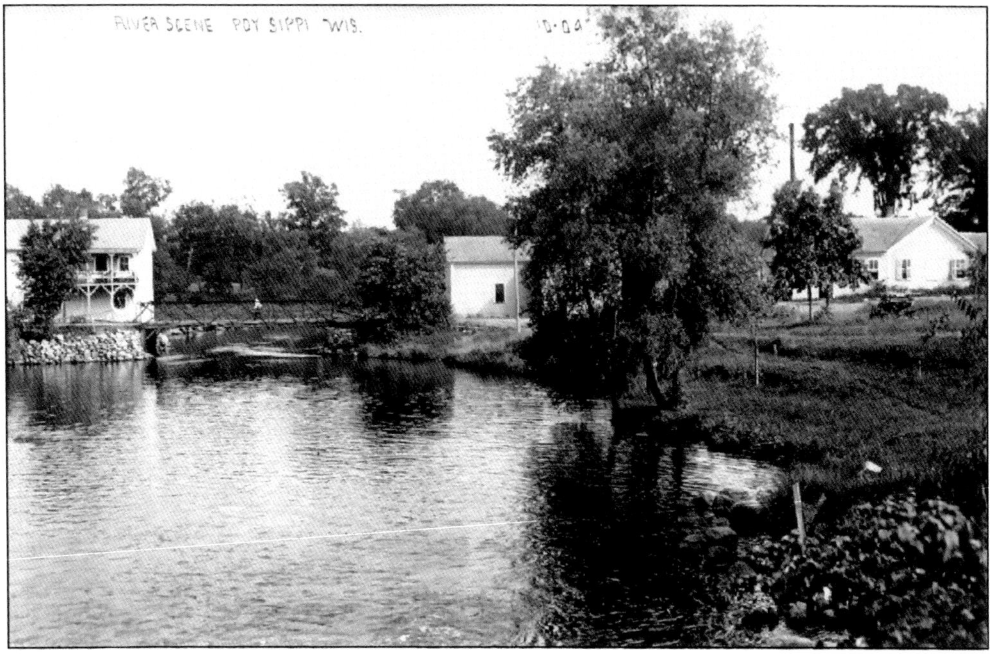


**RIVER SCENE.** This postcard photograph is very similar to the top photograph on page 38; however, it was taken a little farther south, showing more of what was south of the bridge. The building on the far right was the Daisy Dairy.

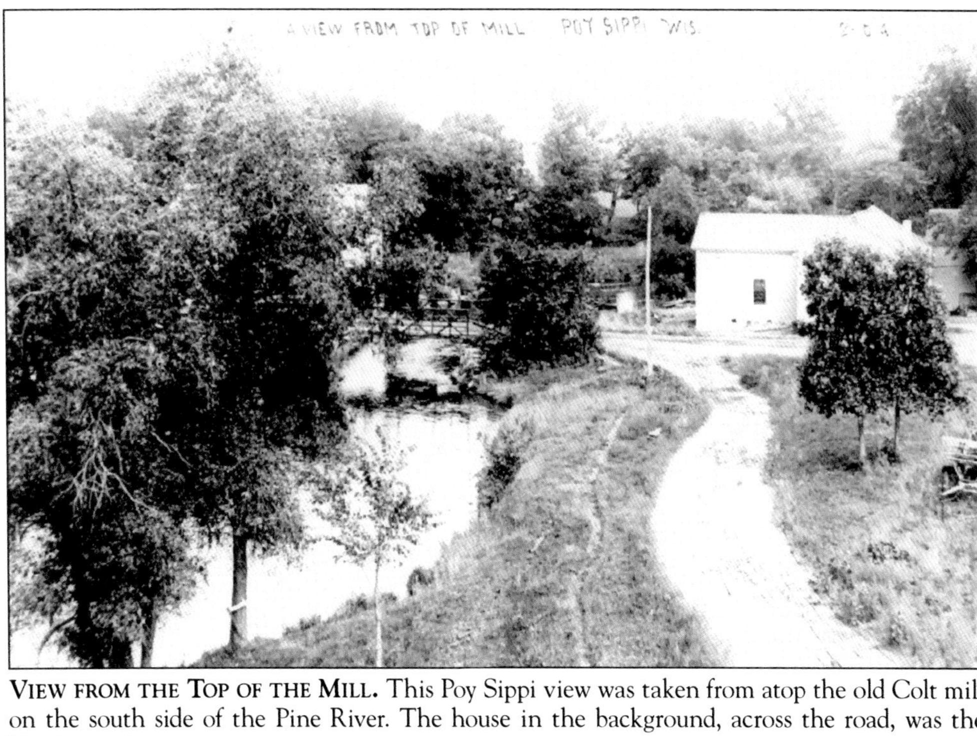


**VIEW FROM THE TOP OF THE MILL.** This Poy Sippi view was taken from atop the old Colt mill on the south side of the Pine River. The house in the background, across the road, was the Vergin residence.

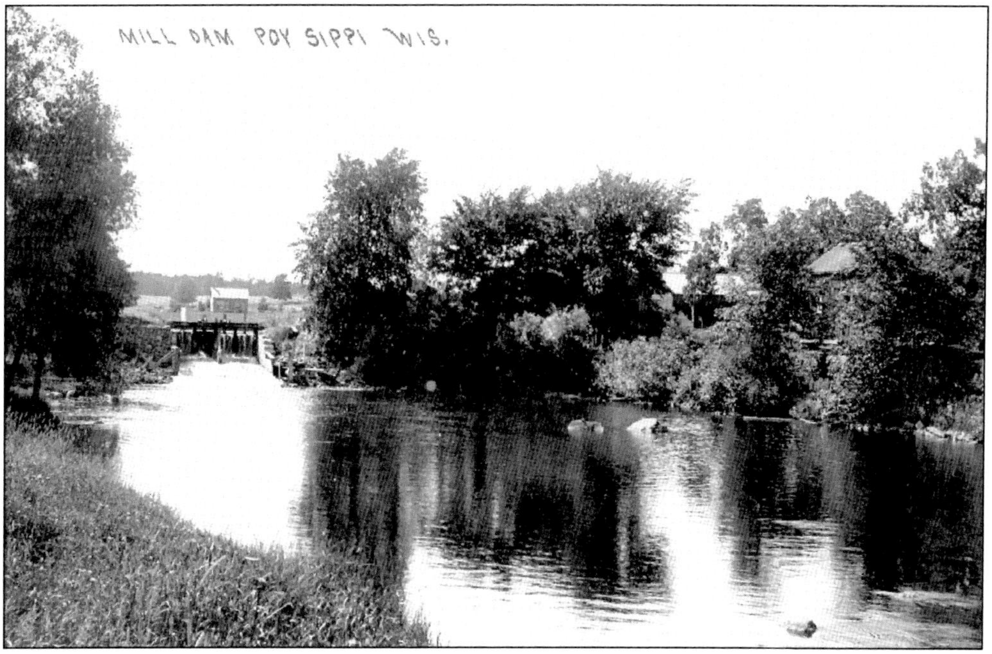


**MILL DAM.** The south dam, seen here from the bridge, powered the mill that is hidden by the trees on the right.

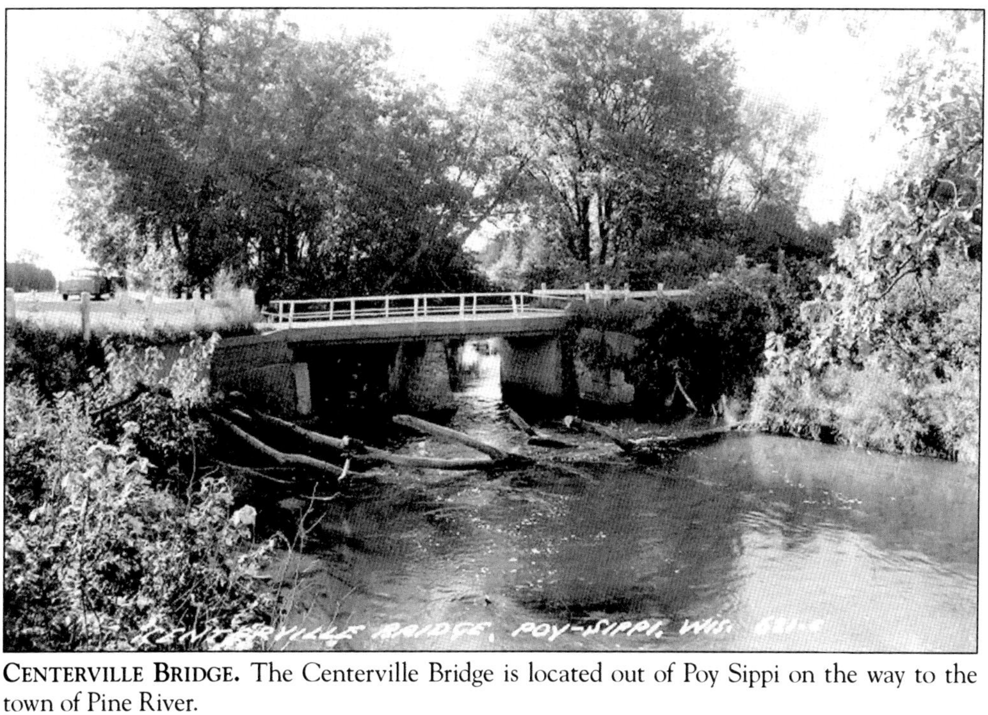


**CENTERVILLE BRIDGE.** The Centerville Bridge is located out of Poy Sippi on the way to the town of Pine River.

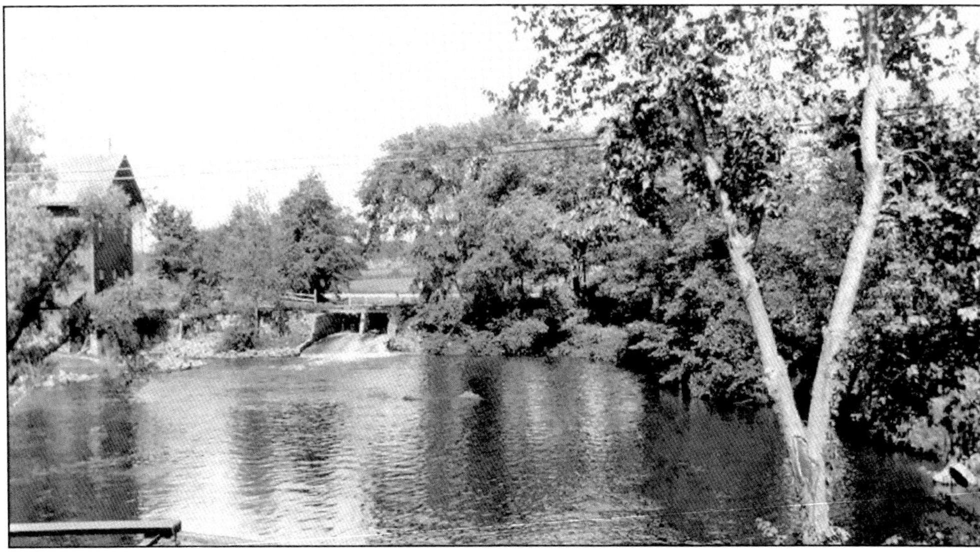

**LOOKING WEST FROM MAIN STREET BRIDGE.** Although this image is similar to the lower photograph, it provides a better view of the dam. The reader also gets a clearer idea of the pond-holding area, which was used to power the sawmill downstream. A walkway over the dam allowed access to the other side of the river. It is still in use today.

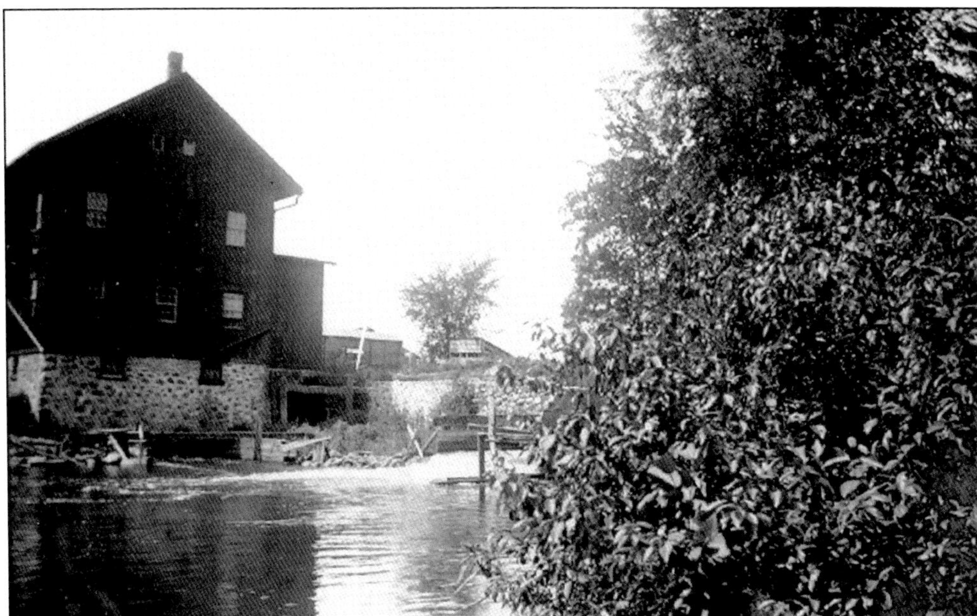

**GRISTMILL.** George Hawley had the foresight to build this gristmill and a sawmill along the Pine River to capture the energy of water. This mill was once owned by Herb Colt, whose family was instrumental in starting several businesses in town over the years. Alfred Olsen and Clarence Gates each also owned the mill at one time. It later burned down in 1975, while Russell Grambsch was the owner. Grambsch had owned the mill for nine years. The Larsen Salvage Company of Weyauwega removed the metal debris, and the rest of the refuse was taken to the Poy Sippi dump. Stored behind the mill were some of the railroad ties for a railroad that never came to be.

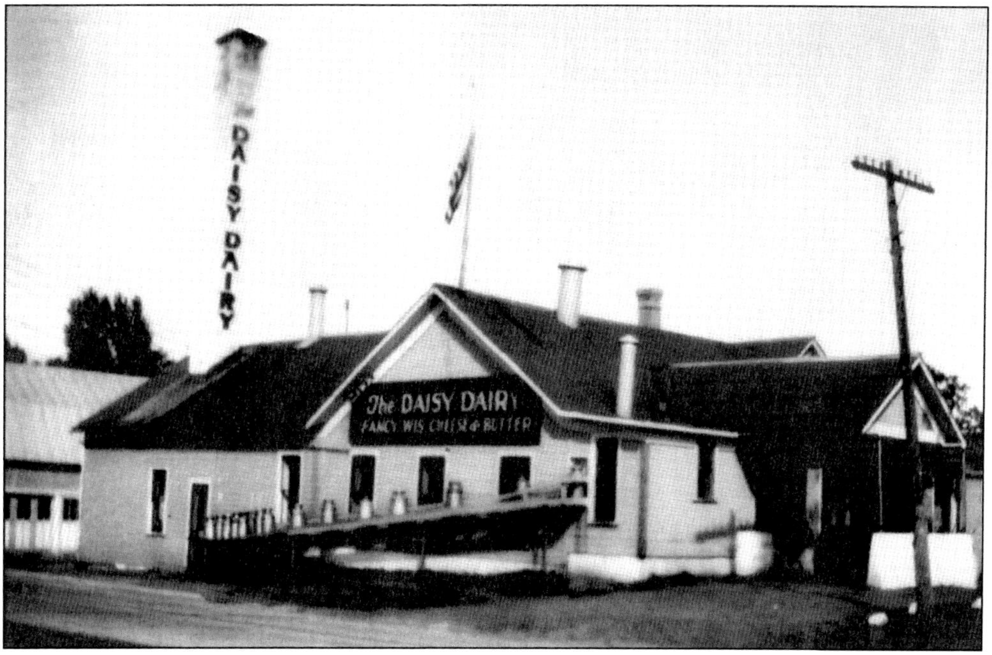


**DAISY DAIRY.** This undated view reveals the dairy, located just south of the Pine River. An apartment building now occupies the site.

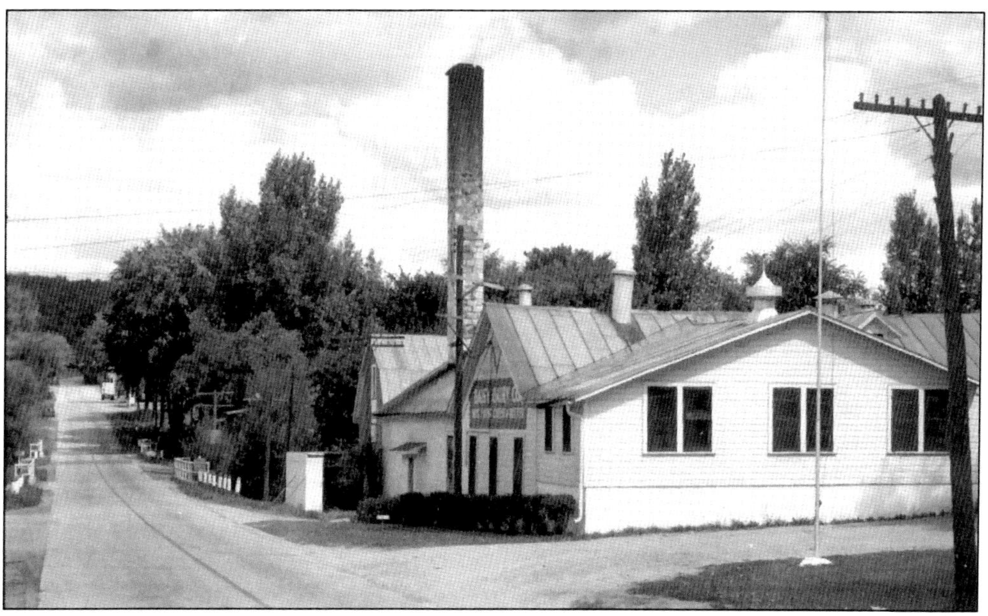

**DAISY DAIRY COMPANY.** The cheese-making company is shown here with the surrounding clean, paved streets and a wider bridge. Note the tin roof and the addition to the building.

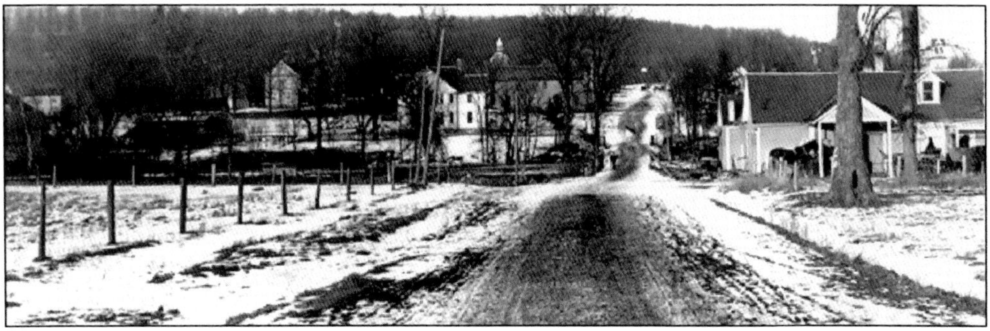

**CHEESE FACTORY.** Photographs of the Daisy Dairy Company (right) are hard to find. This view, similar to the image on page 45, was taken from farther down Main Street and farther from the river. The Paulson mill is on the left, and the Paulson house is in the center.

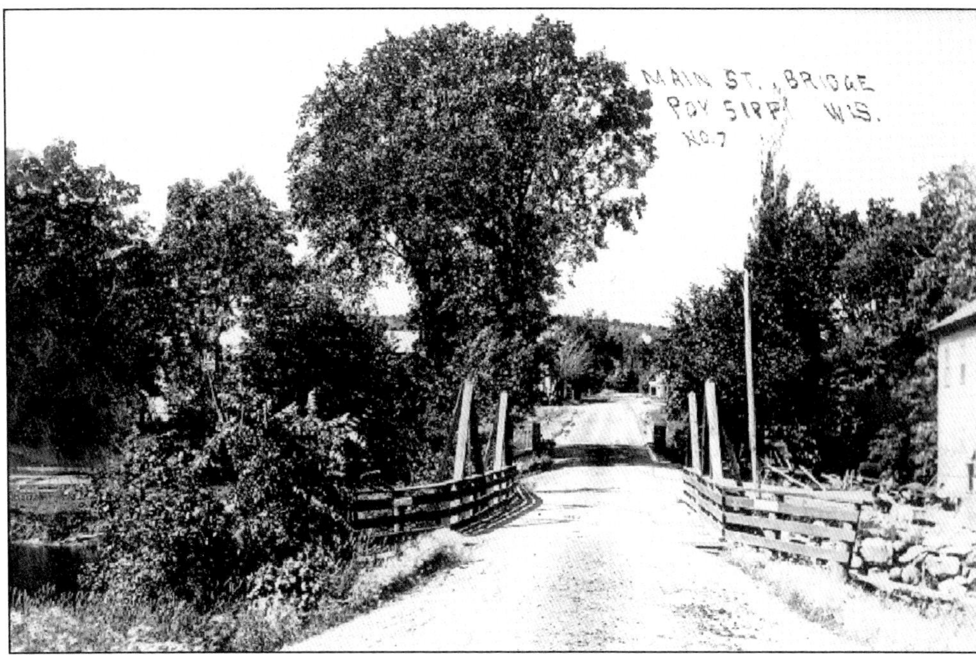


**MAIN STREET BRIDGE.** The bridge over the Pine River is nothing more than a wooden plank and a dirt road in this early-20th-century view.

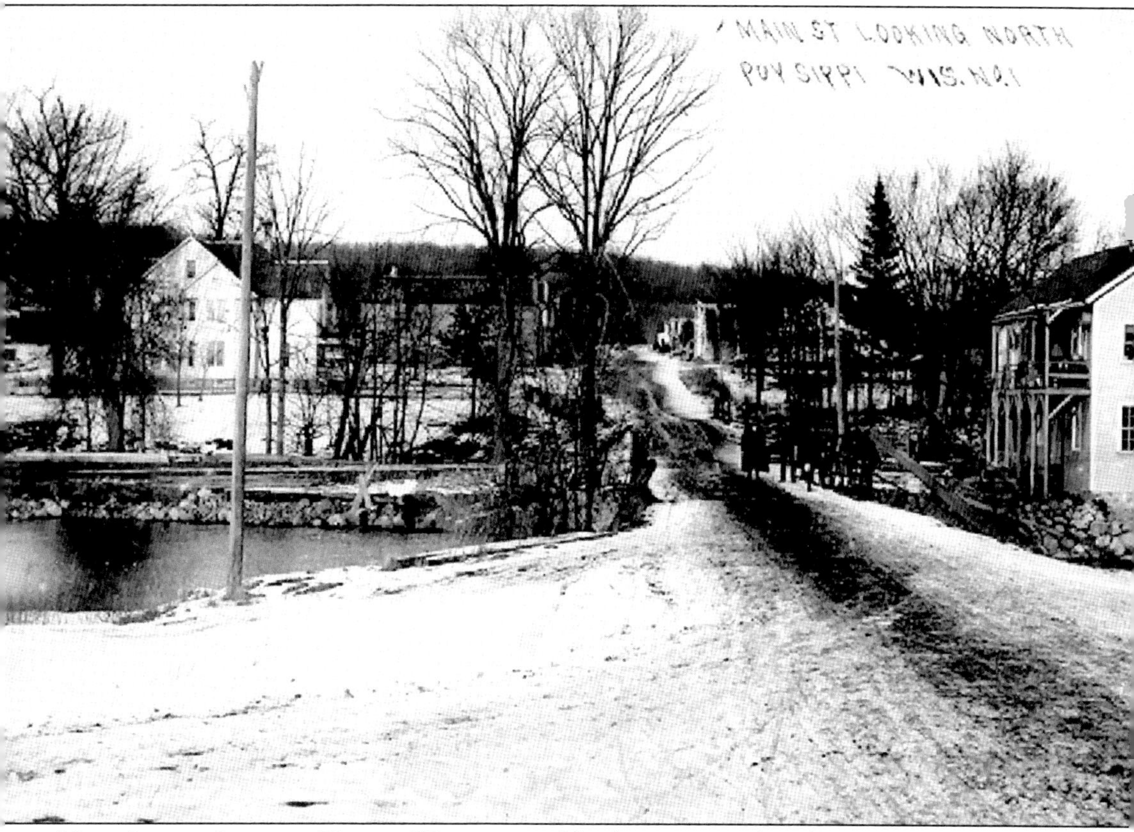


**MAIN STREET, LOOKING NORTH.** Winter scenes like this are remembered by the older people in town. They used to slide down Main Street in long sleds from the hill in the background toward the foreground of the photograph. The Paulson house is the big white one on the left. This postcard view was taken just east of the feed mill owned by the Colts. Herb Safford and Alfred Olsen owned the mill in the late 1920s and early 1930s. The building on the right, in the same period of time, was Nels Jensen's Garage. A bowling alley now occupies the spot from which this photograph was taken.

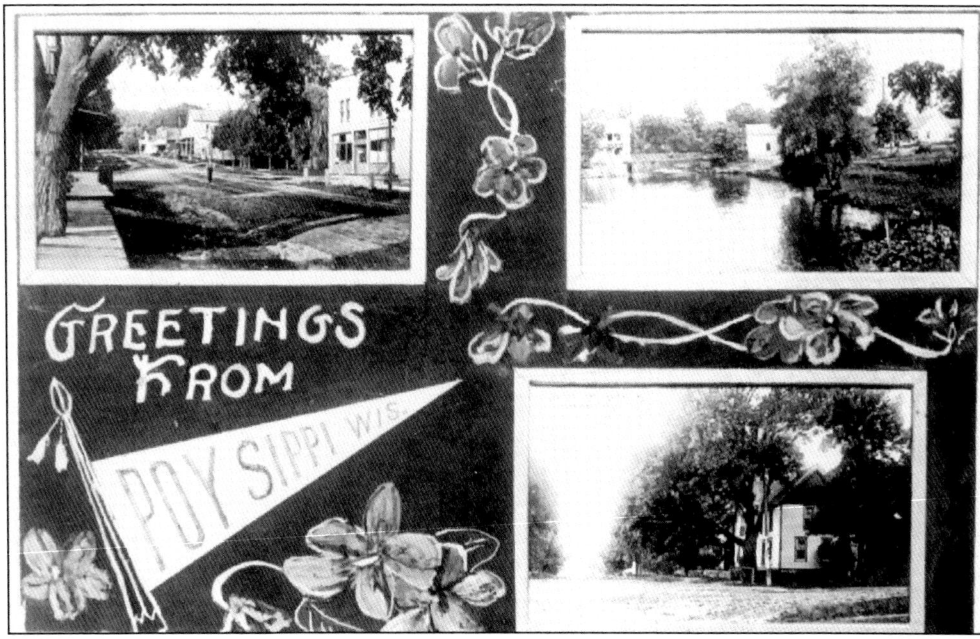


**POSTCARDS FROM POY SIPPI.** It seems like all towns had postcards for sale. Poy Sippi was not any different. Although there was not a big selection, the cards showed different scenes from around 1913 that were of importance to residents. The upper postcard shows, clockwise from the upper left corner, Main Street, the Mill Pond, and the Hawley House. The lower postcard shows, clockwise from the upper left corner, the Mill Pond, Main Street, Colt Mill, Grove School, the Pine River, Paulson's Sawmill, J. E. Wendt Store, and the German Methodist Episcopal Church.

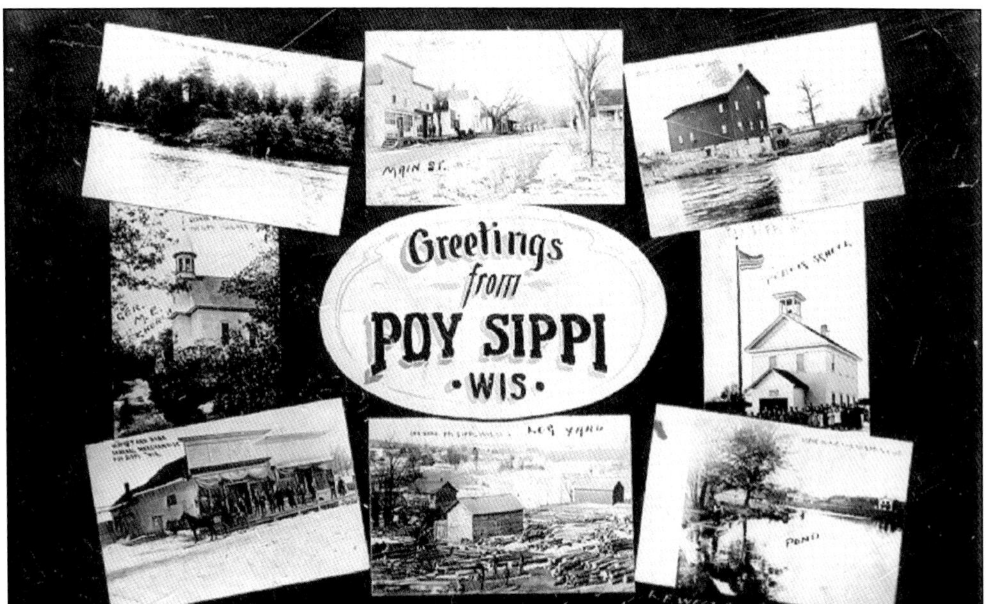

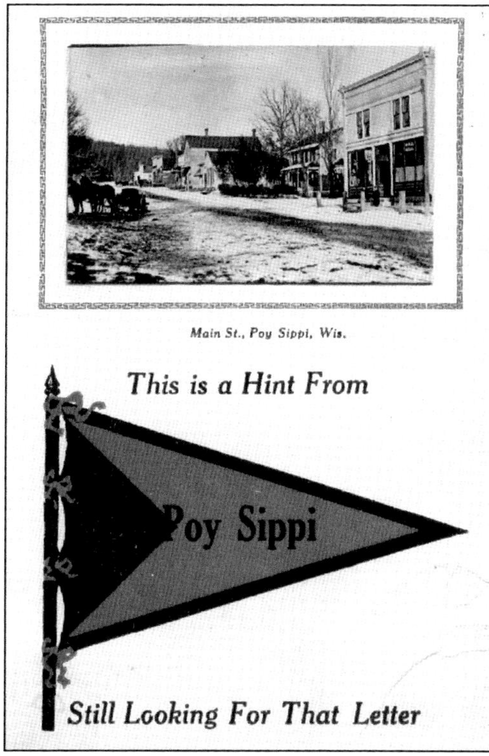


**POSTCARD WITH GAR HALL.** In another sample of a postcard from Poy Sippi, this view shows the east side of Main Street, with the GAR Hall as the building to the far right. Scenes that depicted GAR Halls were popular about 1910 and later.

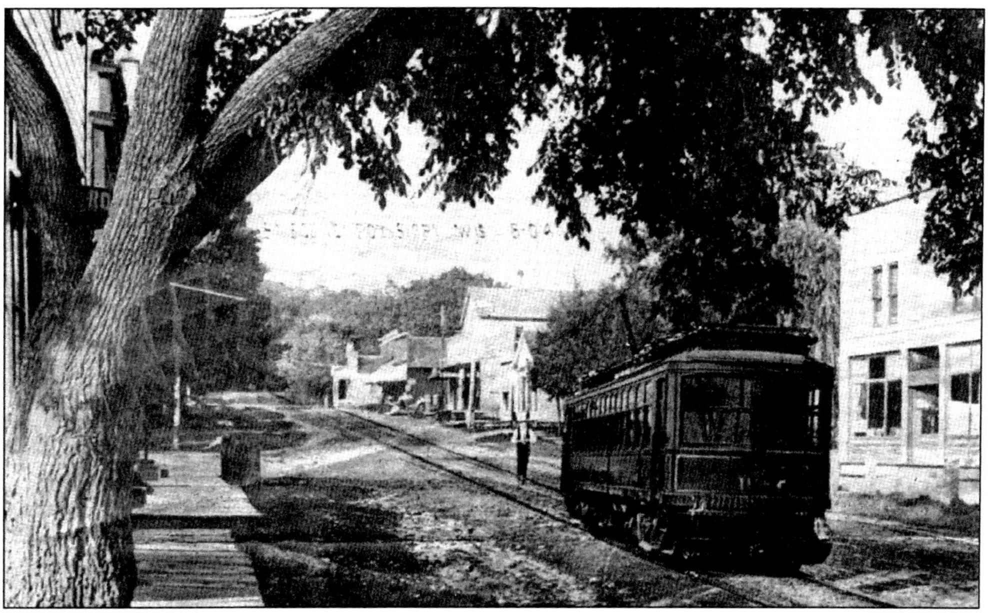

**TROLLEY CAR IN POY SIPPI.** Around 1910, several spoof postcards were made of small communities in the area. This one includes a trolley car incorporated into a photograph of Main Street. There never was a trolley car in town. There had been talk of a Northwest train rail coming to Poy Sippi and a depot being situated in town. That venture failed to materialize, leaving the townspeople sore, as they had invested thousands of dollars. People had also bought shares of the rail, along with tickets for the maiden journey, now worthless.

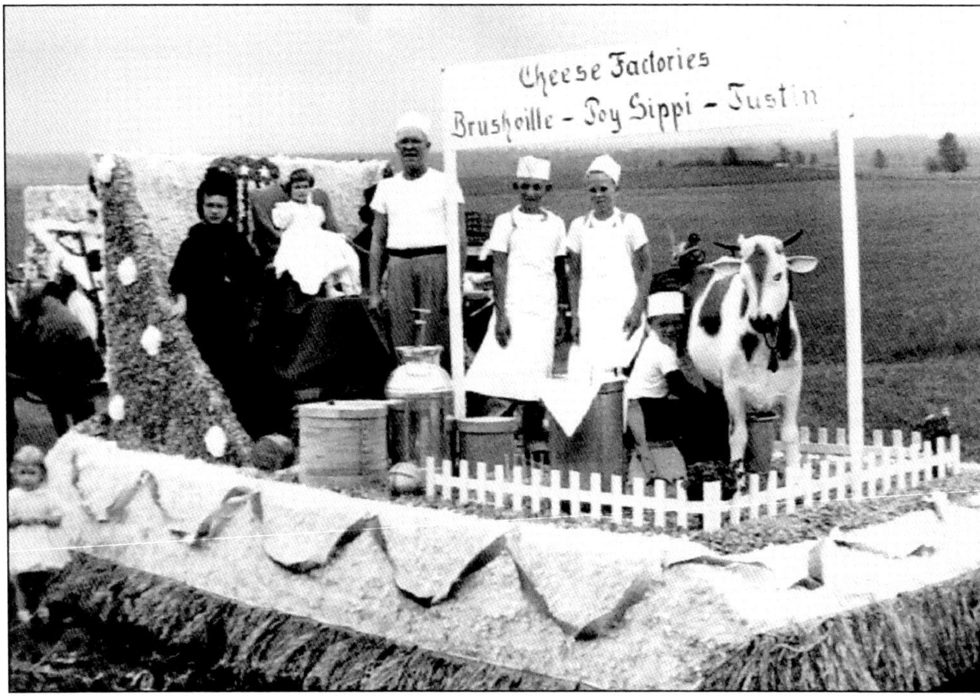


**CHEESE FACTORIES FLOAT.** The Brushville, Tustin, and Poy Sippi cheese makers got together for this float in the centennial parade of 1953. Everson and Sons, Alder Creek Cheese Company, and the Poy Sippi Dairy Cheese are represented here. Those pictured are, from left to right, Jane Everson (little girl standing next to float), one of the Lind girls, unidentified, Elmer Everson, Milford Robbert, Tom Everson, and John Olmstead (pretending to be milking the cow).

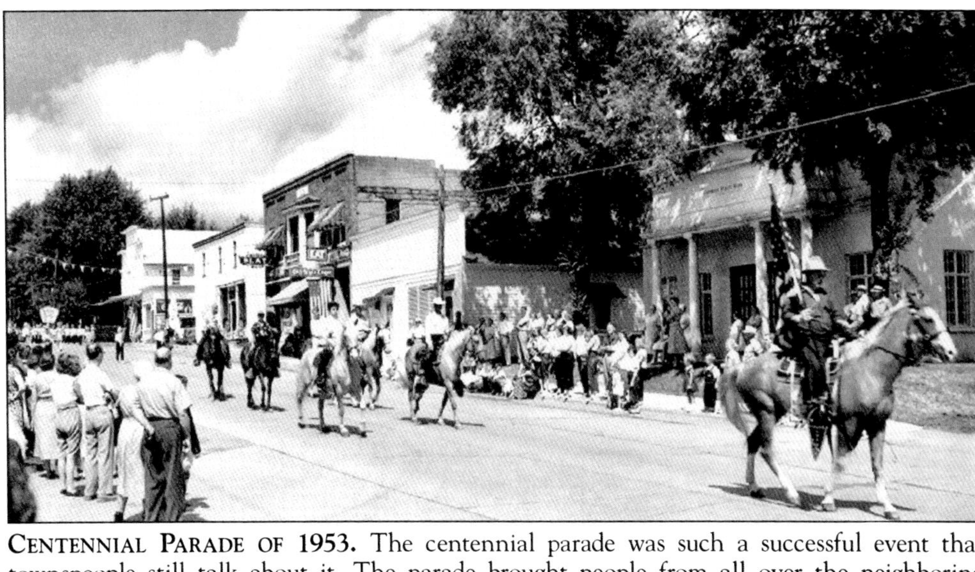

**CENTENNIAL PARADE OF 1953.** The centennial parade was such a successful event that townspeople still talk about it. The parade brought people from all over the neighboring communities. Even the rainstorm that came through later in the day could not dampen their spirits.

*Three*

# The People of Poy Sippi

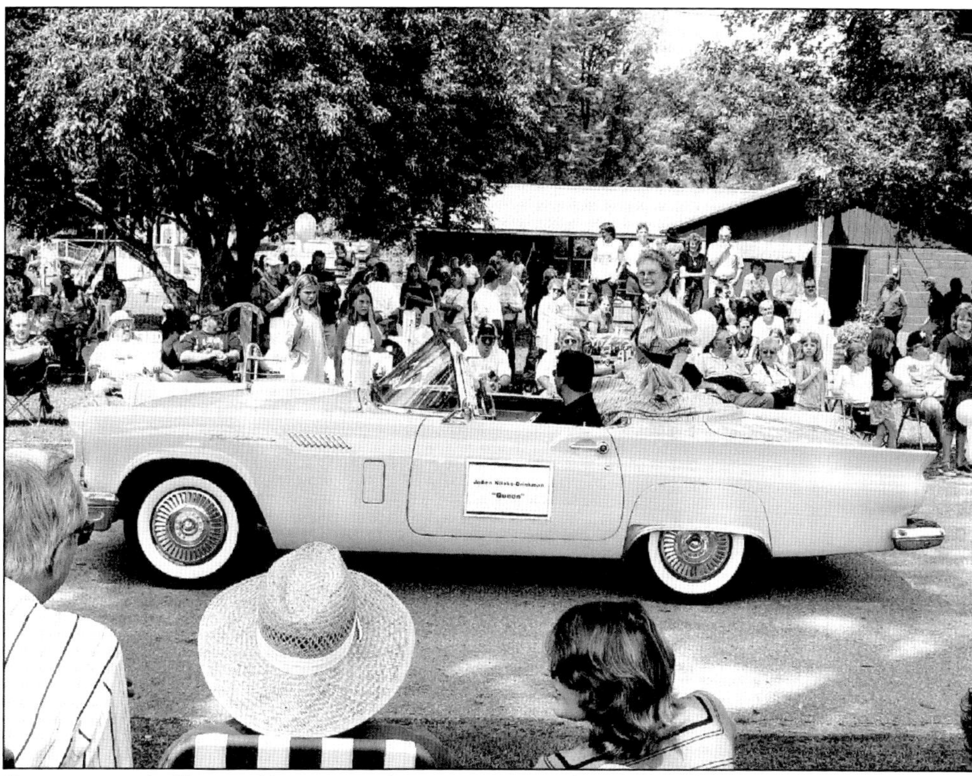

**Queen for 50 Years.** Every town has a queen. And Poy Sippi has Joanne Brinkman. She served as queen for the centennial celebration in 1953 and the sesquicentennial celebration in 2003. Here, she sits on a Ford Thunderbird in the 2003 parade.

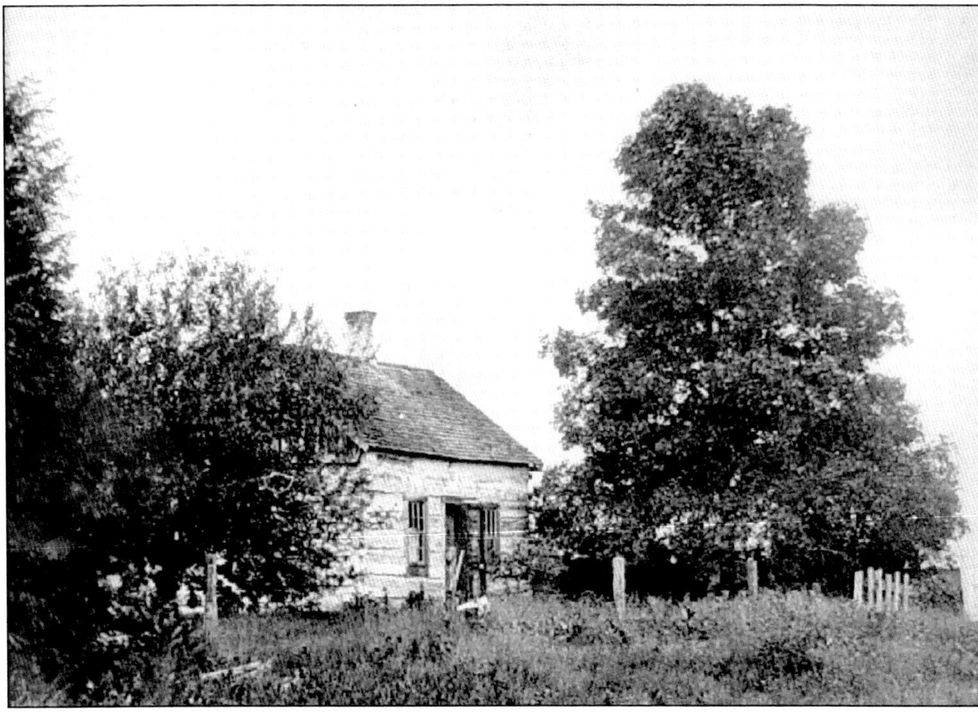

**Jensen Home.** This early-20th-century view depicts the Lars Jensen home, located just out of Poy Sippi. The building has since been remodeled with a second-floor addition.

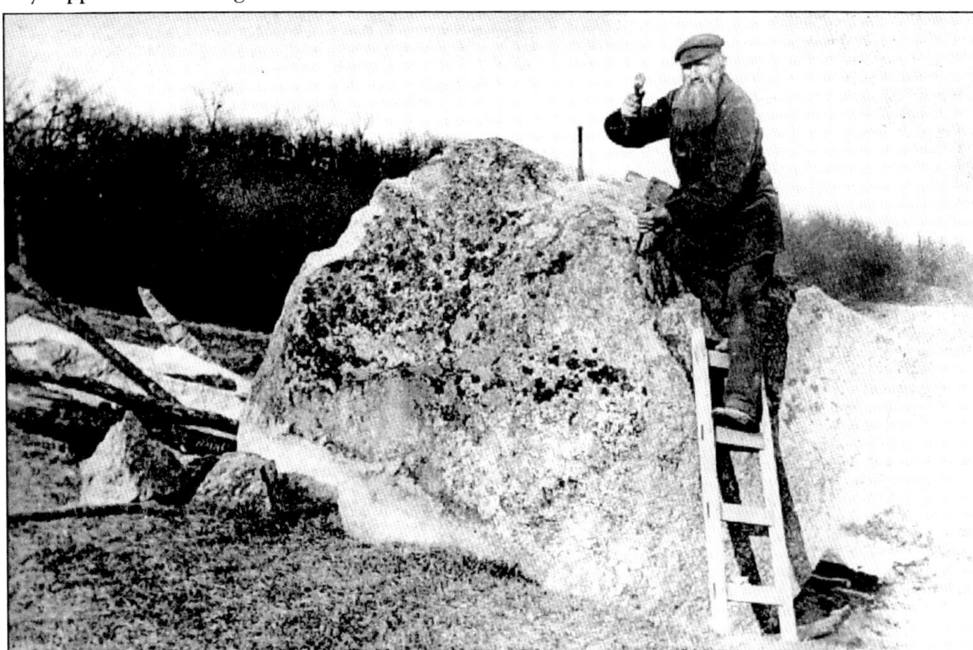

**Stone Cutter.** Hans Henningsen prepares to split the granite rock. He was well known for making granite markers, fence posts, and horse-hitching posts. Many of these are still visible around the countryside. Henningsen lived about a mile west of Poy Sippi.

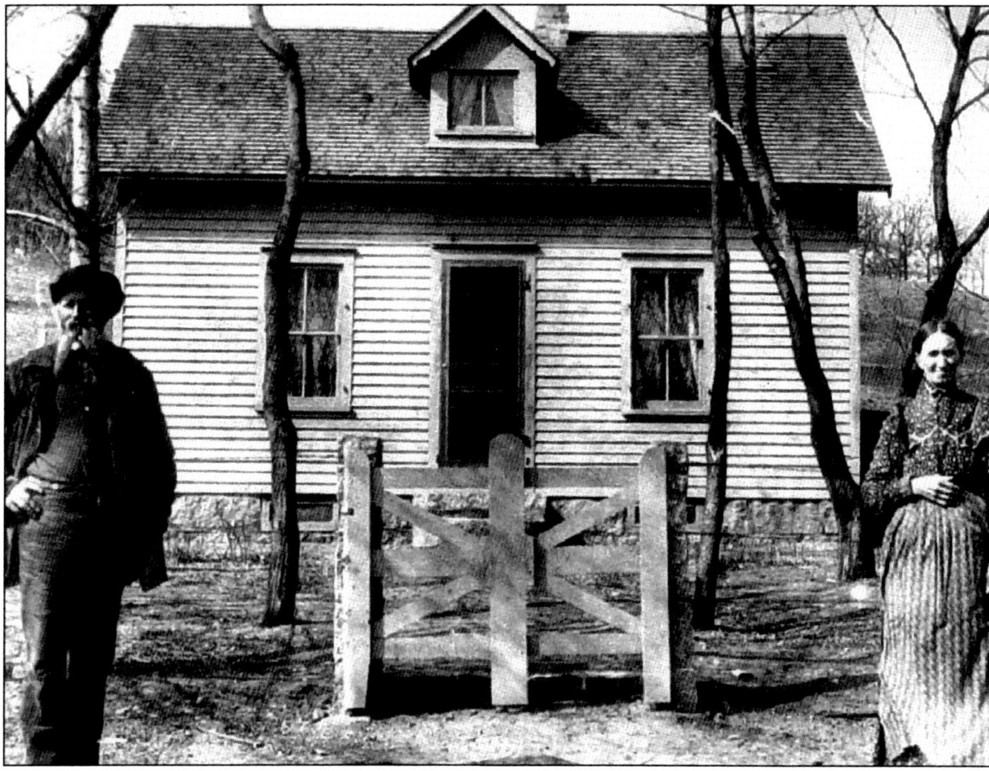

**HENNINGSEN HOUSE.** Hans Henningsen and his wife, Caroline, appear outside the gate to their home. Note the Henningsen-made granite fence posts on each side of the gate.

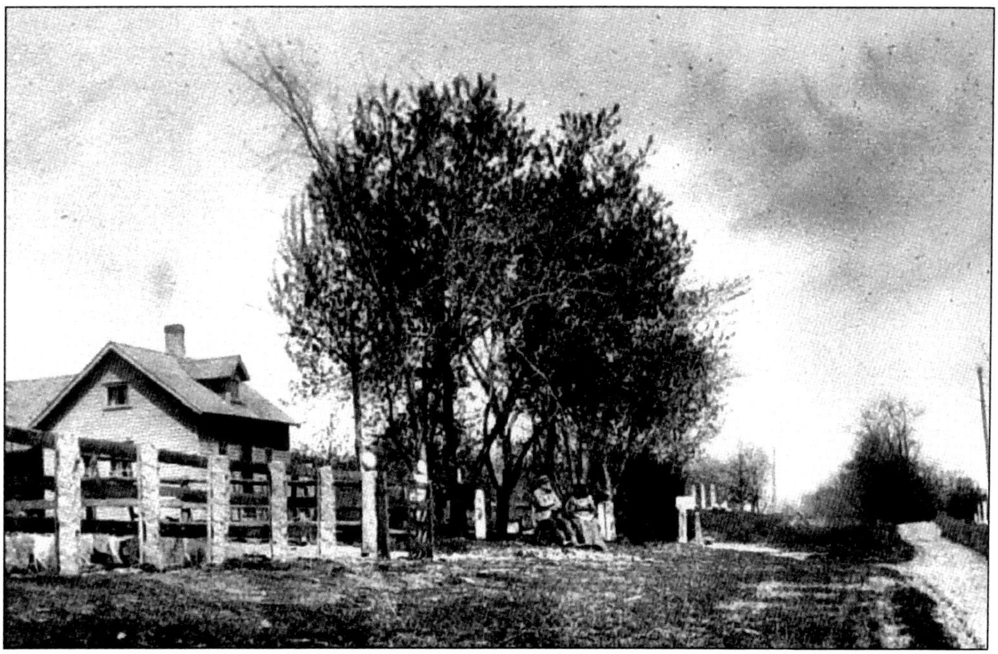

**HENNINGSEN'S HOUSE.** The Hans Henningsen home stood west of town on Badger Road. Here, Hans and Caroline sit for a photograph.

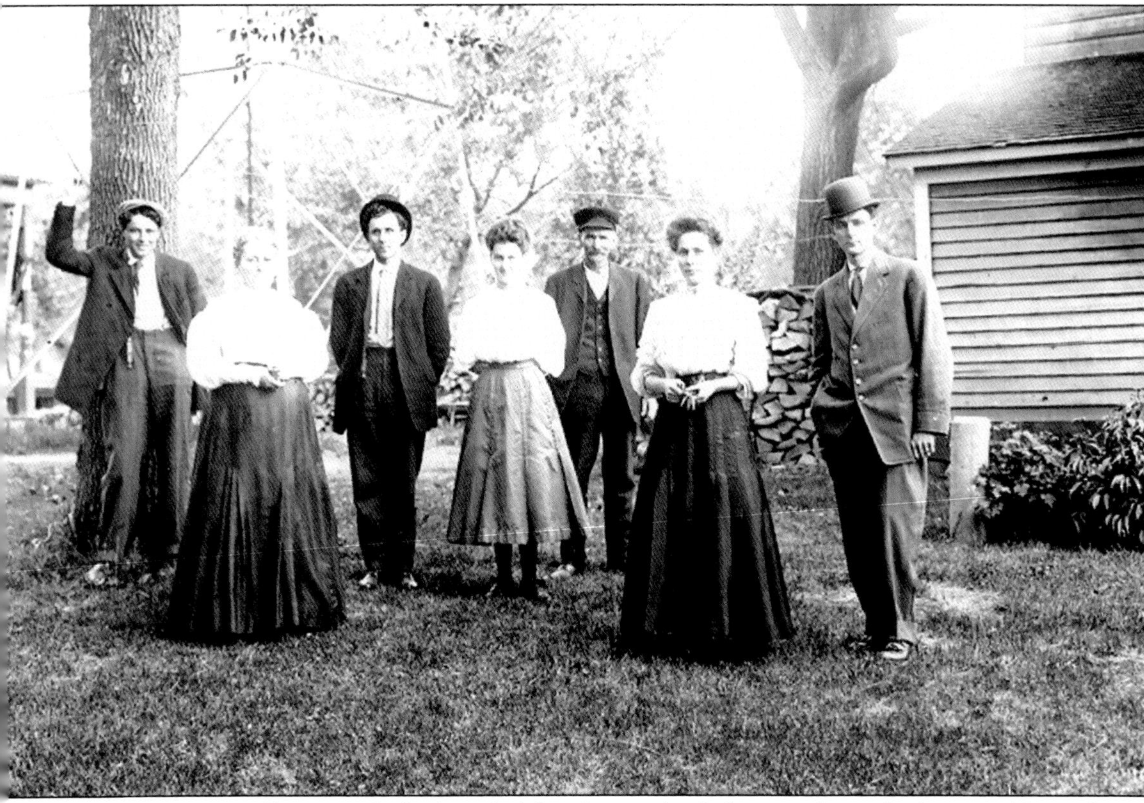

**COLT FAMILY.** Shown in the backyard of their home, the Colts were shirttail relations of Samuel Colt of pistol fame. From left to right are Chet, Amanda, Lyman, Bessie, Herb, Flavia, and Riley. Herb Colt was the owner of the gristmill. Riley Colt was one of the area's favorite musicians. He was also the grandson of Riley P. Colt, captain of Company H of the 18th Wisconsin Infantry during the Civil War. Riley P. was also one of the first store owners in Poy Sippi, opening the Colt General Store in 1850. He later became the postmaster and justice of the peace. Riley P.'s sword that he carried in the Civil War is still in the hands of one of the locals.

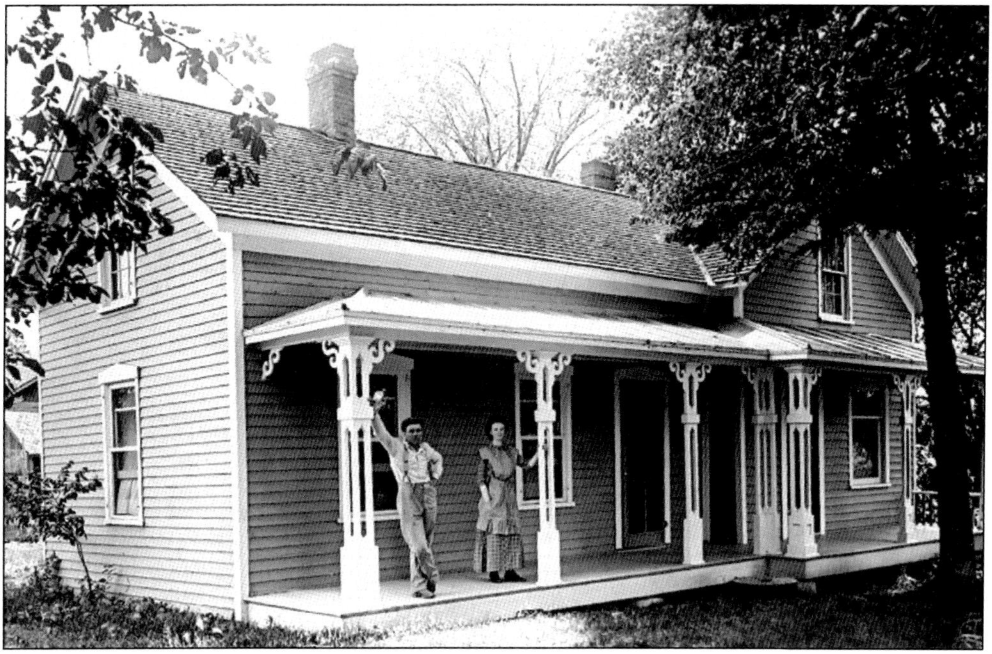

**COLT HOUSE.** Lyman and Bernice Colt are pictured here. Lyman was the son of Herb and the brother of piano player Riley Colt. Bernice Skinner Colt was a *Berlin Journal* correspondent from Poy Sippi. The home was located on the east side of Main Street near the river.

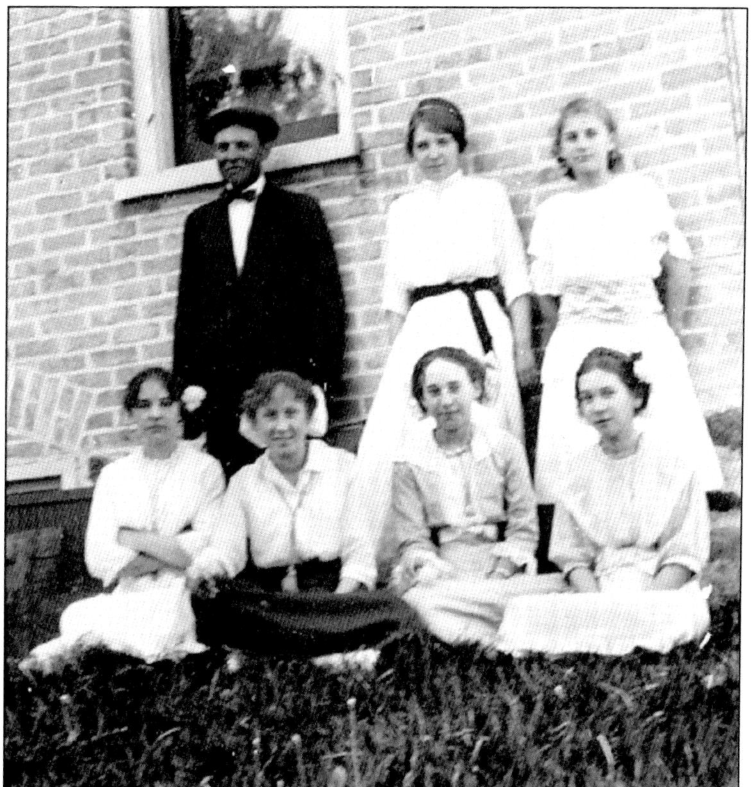

**SOME OF THE YOUNG PEOPLE.** Posing for a photograph, from left to right, are (first row) Della Zabel Kopityke, Lona Zabel Zemple, Genivieve Campfield Mehr, and Lottie Gleffe Birkholtz; (second row) Louis Wendt, Irma Wendt Zabel, and Ruth Blaisdell Boyson.

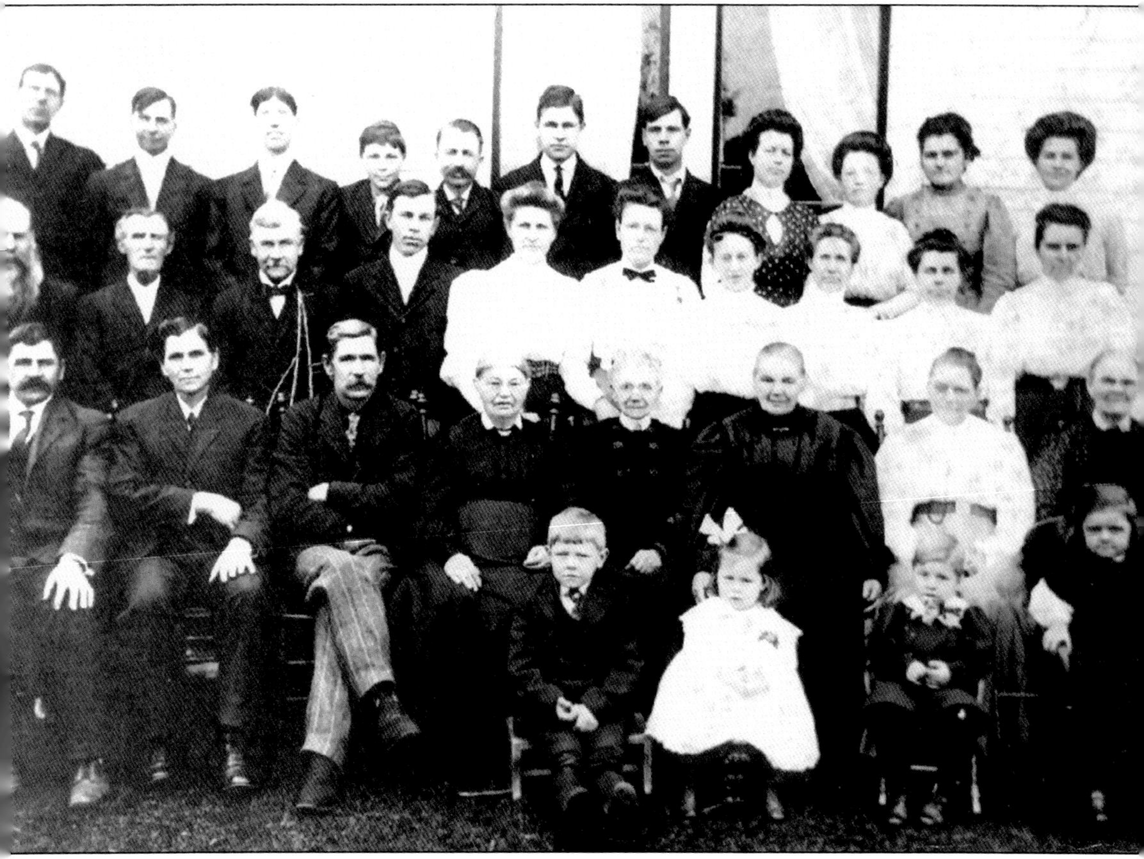

**REUNION PHOTOGRAPH.** In this photograph are some of the descendants of the early families of Poy Sippi. Pictured here, from left to right, are the following: (first row) Clarence and Helen Grambsch, Harold Strehlow, and Mabel Tuma; (second row) Herman Grambsch, Otto Grambsch, Gust Grambsch, Augusta Culver, Ann Wendt, Louise Pohl, Pauline Lindekugel, and Mrs. Rates; (third row) Mr. Rates, William Wendt Sr., William Lindekugel, Frank Lindekugel, Minnie (Mrs. Herman) Grambsch, Amelia Wendt, Amelia Lindekugel, Emma Byholdt, Lydia Strehlow, and Nettie Buettner; (fourth row) George Wendt, Herman Lindekugel, Will Wendt, Alvin Grambsch, Henry Strehlow, Rhinold Grambsch, Ed Lindekugel, Mabel Stumpner, Anna Rickert, Iva Wendt, and Etta Tuma.

**GRANT BOYSON FOR CLERK.** This card promotes Grant Boyson for Waushara County clerk; he won the election.

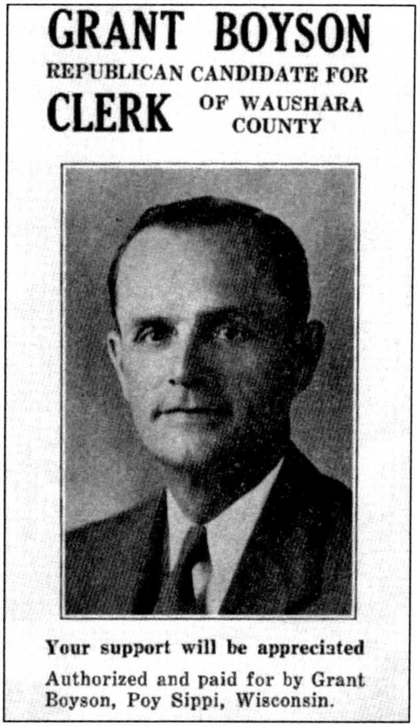


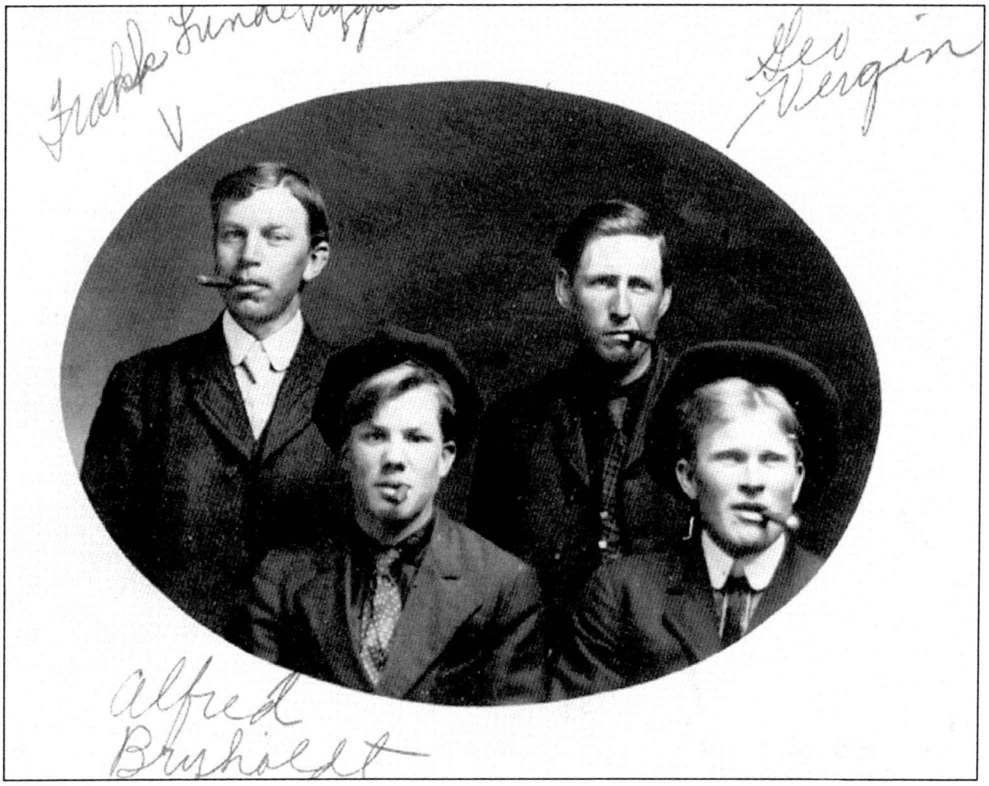


**FOUR MEN.** Posing here, from left to right, are Frank Lindekugal, Alfred Bryholdt, George Vergin, and unidentified.

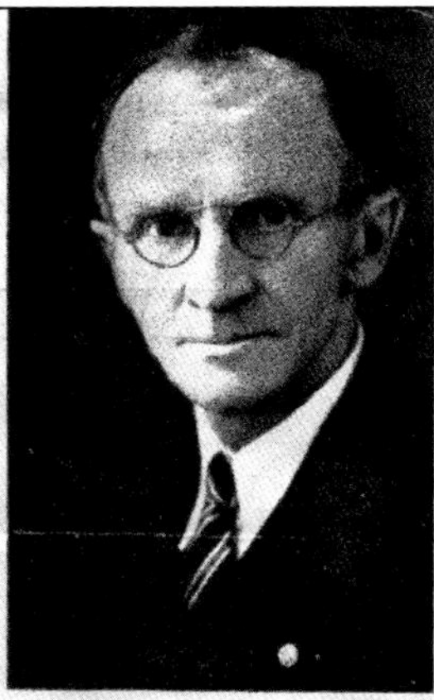

**Arthur Roegner, Director**

Mr. Arthur Roegner has been a stockholder of the Farmers State Bank for the past five years, and has been a director for more than three years.

Mr. Roegner is widely known through his connection with and operation of the Daisy Dairy factory during the past eight years.

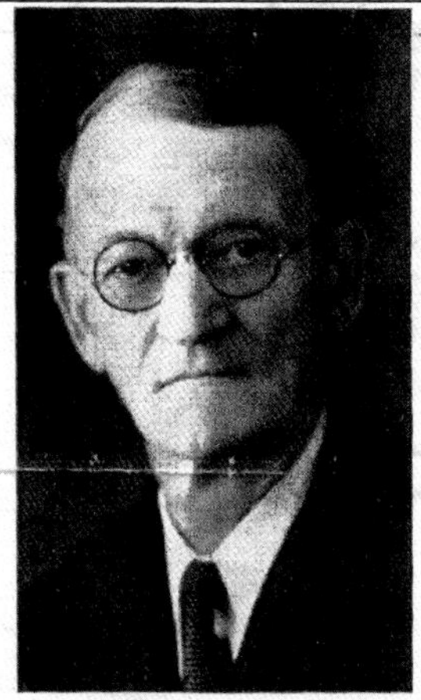

**W. H. PAULSON, Director**

Mr. W. H. Paulson, a resident of this vicinity practically all his life and for 40 years identified with the Paulson Grist Mill and Sawmill in which connection a great many people know him, has been a stockholder of the Farmers State Bank since its organization in 1915, and has been a director of the bank for more than five years.

Mr. Paulson has the distinction of being our oldest director, having passed the three-quarter century mark with a margin of three years.

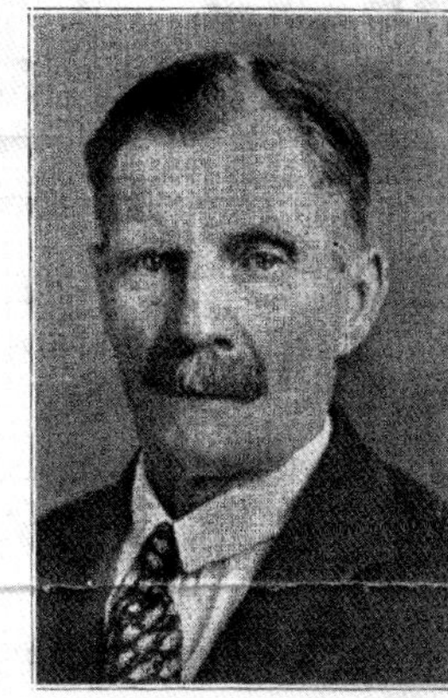

**FRANK BLAISDELL**

Mr. Frank Blaisdell has been a stockholder of this bank since its organization, has been a director for more than eight years, and vice president for the past five years.

Mr. Blaisdell is also president of the Poy Sippi Telephone Company, having served in that capacity for many years.

THREE BUSINESSMEN. These photographs, taken from the 1933 and 1934 *Farmers State Bank Booklets*, show three area businessmen. The man on the left is Arthur Roegner, owner of the Daisy Dairy. In the center is W. H. Paulson (likely Walter Hans), owner of the gristmill and sawmill. On the right is Frank Blaisdell, owner of the Poy Sippi Telephone Company.

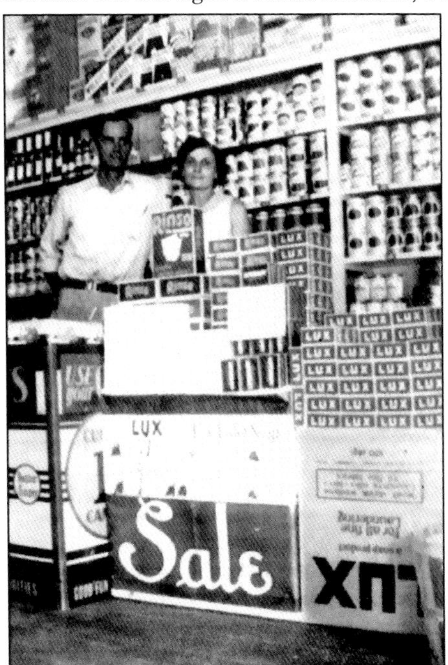


BOYSON STORE IN POY SIPPI. Grant and Ruth Boyson are pictured inside the Boyson Store before it burned down in 1931. From the looks of it, there was quite a sale on Lux soap.

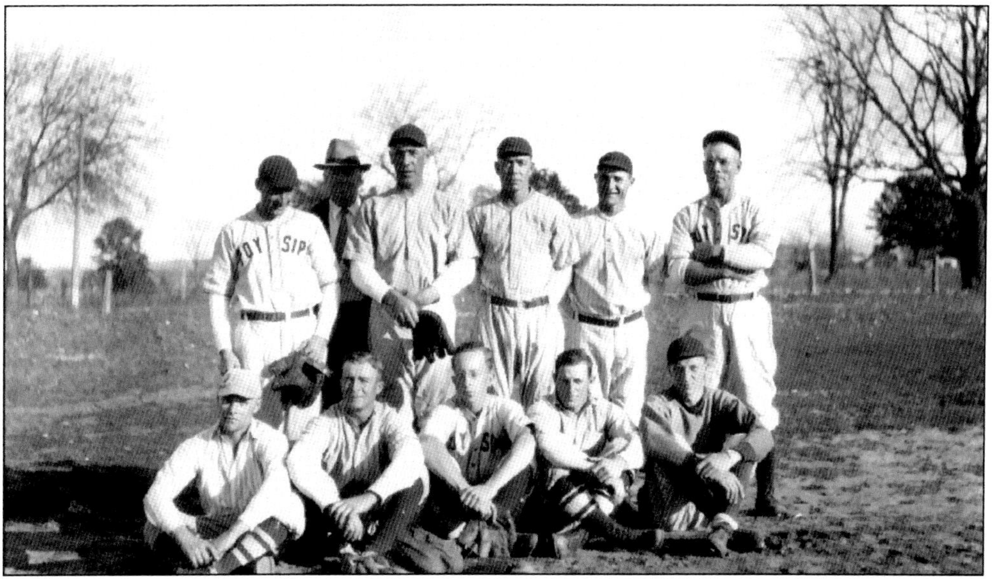


**POY SIPPI BASEBALL TEAM.** These two photographs depict the Poy Sippi baseball team in the late 1920s.

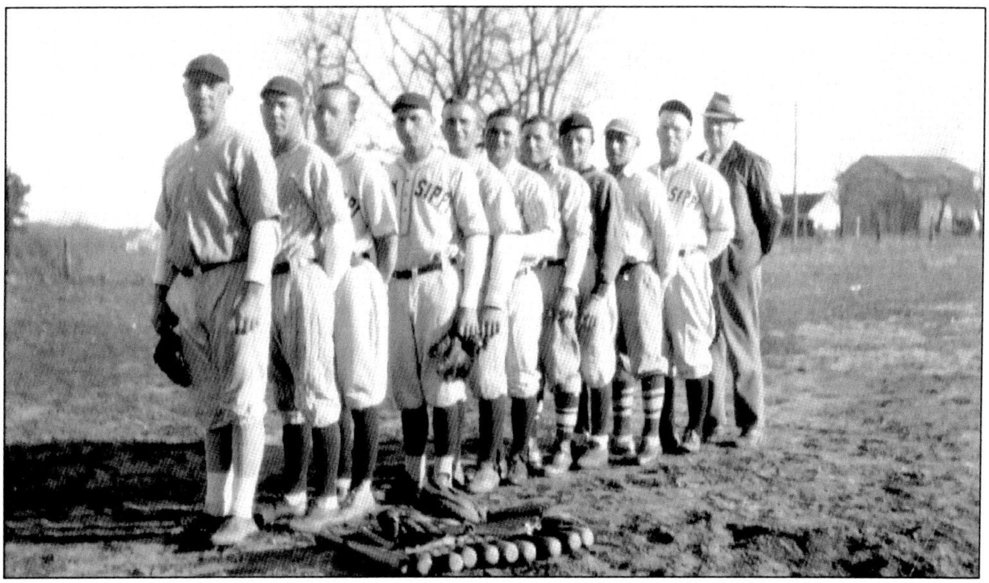

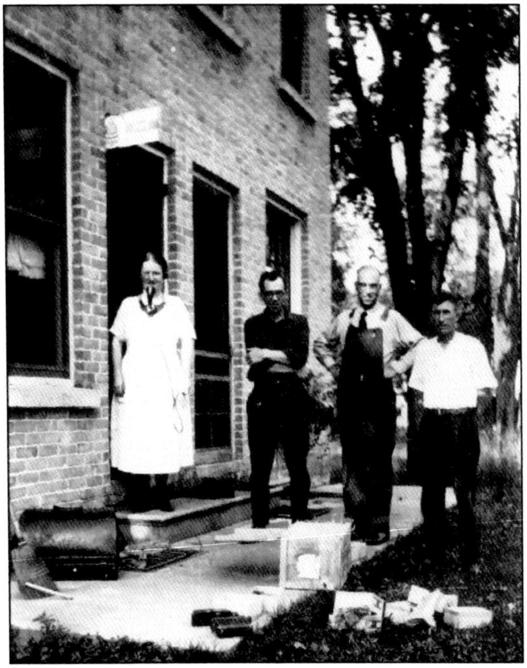

**POY SIPPI TELEPHONE COMPANY.** The Poy Sippi Telephone Company operated in a yellow brick building just west of the Liberty Street and Main Street intersection. Shown here are, from left to right, Elsie Baldmine, Jim Peterson, and two unidentified workers. Cicely Blaisdell began working at the phone company when she was just 14 years old and stayed on for 37 years, during which time she received the death notifications from World War I. She also received all the birth and death calls for three generations. The telephone company was once located above the hardware store. It was later sold to George Dobbins.

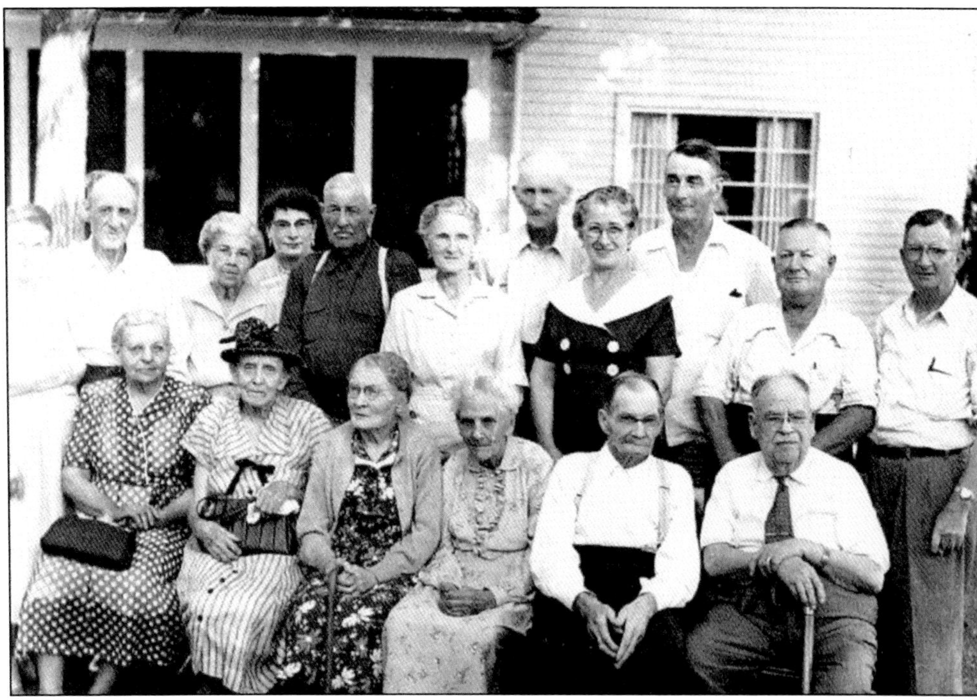

**CENTENNIAL PHOTOGRAPH FROM 1953.** This photograph shows some of the descendants of the town's pioneers. Pictured here, from left to right, are the following: (first row) Lattie Morrow, Jessie Dodd, Edith Blaisdell Skinner, Belle and Frank Blaisdell, and Frank Briggs; (second row) Mr. and Mrs. Albie Culver, Luta Blaisdell, Cicely Blaisdell Kissinger, Louie Stratton, Clavia Culver Winge, William Winge, Frances Culver, W. M. Bens of St. Paul, Minnesota, George Campfield, and Cliff Montgomery.

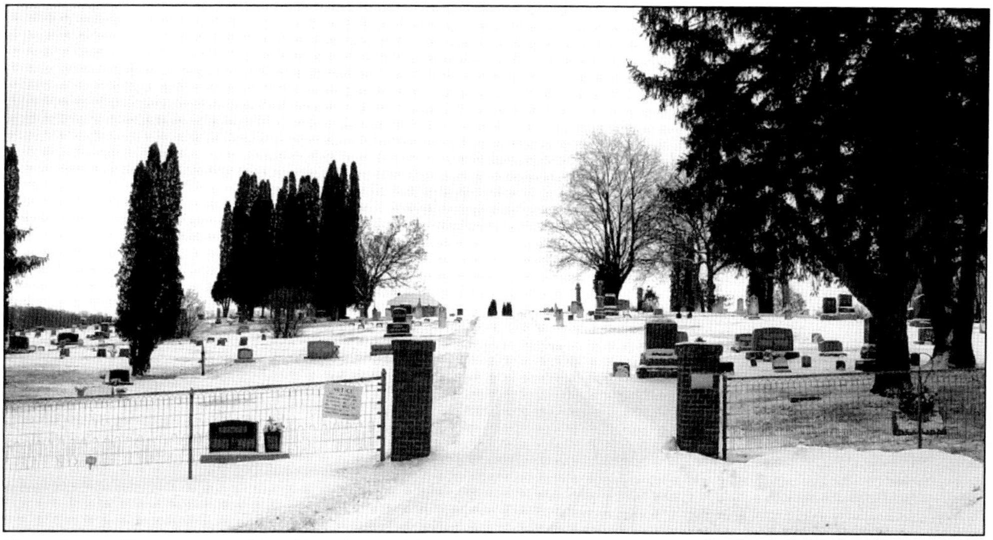

**POY SIPPI CEMETERY.** The Poy Sippi Cemetery is the interment place of many of the town's settlers. The cemetery holds many Civil War veterans' graves, as well as many of the early businesspeople who gave Poy Sippi its start. Located south of town on County Trunk SS, it is about two miles from Main Street. On Memorial Day, known as Decoration Day years ago, citizens marched in a parade from town to the cemetery to decorate the graves of its soldiers. This tradition started in 1866 and continued for many years.

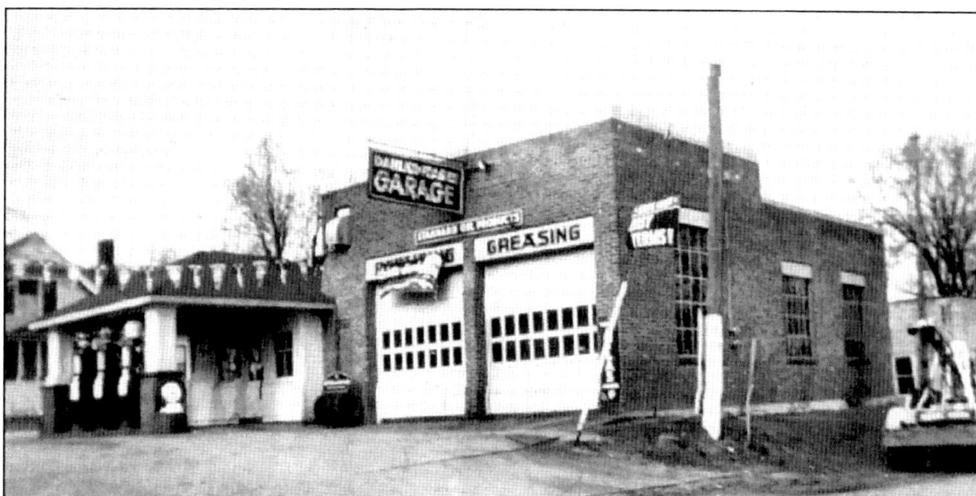


**GARAGE.** The garage on the northeast corner of Commercial and Main Streets is still in business. Although it has changed hands, the garage part of the building is much the same. The gas station portion has been removed, and a new office and waiting room have been added. There are no longer any gas pumps.

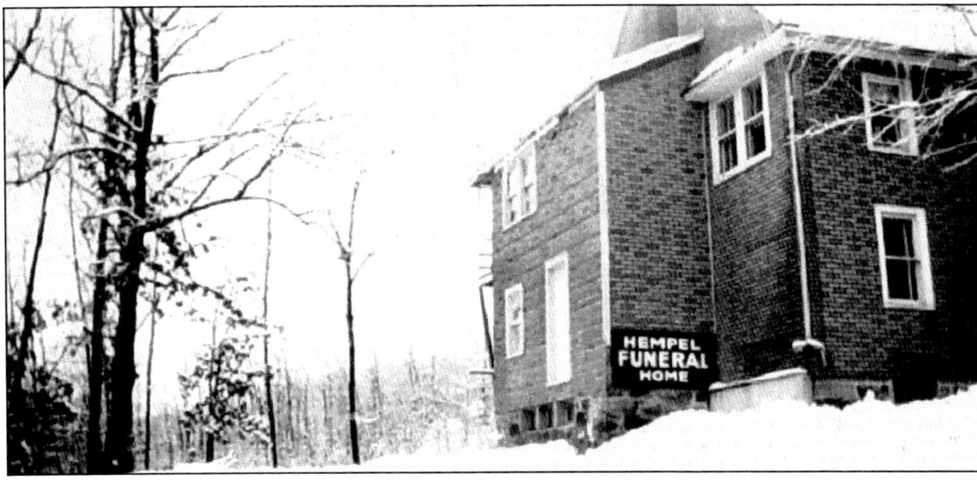


**HEMPEL FUNERAL HOME.** In the 1940s, this funeral home stood on the hill overlooking the town from the north. It was located in the building once known as the Evangelist Lutheran Church until Raymond Hempel bought the church for his business. The structure included upstairs apartments in addition to the first-floor funeral home. It later became the site for a new church.

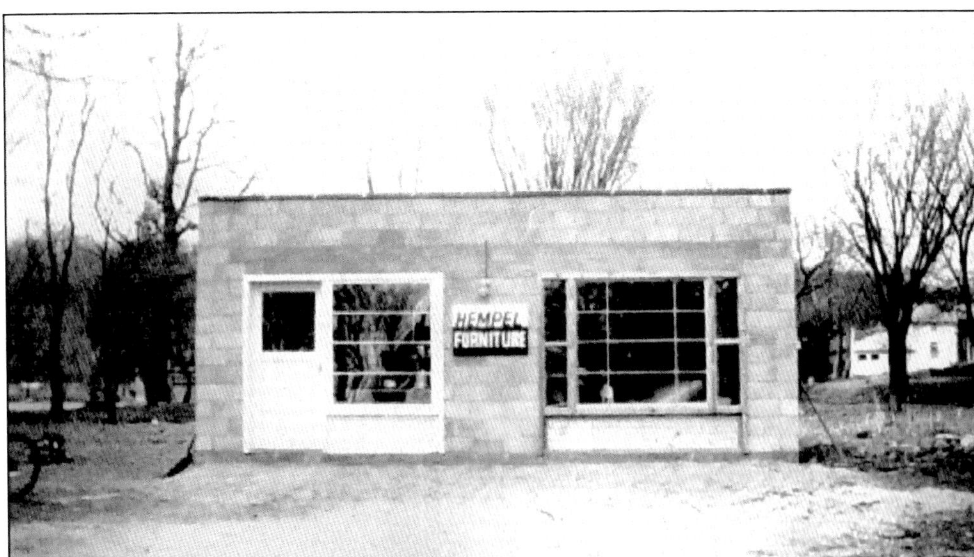


**HEMPEL FURNITURE STORE.** This block building was built in the early 1950s by Raymond Hempel, who used it as a furniture store and later as a combined furniture store and funeral home. He moved his funeral business from the building on the hill to this new building. It was eventually sold to the Holly Funeral Home, which is still in business there.

# *Four*

# THE CHURCHES AND SCHOOLS OF POY SIPPI

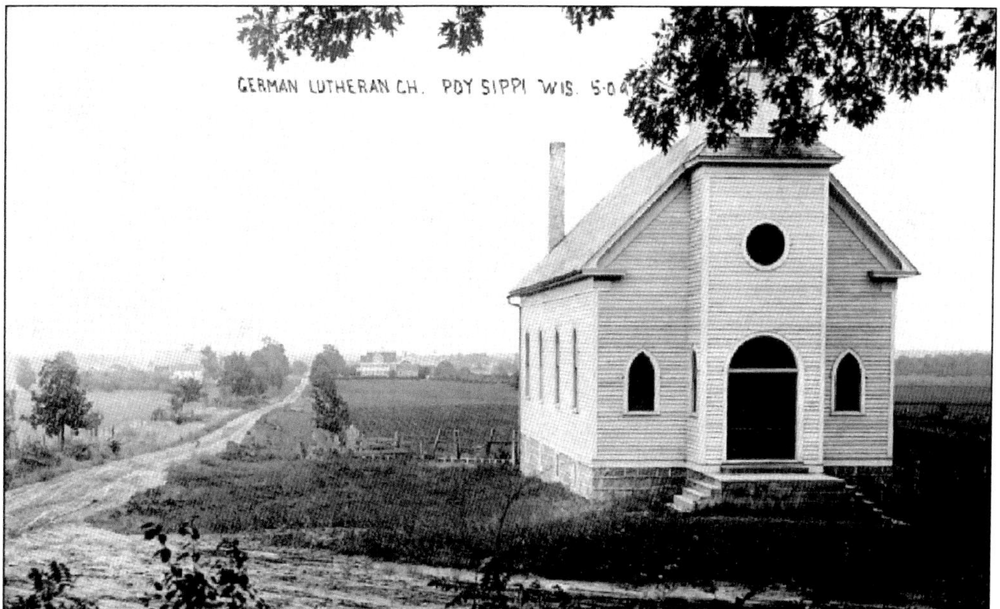


**GERMAN LUTHERAN CHURCH.** Built on the north hill overlooking Poy Sippi, this church was finished by the fall of 1899. It has since been replaced with another church. In all, there were seven churches in town. This view also shows the road to Tustin and the countryside east of Poy Sippi.

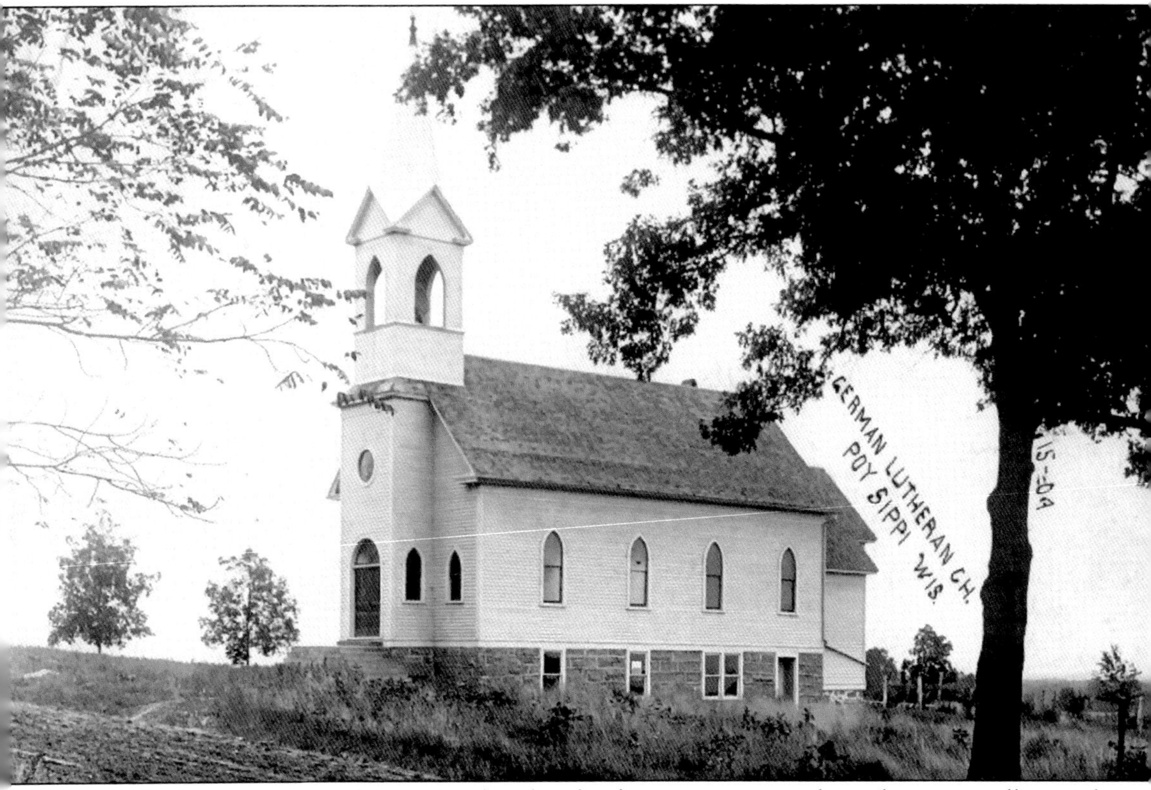


**GERMAN LUTHERAN CHURCH.** The church, shown as new in this side view, really stood out against the countryside. The congregation formed in 1897, and the church was built by Allie Hutton. Many people, as they passed through Poy Sippi, remembered the old structure as a landmark.

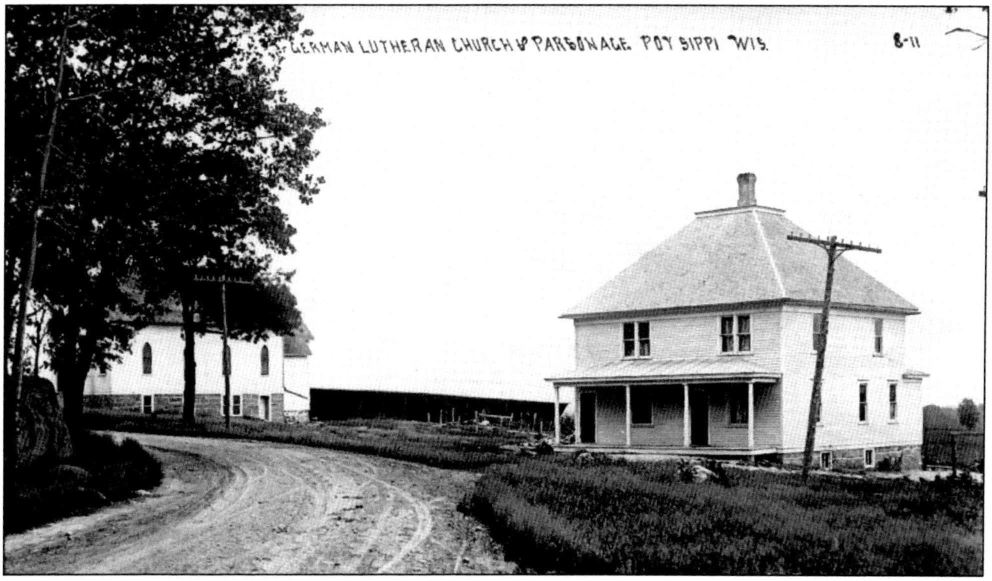


**CHURCH AND PARSONAGE.** The church in the background is the same as the one shown in the previous two views. This time, however, the parsonage is seen to the south of the church. Built by Allie Hutton in 1910, the parsonage still stands, but the road has been built up about 15 feet in front of it.

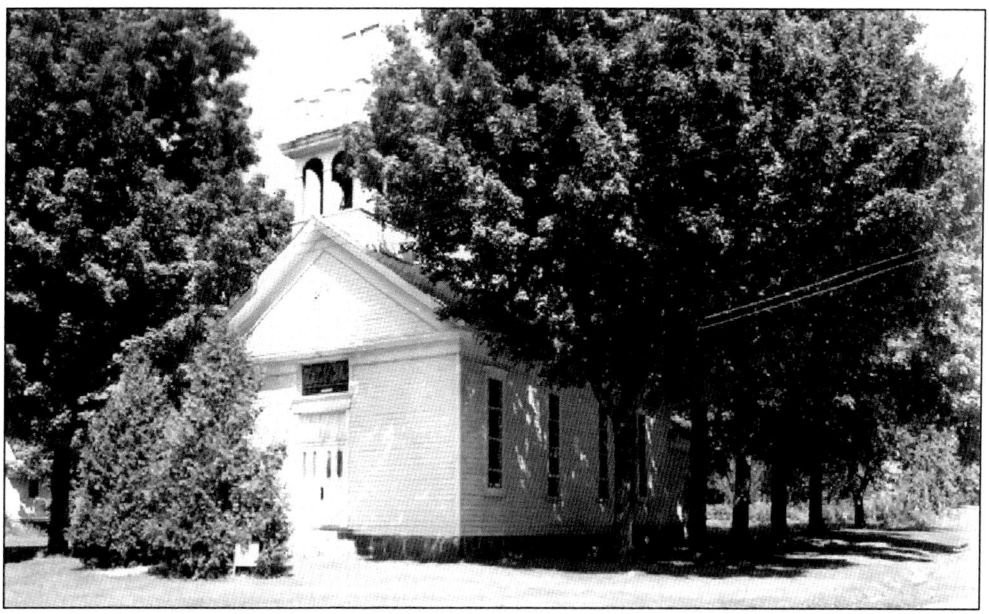

**CATHOLIC CHURCH OF POY SIPPI.** In May 1920, Fr. Roland Ahearn asked for permission to start a Catholic church in Poy Sippi. After four Sundays of masses held in June, attendees decided to have a parish called the Scared Heart Parish. The new members immediately began to pledge money for the purchase of the Congregationalist church building.

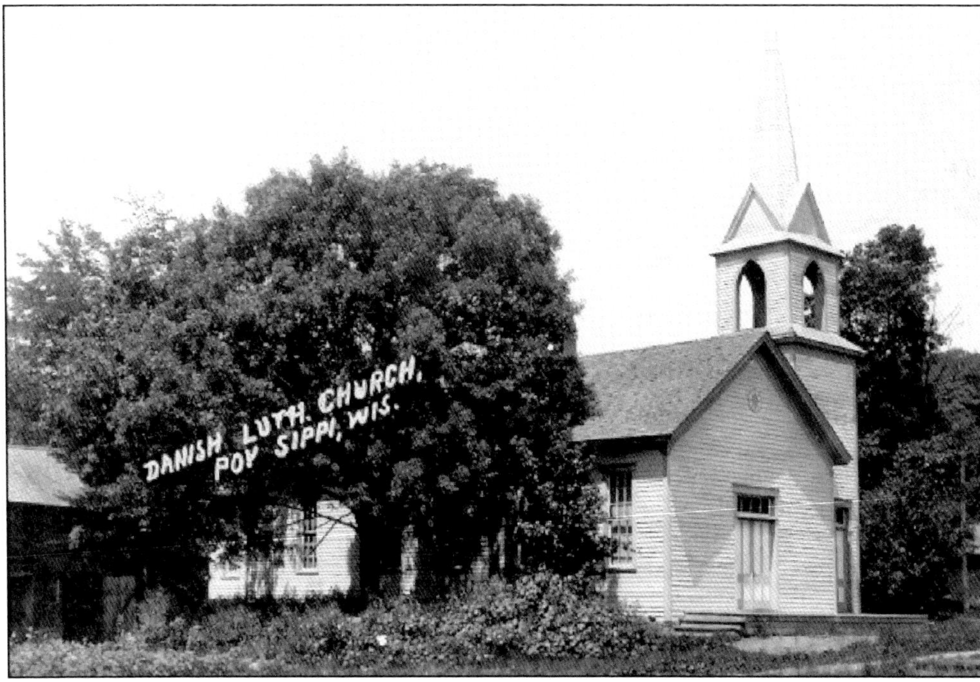


**DANISH LUTHERAN CHURCH.** With the town's many ethnic backgrounds came many different churches. The Danes had their own Lutheran church, and the Germans had theirs. This congregation started in 1875.

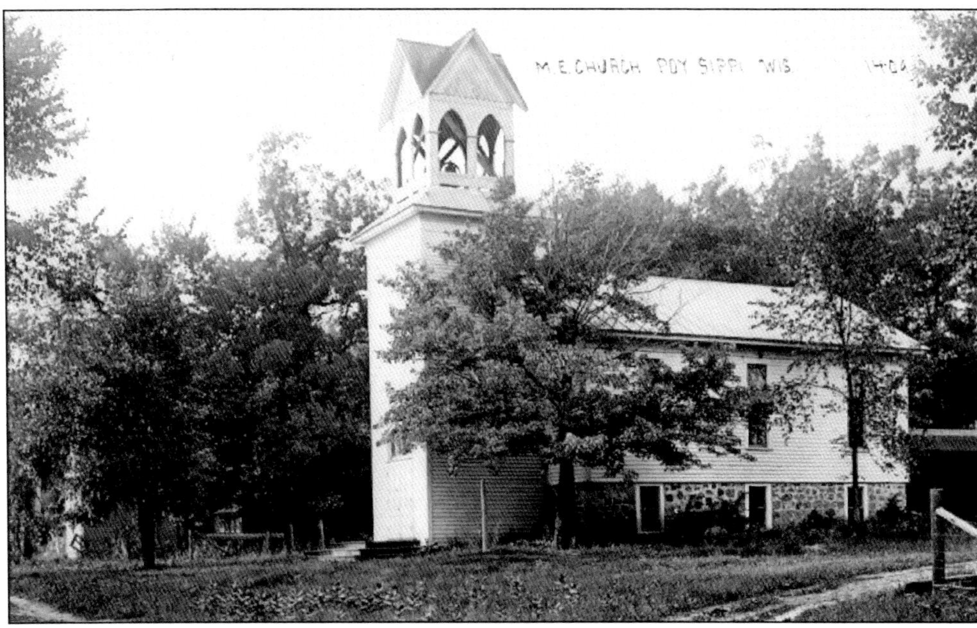


**METHODIST EPISCOPAL CHURCH.** The Methodist church was built around 1878. The congregation had previously shared a church but decided to build its own. During a depression that some say was worse than the crash of 1929, money was hard to come by. George Hawley offered to have the logs cut at his mill. The basement was then dug out by hand, the basement walls built, and the church erected.

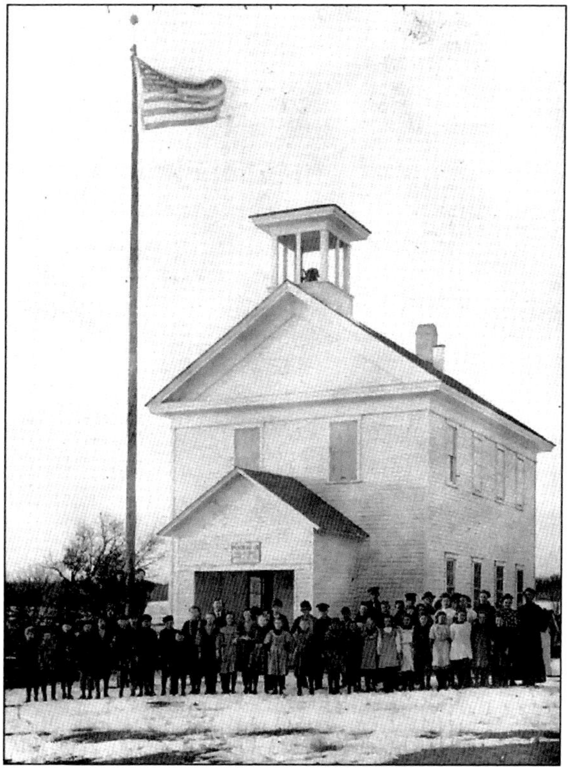

**PUBLIC SCHOOL OF POY SIPPI.** Children are lined up for a photograph in front of the Poy Sippi School. This school served grades one through ten and was located on County Trunk H. Built in 1854, it was used until the brick schoolhouse was built in 1921.

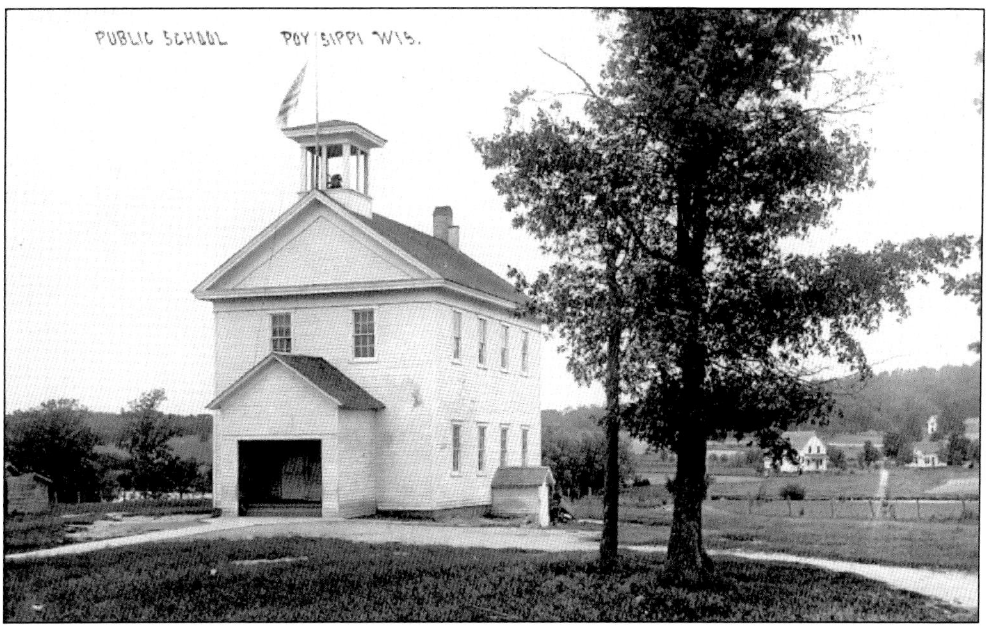


**POY SIPPI PUBLIC SCHOOL.** The old school along the Pine River is shown amongst the openness of the town's west side about 1908. The area behind the school remains fairly similar today, except for a few more homes and a park. This was actually the second school in Poy Sippi. The first held classes in a shanty during the early years. The school hand ringer, used by the teacher to get the attention of the children, still belongs to a family in town.

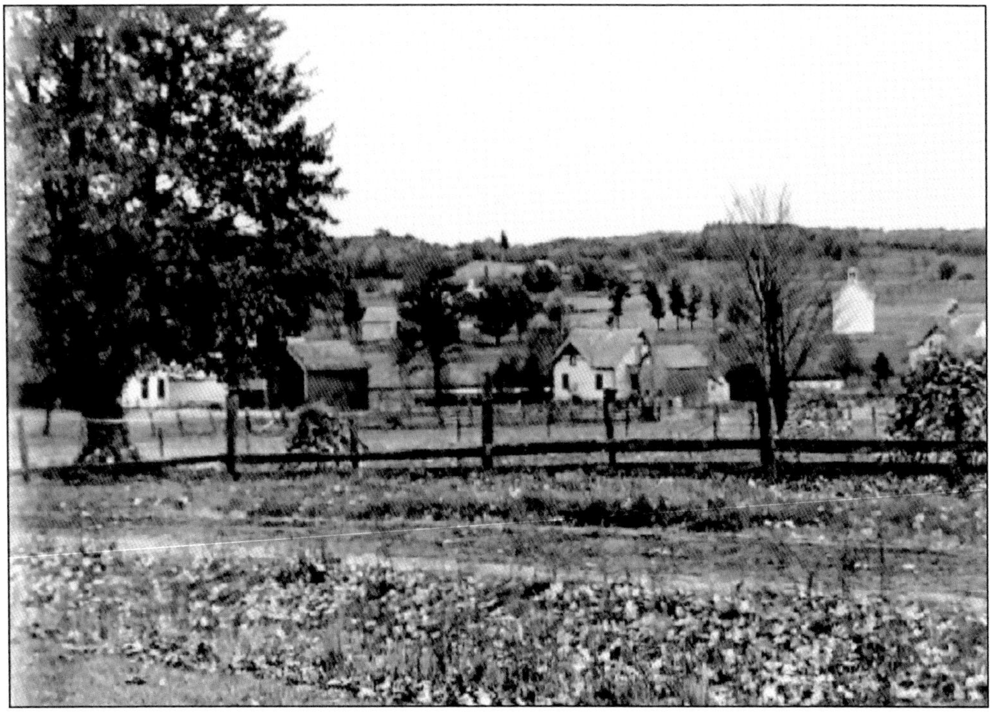

**Overlooking Pine River at School.** The Pine River can barely be seen running through the center of the photograph. The large white building to the right is the back side of the Poy Sippi Schoolhouse. In the foreground is the countryside just west of Main Street.

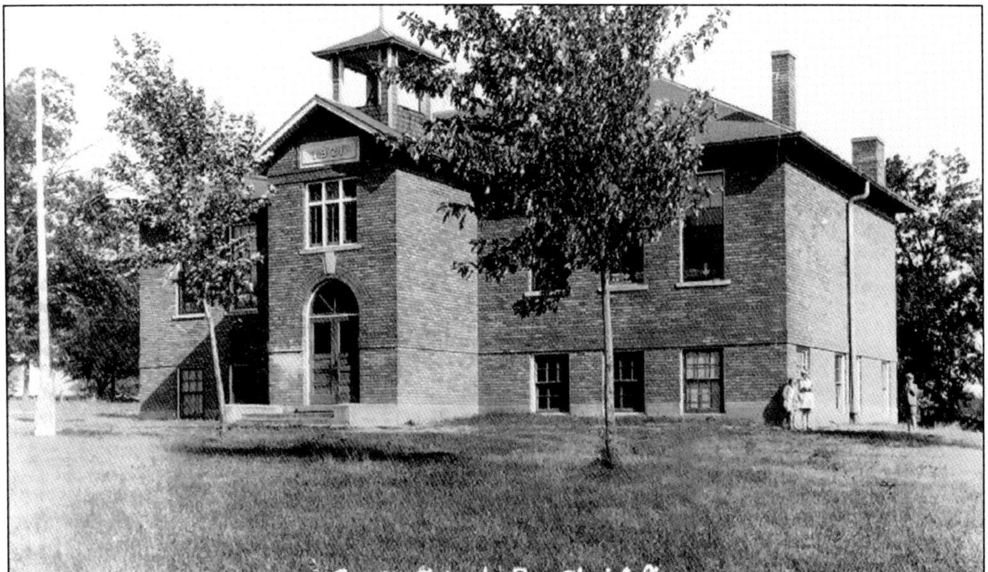


**Poy Sippi Grade School.** This structure was the third grade school built in Poy Sippi throughout the years. Constructed in 1921, the school served grades one through four on the north side and five through eight on the south side. The gymnasium, restrooms, and stage were located in the basement. The building has since been torn down, and the Poy Sippi Library stands in its place.

*Five*

# THE MILITARY IN POY SIPPI

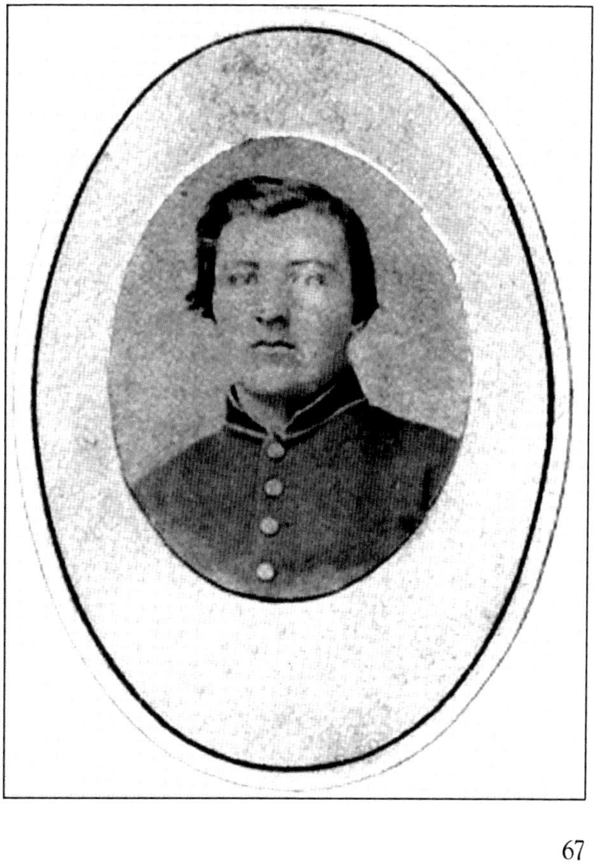

**DANIEL WIGGIN CATE.** A resident of Auroraville, Daniel Wiggin Cate enlisted in the 30th Wisconsin Volunteers, Company H, when he was 19 years old. The 30th was involved with the Great Sioux Massacres in Minnesota during the Civil War. Using the Native Americans as a diversion, the Confederates forced the Union to fight on another front, thereby taking pressure off the East. The 30th Wisconsin was instrumental in rounding up the rebel Sioux. Cate survived the war and finished out his life in Auroraville, where he was a member of the Good Templars and the Grange and the secretary-treasurer of the cheese factory. He farmed profitably for 28 years. Cate is buried in the Pine Grove Cemetery in Auroraville. Descendants of the Cates, credited as early settlers, still live in Auroraville.

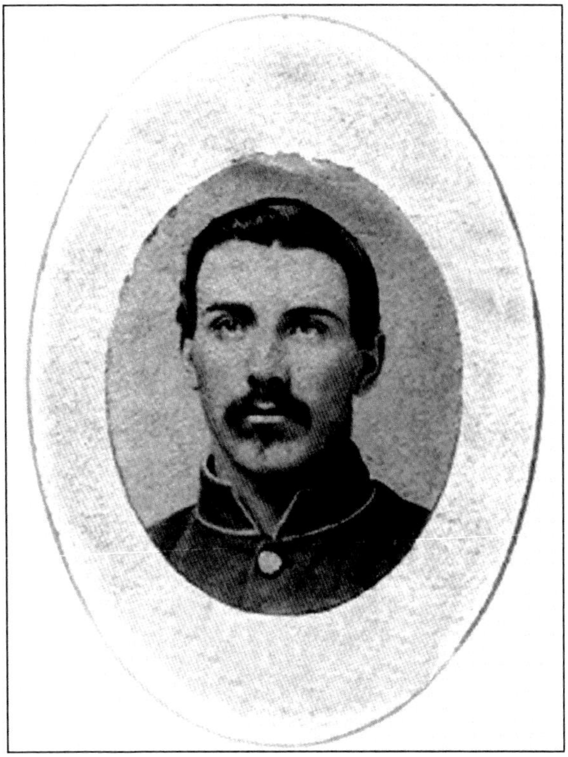

**SYLVESTER SHUMWAY.** The son of Joel and Margaret Shumway, Sylvester was with the 30th Wisconsin, Company H, as well. The family eventually owned a whole section north of Auroraville. Sylvester survived the war and is buried in the Poy Sippi Cemetery.

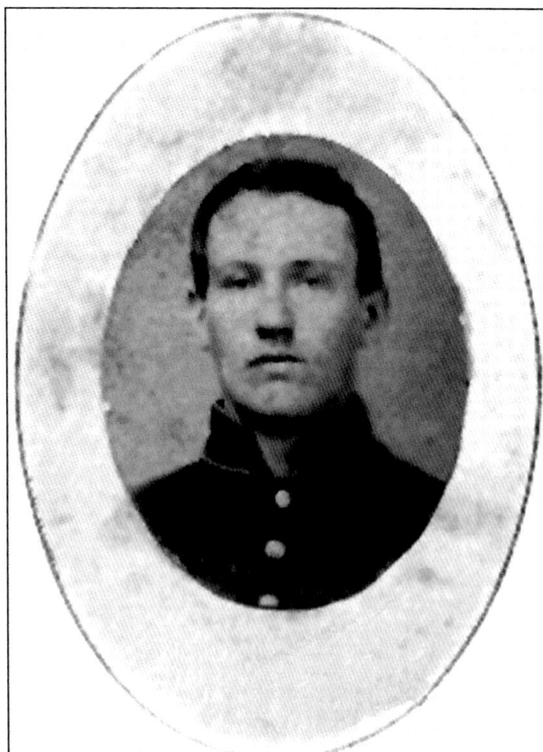

**THOMAS MOON.** Thomas Moon enlisted in the 30th Wisconsin, Company H, from the small town of Mount Morris, west of Auroraville. He survived the war.

**WILLIAM MATHEWS.** Another member of the 30th Wisconsin, Company H, William Mathews was from the town of Leon and served as a wagoner for the unit. He was discharged because of a disability on March 27, 1865, and is buried in the Poy Sippi Cemetery. Other Mathews family members who fought in the 30th were James, a private, and Nathan, who served as a corporal. Joseph Mathews was commissioned a second lieutenant and later turned down the rank of first lieutenant.

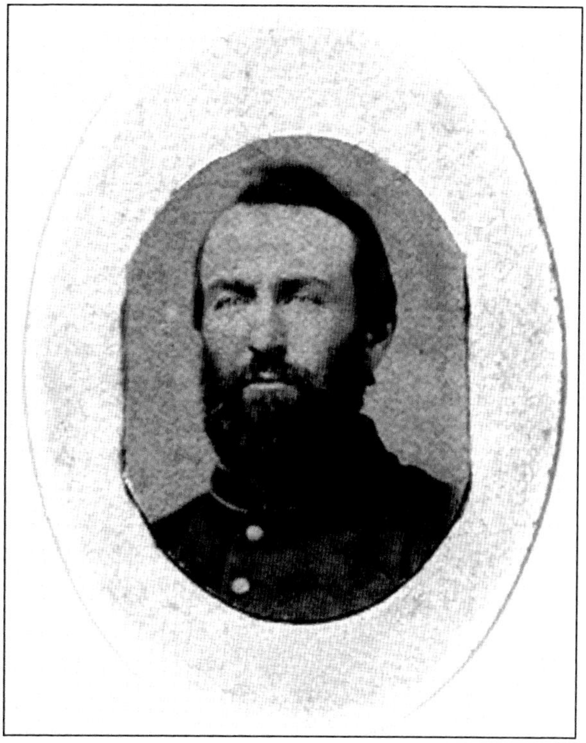

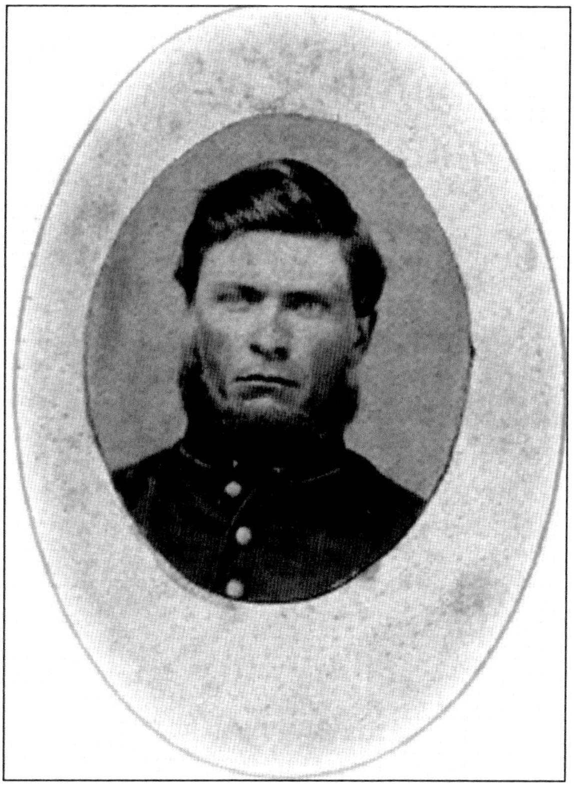

**JOHN S. BOUTWELL.** John S. Boutwell enlisted in the 30th Wisconsin Infantry, Company H, and served from August 21, 1862, to September 20, 1865. After the war, he returned to Auroraville, where he was active in the Methodist church.

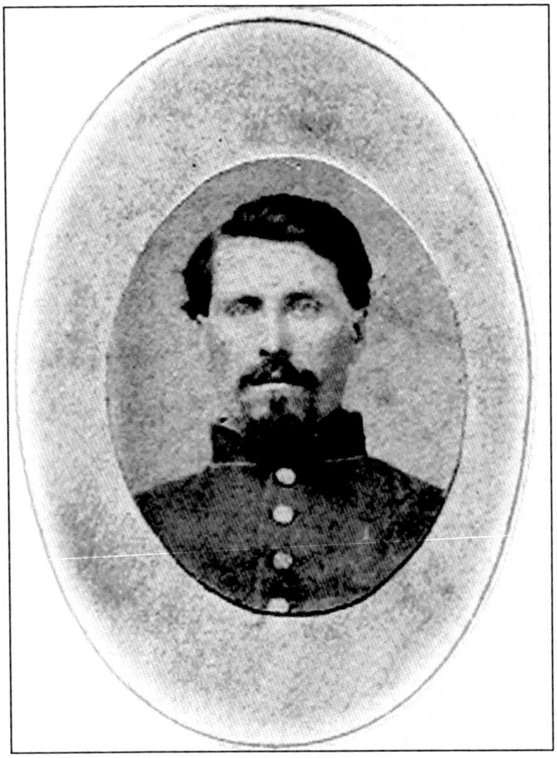

JOHN MATHIAS. A Saxeville resident, John Mathias enlisted on August 21, 1862. He served through the war with the 30th Wisconsin, Company H, and was mustered out with the regiment on September 20, 1865. Mathias is buried in the Poy Sippi Cemetery.

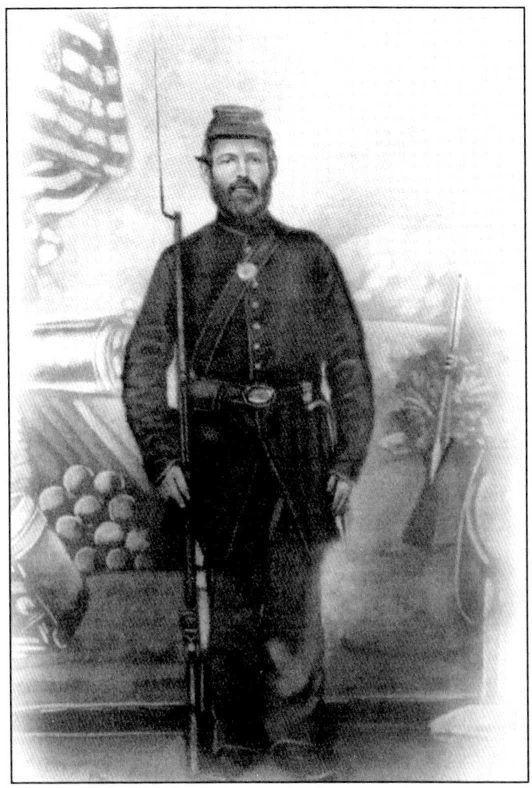

FRANKLIN BLAISDELL. This charcoal drawing portrays Franklin Blaisdell with his rifle in front of a painted backdrop, a popular way of having one's photograph taken or portrait painted. Blaisdell fought in 17 major engagements and skirmishes in the Civil War without suffering a scratch. He fought in the 8th Wisconsin Infantry—the "Old Abe" Eagle Regiment. The unit had an eagle as a mascot that went into battle alongside the men. Both Blaisdell and the eagle survived the war. Blaisdell returned to Poy Sippi to farm and is buried in the Brushville Cemetery.

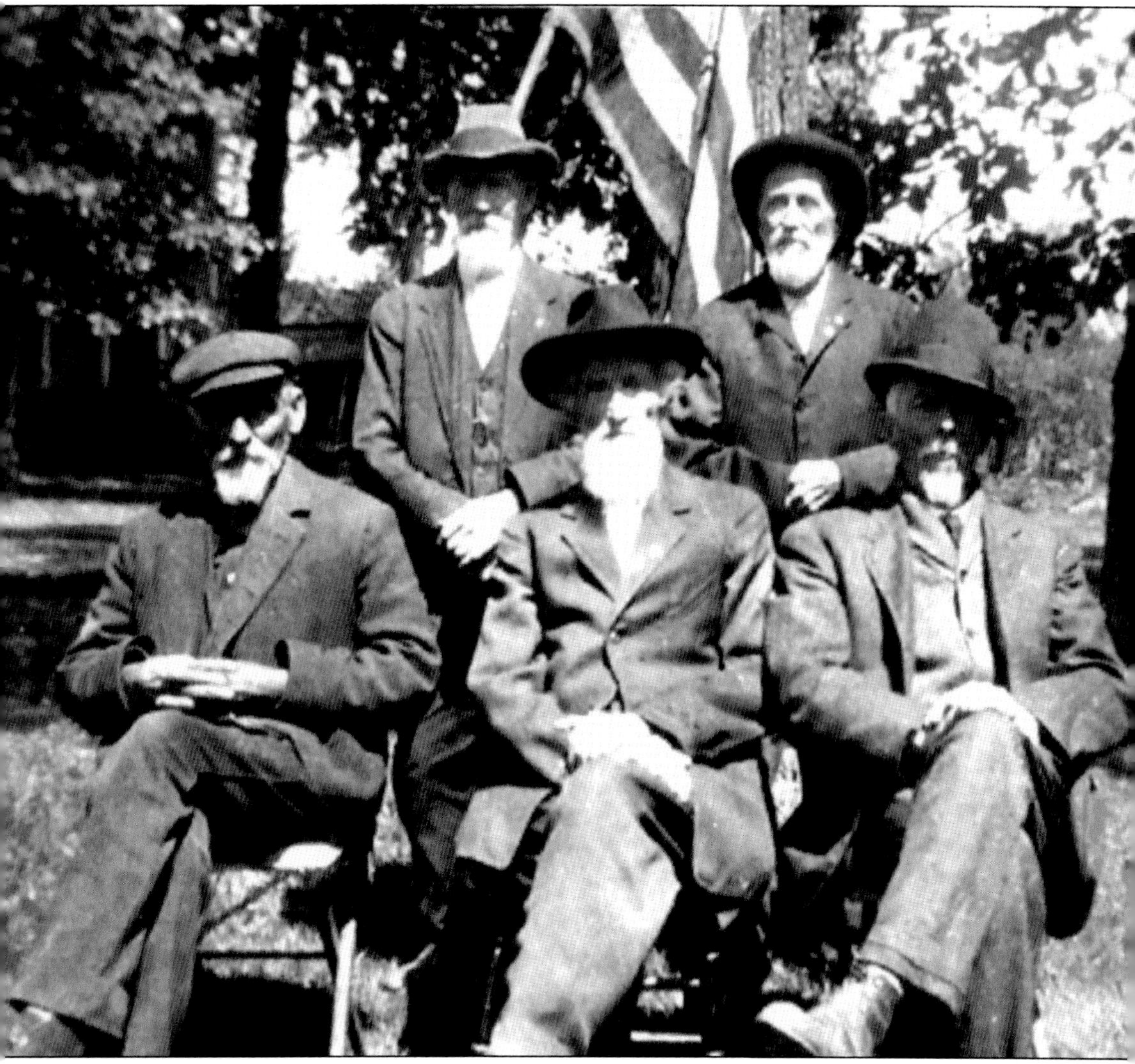

**JAMES EWING GAR POST NO. 231.** The last five survivors of the Poy Sippi James S. Ewing Grand Army of the Republic Post No. 231 are shown in front of the post flags. Pictured here, from left to right, are the following: (first row) Edgar Brewster, John McCue, and Fred Hawley; (second row) John McGregor and Dave Kimball. Notice the GAR lapel pins worn by three of the veterans. James S. Ewing married Elizabeth "Betsy" about 1838 and attended medical school in Fairfield, New York. He practiced medicine in Pittsfield, Vermont, for 11 years, some of that with a Dr. Barlow. He came to Wisconsin in 1847 and spent the winter in (Mapes) Ripon, where he taught school. After a short service as an assistant surgeon for the 5th Wisconsin Infantry during the Civil War, Ewing came back to farm in the town of Leon in Waushara County. He practiced medicine almost to his dying day, November 6, 1877. His grave has been decorated for years by the community on Memorial Day.

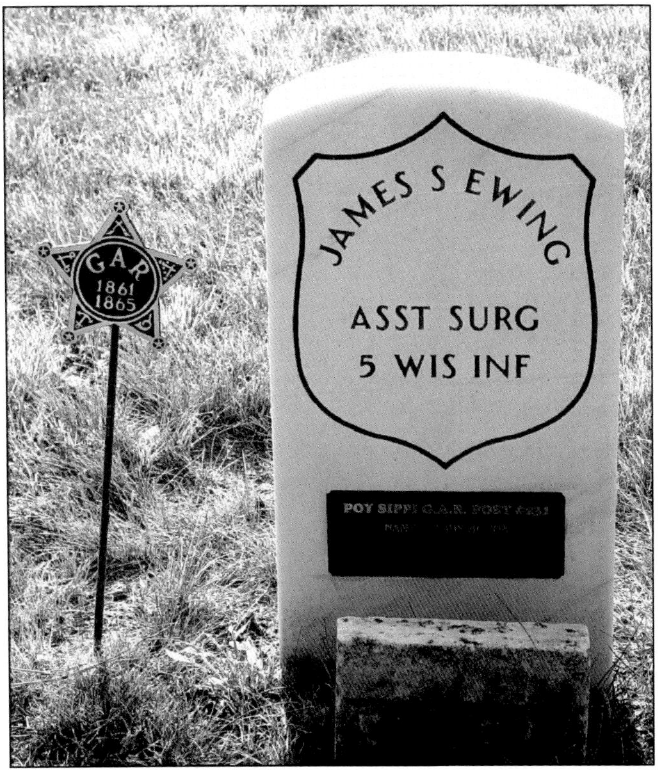


**JAMES S. EWING'S GRAVE.** This is the grave of a man who was held in high regard by his fellow Civil War veterans. In addition, as the doctor of Poy Sippi, he was well liked and respected. Ewing's grave site has finally been decorated in a manner due him for all his work during the Civil War and in the community. Until recently, all that marked his grave was a stone bearing only his initials. Through the efforts of the Sons of Union Veterans of the Civil War Camp No. 8, a new headstone marker and flag holder have been placed at his grave.

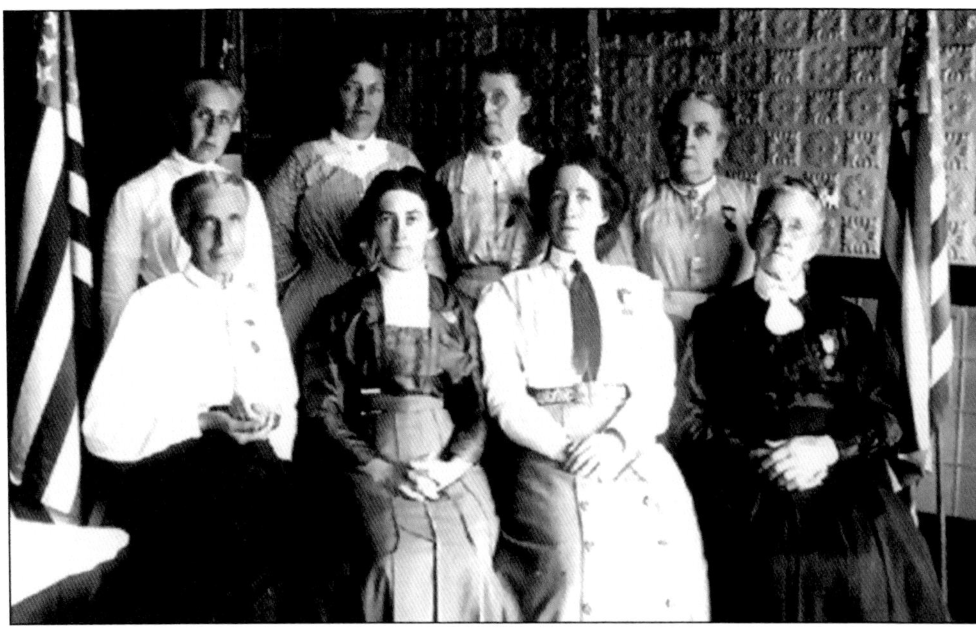

**GAR WOMEN'S AUXILIARY.** Taken inside the GAR Hall, this photograph shows the Women's Relief Corps. Pictured are the following members, from left to right, (first row) Mrs. Shepard, Clara Hanson, Emma Wagoner, and Lucy Warner; (second row) Carrie Horn, Anna Clark, Mrs. Holsworth, and Min Georgeson. Wearing Women's Relief Corps badges, they are positioned next to the 48-star flags.

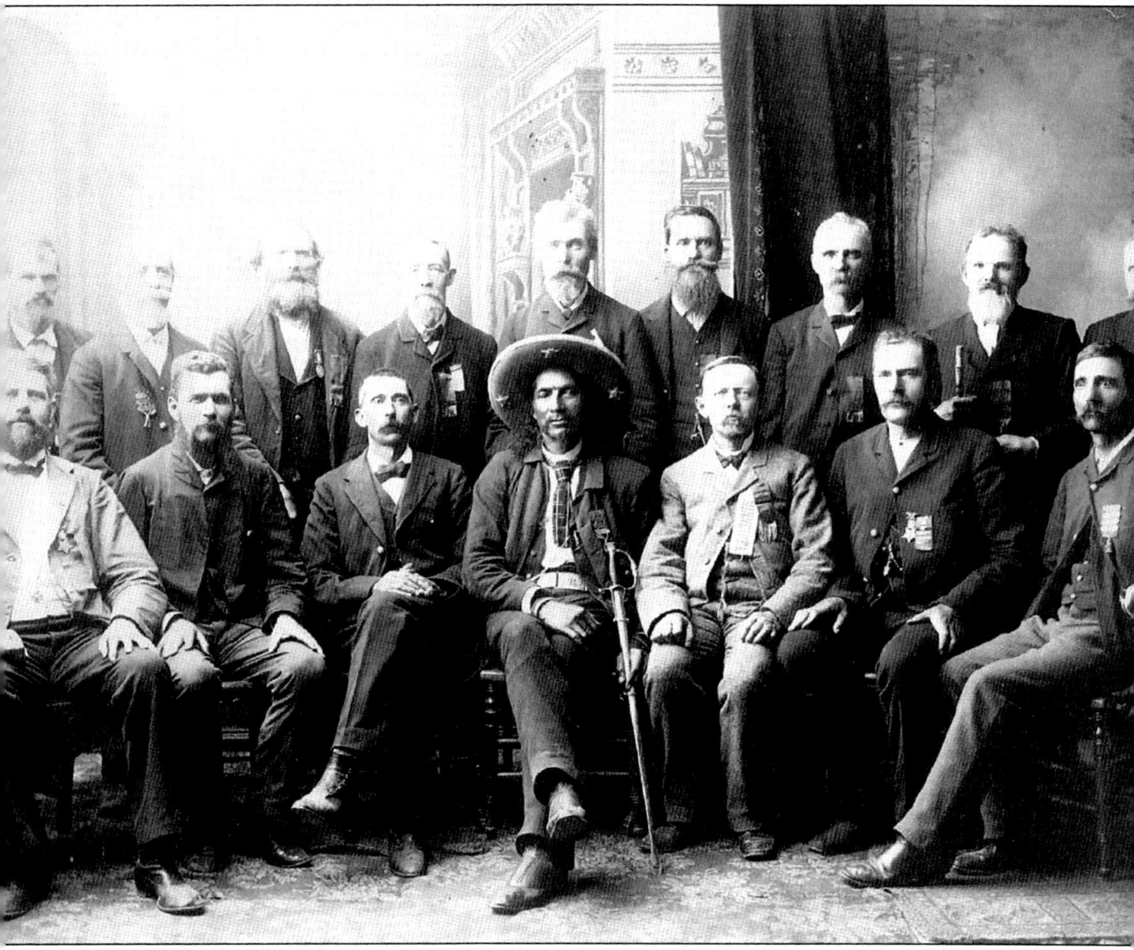

**Poy Sippi GAR.** This photograph, although its date is unknown, bears significant historical value. Notice the man on the far right of the first row. He wears a GAR canteen, which served as a souvenir for GAR reunions, and a ladder badge. He may be John McCue of Poy Sippi. The man with the hat in the center is Steve Nicholas, called "Steve Nick," an American Indian. Nick was a direct descendant of King Philip, famous during the French and Indian War. He tried to enlist in Company K of the 21st Wisconsin Infantry but lost out in a lot drawing. He then enlisted in the 1st Wisconsin Infantry from Ripon. Known for his fearless fighting and patriotism, Nick was a distinguished soldier. Indeed, his position in the seating arrangement suggests a place of honor. The man fourth from the left in the second row is John McGregor, a well-known Poy Sippi resident and the second to last to die as a Poy Sippi Civil War veteran.

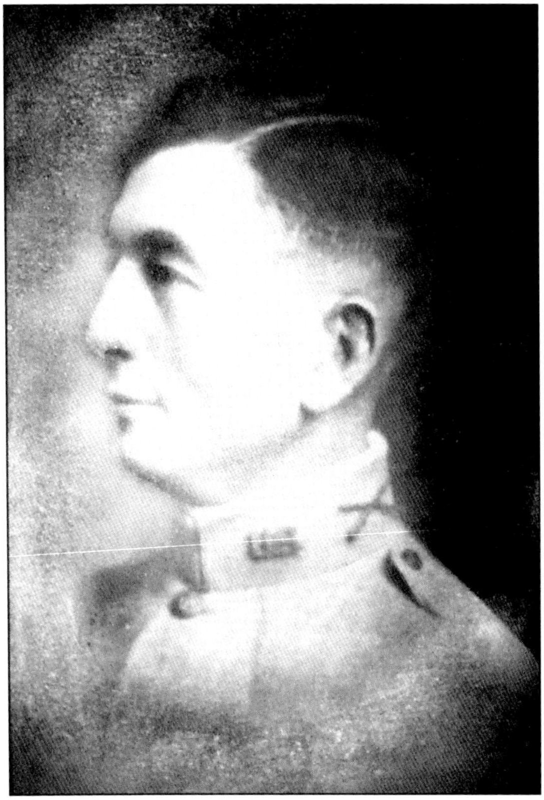

**Frank B. Inda.** As in any war, the Poy Sippi men stepped forward. Frank Inda, shown here in his World War II uniform, served as a lieutenant in Company L of the 5th Infantry of the Wisconsin National Guard. He returned to Poy Sippi after the war. In 1920, the Inda family, along with several others, was instrumental in starting the Sacred Heart Catholic Church in Poy Sippi.

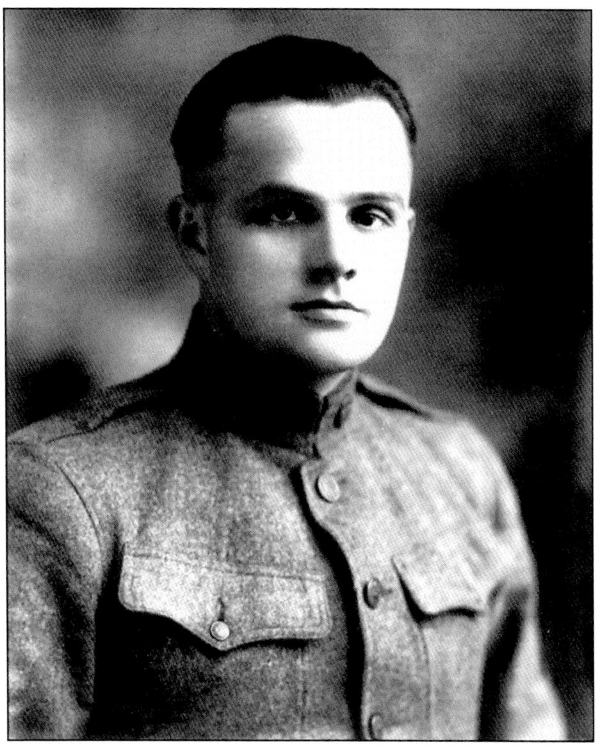

**Grant Boyson.** One cannot think of Poy Sippi without also thinking of Grant Boyson. Born on May 15, 1897, Boyson led an interesting life. Pictured in his World War I uniform, he fought in several of the war's major battles in France, where he was an interpreter. He also ran telegraph wire to the front lines. Throughout the years, Boyson managed a hotel, ran a men's clothing store, worked for J. I. Case in Racine, swam with *Tarzan*'s Johnny Weissmuller, trapped muskrats, and played violin. He was even scouted by the Chicago White Sox.

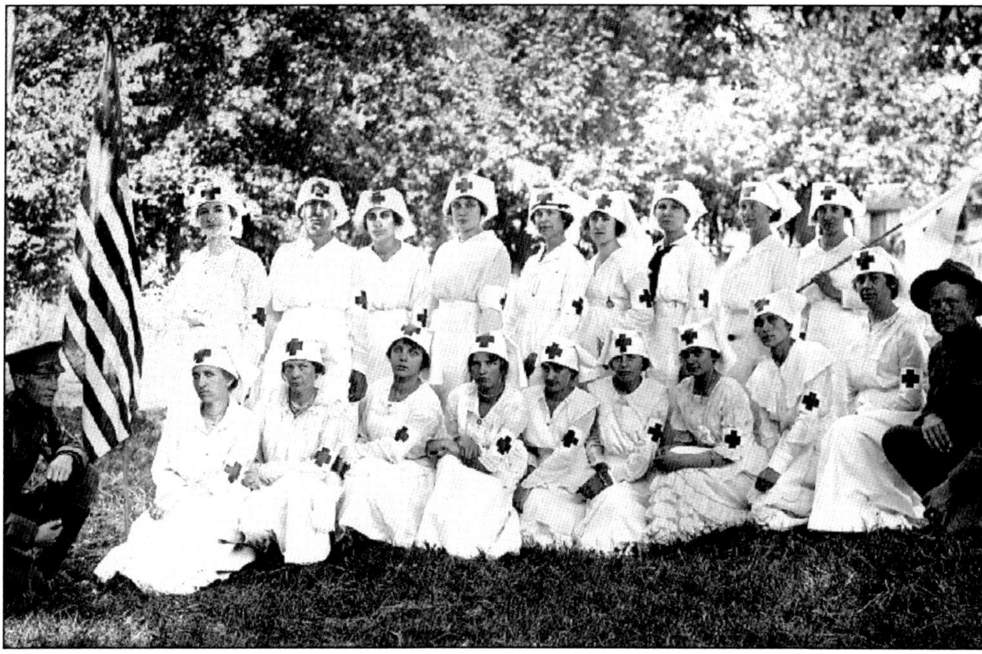

**RED CROSS NURSES.** These young women are dressed in Red Cross uniform costumes for the parade on July 4, 1917. Two soldiers helped them practice for the parade: Clyde Diggles (left) and Bob Becker (right). The women marching, from left to right, are as follows: (first row) Maude Vergin Beck, Gertrude Christiansen, Marie Brewster Mirrell, Velma Harper (telephone operator for many years), Fern Bowen, Laura Ziegenhagen, Stella Peterson, Sylvia Becker Kolpin, and Ella Barrington; (second row) Bernice Skinner Colt, Annie Christianson, Cicely Blaisdell, Mable Jergensen, Fern Bowen Rubin, Clara Baxter Mitchell, Elsie Stratton, and Avis Peterson.

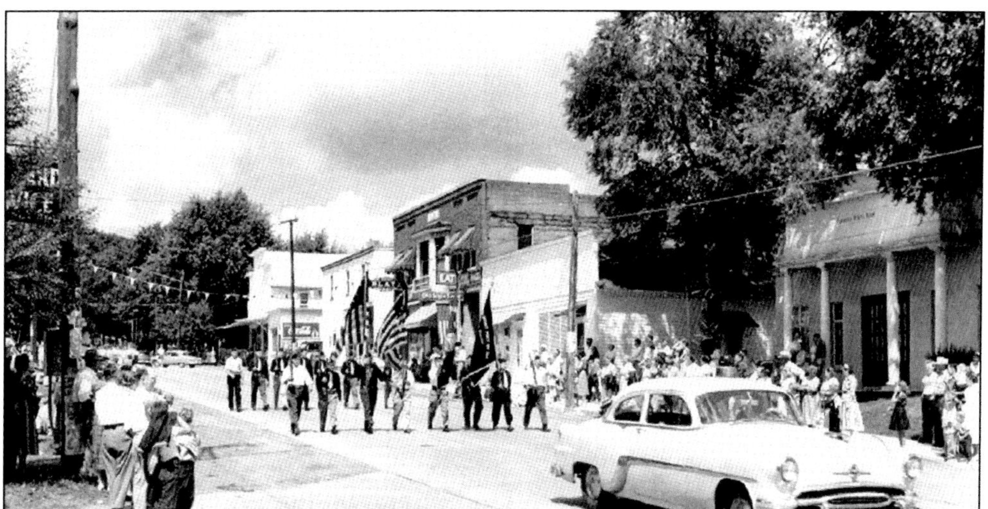

**POY SIPPI AMERICAN LEGION.** During the centennial parade of 1953, the Poy Sippi American Legion passes the Farmers State Bank, located on the northeast corner of Liberty and Main Streets.

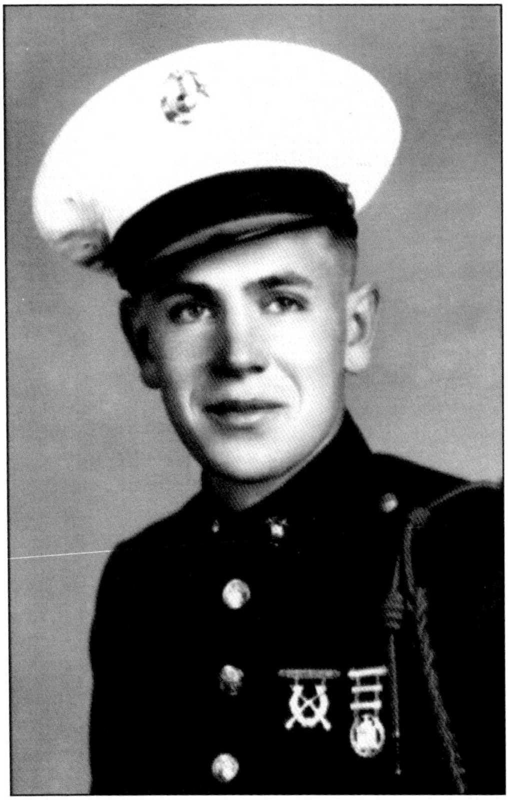

**MELVIN WENDT.** Melvin Wendt, shown in his Marine uniform, was the first of the town's soldiers killed during World War II. The American Legion Post No. 514 was partially named in his honor. Also using the name of a Poy Sippi soldier killed in action during World War I, the post was called the Anderson-Wendt Post. It has since been disbanded.

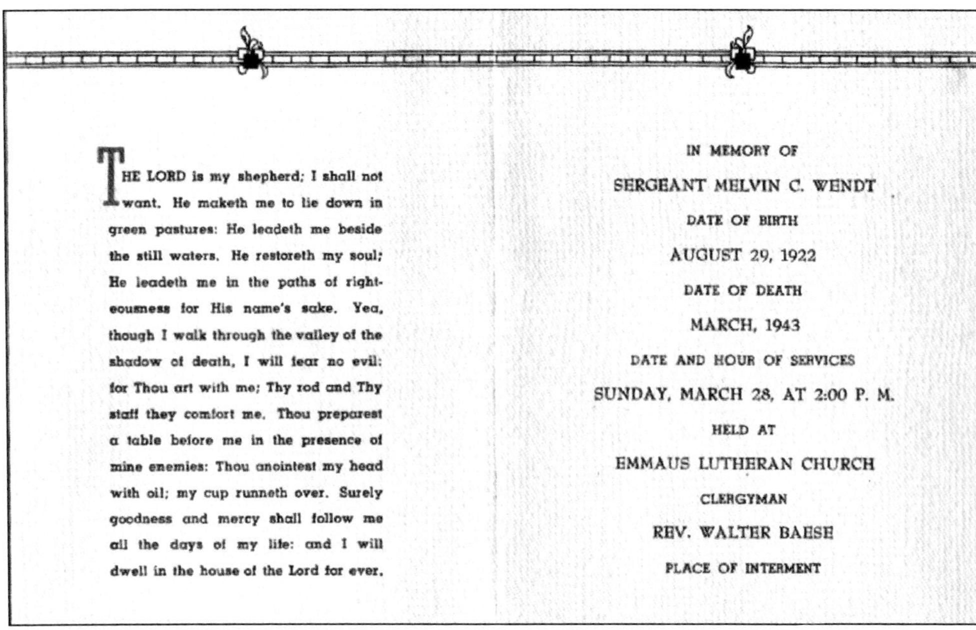

THE LORD is my shepherd; I shall not want. He maketh me to lie down in green pastures: He leadeth me beside the still waters. He restoreth my soul; He leadeth me in the paths of righteousness for His name's sake. Yea, though I walk through the valley of the shadow of death, I will fear no evil: for Thou art with me; Thy rod and Thy staff they comfort me. Thou preparest a table before me in the presence of mine enemies: Thou anointest my head with oil; my cup runneth over. Surely goodness and mercy shall follow me all the days of my life: and I will dwell in the house of the Lord for ever.

IN MEMORY OF

SERGEANT MELVIN C. WENDT

DATE OF BIRTH

AUGUST 29, 1922

DATE OF DEATH

MARCH, 1943

DATE AND HOUR OF SERVICES

SUNDAY, MARCH 28, AT 2:00 P. M.

HELD AT

EMMAUS LUTHERAN CHURCH

CLERGYMAN

REV. WALTER BAESE

PLACE OF INTERMENT

**MELVIN WENDT'S FUNERAL CARD.** Sgt. Melvin Wendt enlisted in the service on September 17, 1940, and fought in both the Atlantic and Pacific theaters during World War II. He worked as an operator in Iceland for ten months and served for three months in New Zealand, where he was killed in a tank accident.

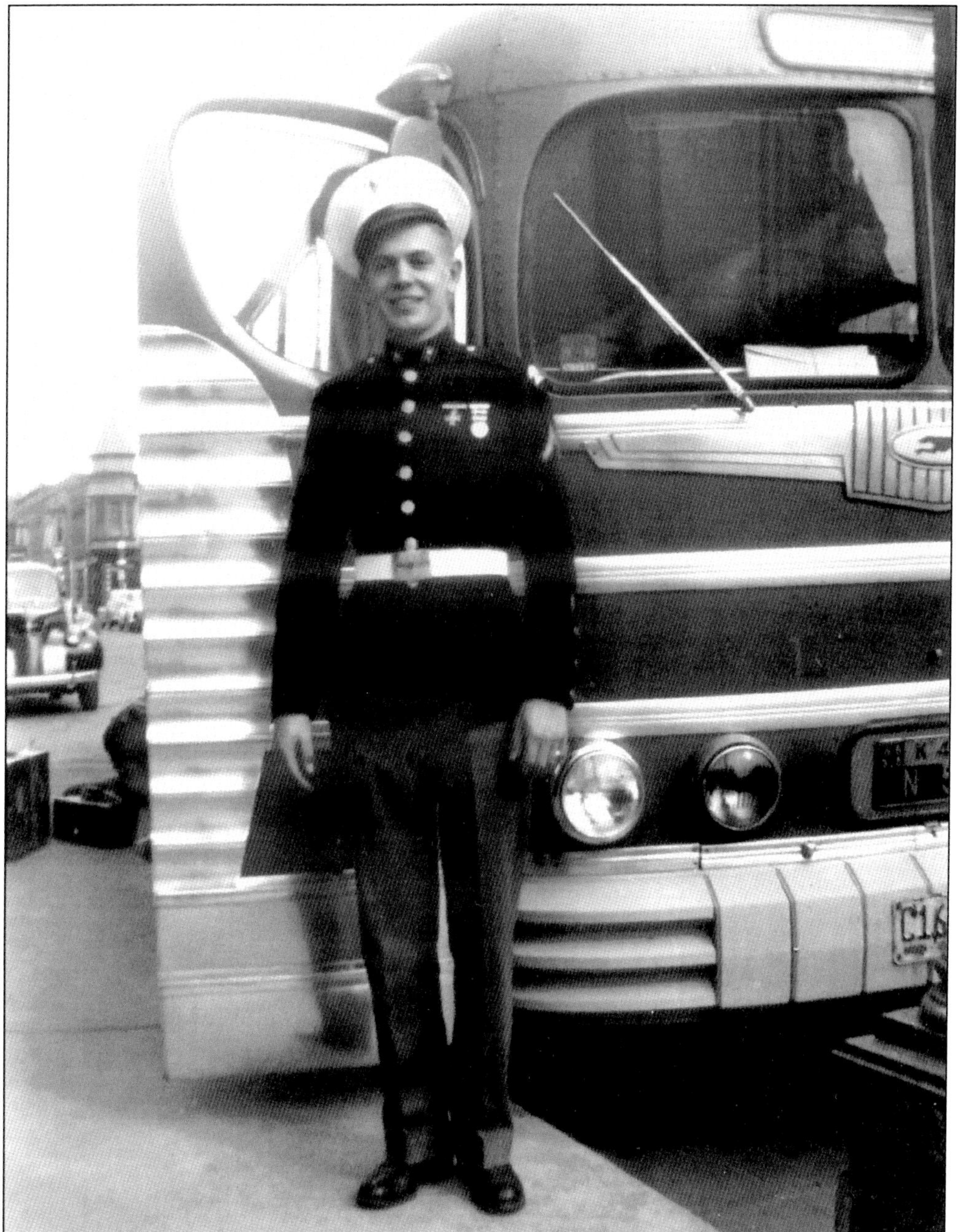

**MELVIN WENDT LEAVES FOR SERVICE.** This photograph was taken in Berlin, Wisconsin, just before Melvin Wendt boarded to return to his unit. Many of the soldiers from World War I and II boarded buses in Berlin as they left home for war.

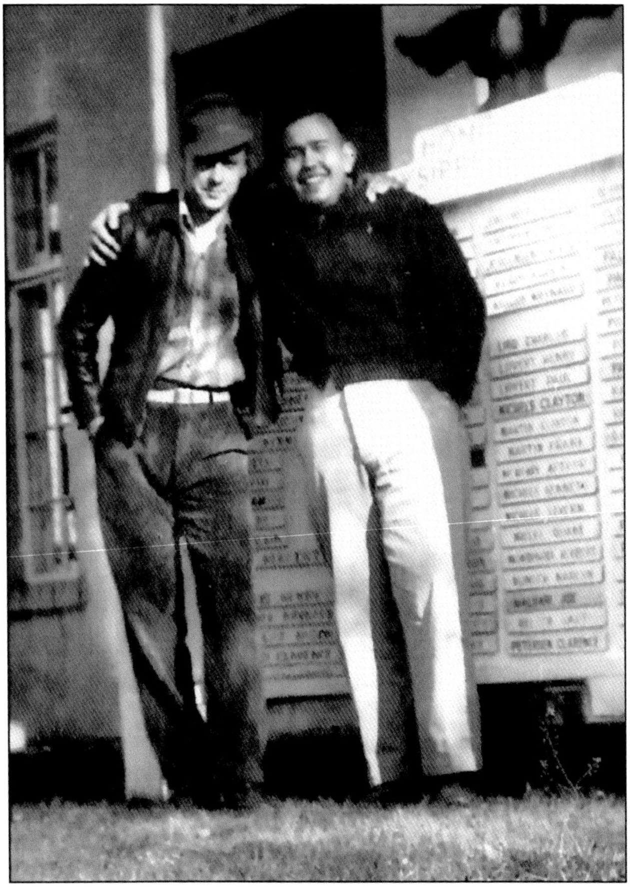

**HONOR ROLL OF POY SIPPI.** Many towns display a board with the names of their citizens who served during World War II. Poy Sippi is one of these towns. Shown with the board are Floyd Vergin (left) and Lothar Sattler. In the early 20th century, Sattler's father, Bill, returned to Germany to find a wife. While he was in Germany, World War I broke out and he was forced to fight on the German side. After the war, he came back to Poy Sippi. He is remembered as the man who set his watch at the telephone office every day and who took care of the U.S. flag. He would remove his hat and take the flag down with the utmost respect.

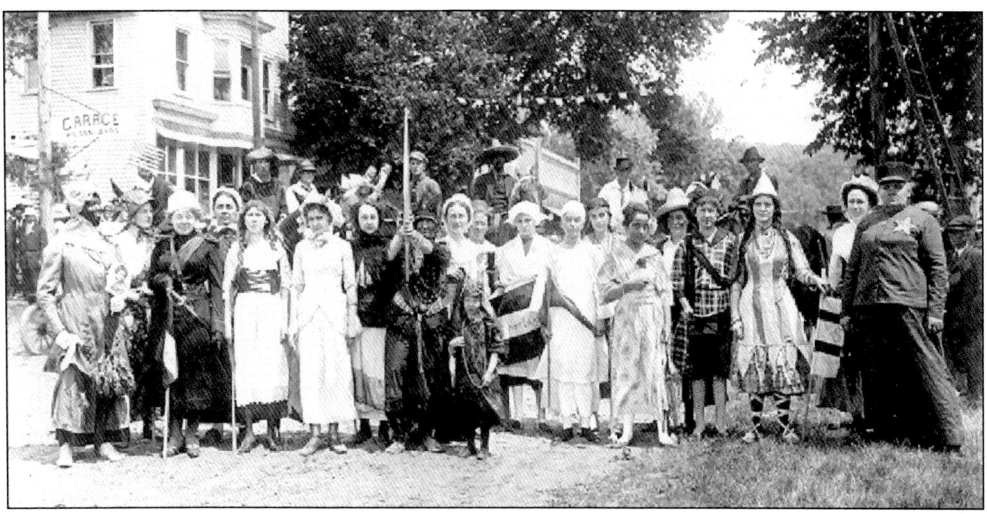

**FOURTH OF JULY.** The children would dress up for the Fourth of July parade. In this photograph, Bernice Skinner Colt is second from the left. Elsie Stratton is in the second row, behind the child. Holding the banner in the center is Ruth Blaisdell Boyson, and two girls to the right of her is Cicely Blaisdell, wearing the American Indian headband. "Mexican Bill" Childs sits on horseback with the sombrero. A great horseman, he was known throughout the state.

# Six

# BRUSHVILLE

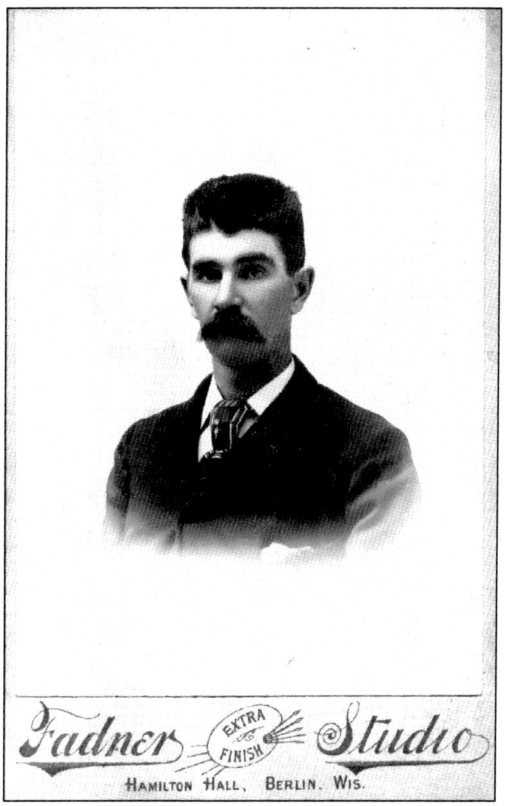


**HERMAN BRUSH.** The Herman Brush family has been credited with settling Brushville. Initially consisting of only a log cabin school, cheese factory, sawmill, and blacksmith shop, Brushville was indeed a small community. Brush and his wife, Caroline, bought the property as a quarter-section of land from John Fitzgerald on May 26, 1853. Fitzgerald, who had bought the parcel from the federal government, had only owned the land for a month. On October 28, 1863, Brush sold off about one-and-a-quarter acres to the Brushville Cemetery Association of Bloomfield in Waushara County for $30. The land was divided up, as more families moved to the area north of Poy Sippi. Although this photograph was marked "Herman Brush," it is not known whether this is the Herman Brush who first bought the land constituting Brushville or his son. The style of the photograph suggests it is the son.

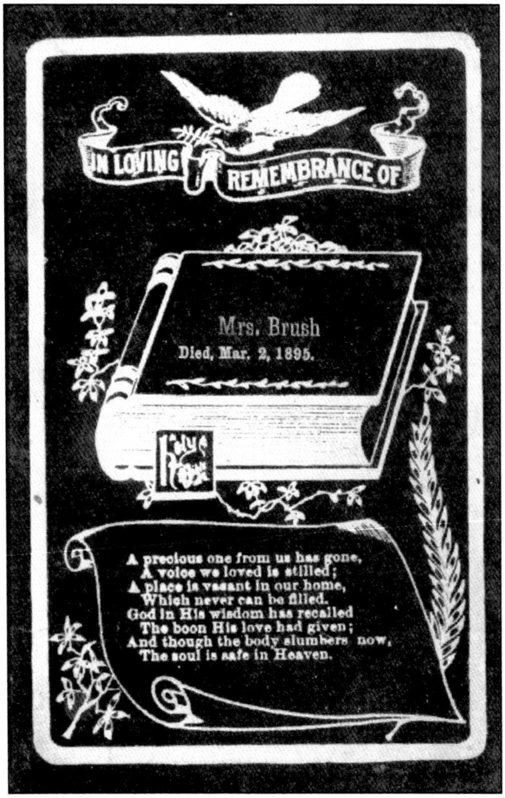


**Funeral Card for Mrs. Brush.** Shown here is the 1895 funeral card for Arozina Brush.

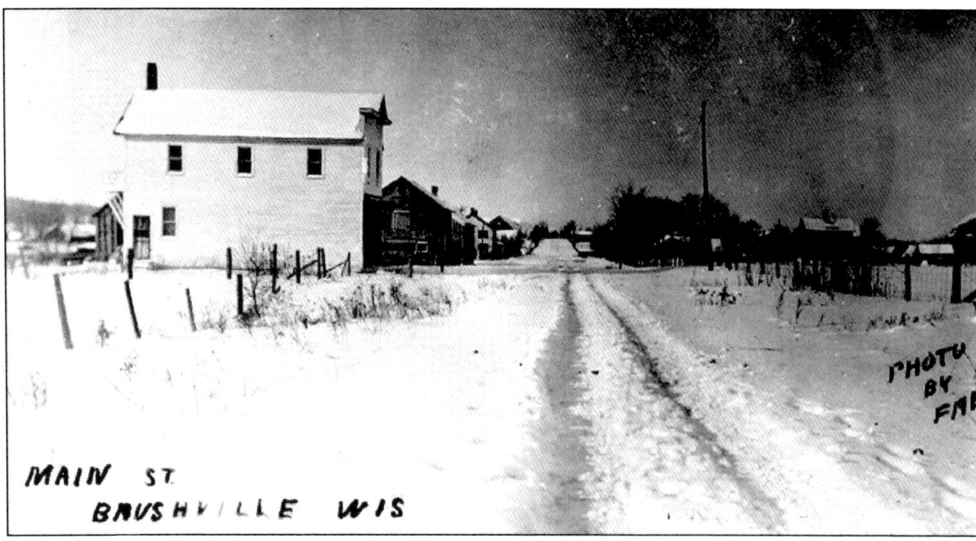


**Main Street, Brushville.** The buildings, from left to right, are Edward Velte's Store (the white building), a warehouse for the cheese factory, the cheese factory, the Brush Hotel (or, as some locals remember, the Stagecoach Inn), Herman Zabel's farm, William Zabel's farm (on the right), and the Deppe farm. The stagecoach ran from Waupaca to Berlin, with the Stagecoach Inn as one of its stops. This street is now County Trunk M.

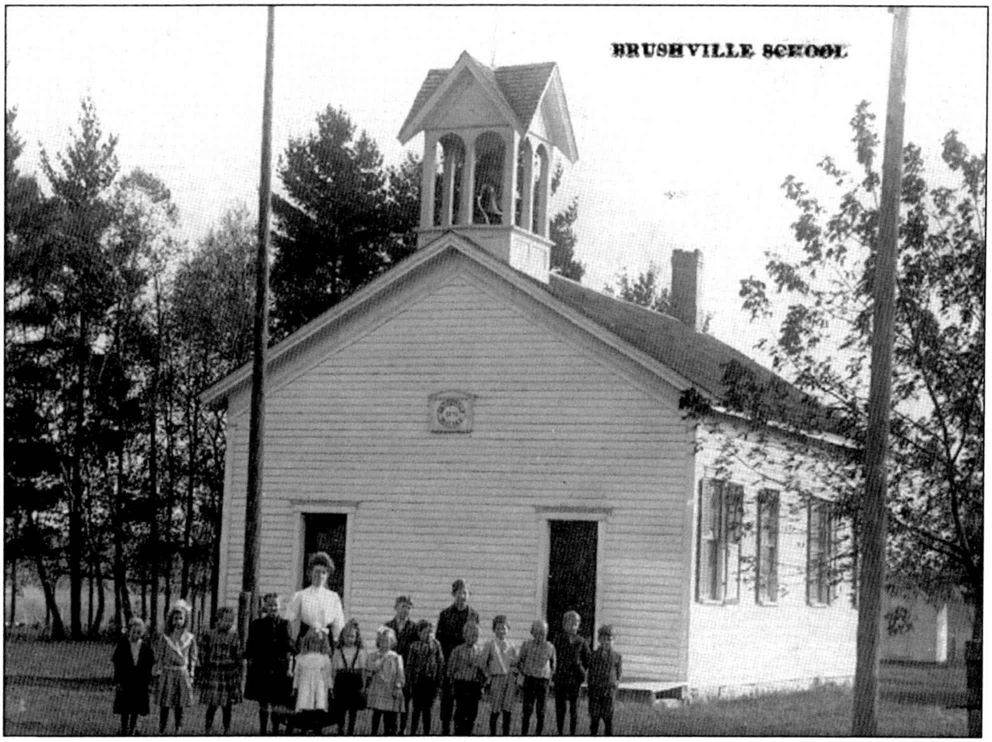


**BRUSHVILLE SCHOOL, 1906 OR 1907.** Bernice Skinner Colt is the teacher in this view. Two of the identified students are Cicely Blaisdell, second from the left, and Ruth Blaisdell, fifth from the left.

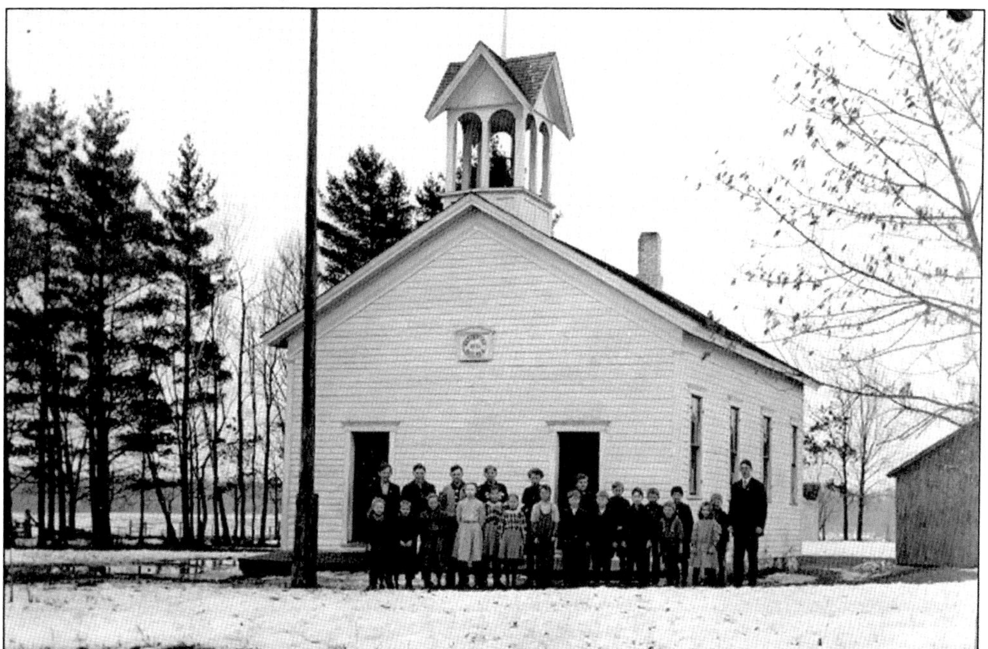

**BRUSHVILLE SCHOOL, 1912.** A male teacher poses with his students at the Brushville School in 1912.

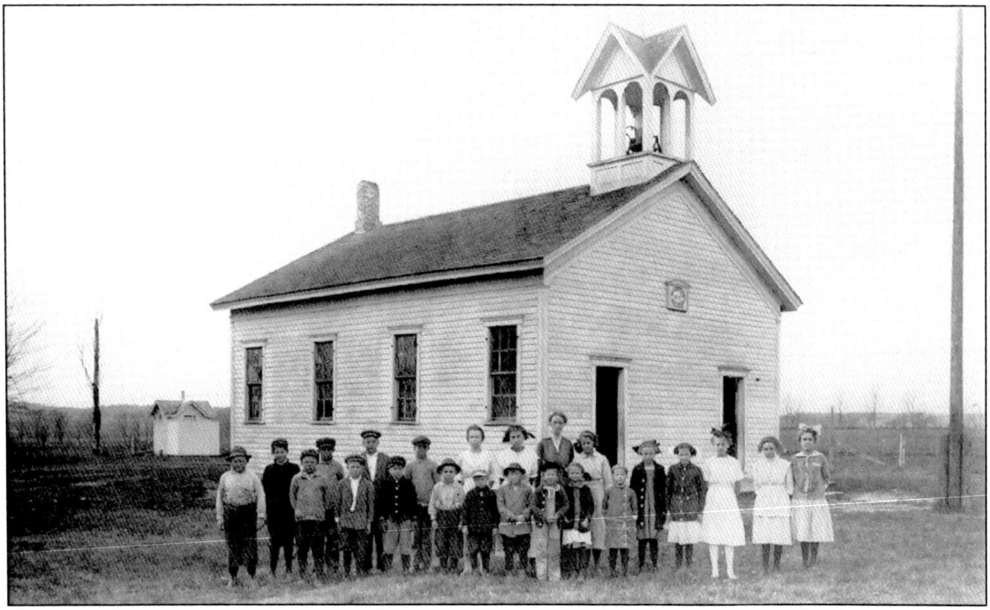

**BRUSHVILLE SCHOOL, 1913.** The students are Edward Howard, Alvin Ziegenhagen, Bill Godson, Bill Ziegenhagen, Irene Howard, Cicely Blaisdell, Jennie Nelson, Dorothy Byrholdt, Edward Kissinger, Louis Ziegenhagen, Harry Godson, Harold Strehlow, Ward Kissinger, Louis Walters, Leonart Sattler, Della Godson, Evelyn Wendt, Floria Godson, Iva Howard, Ruth Blaisdell, Laura Ziegenhagen, and Gertrude Handrich.

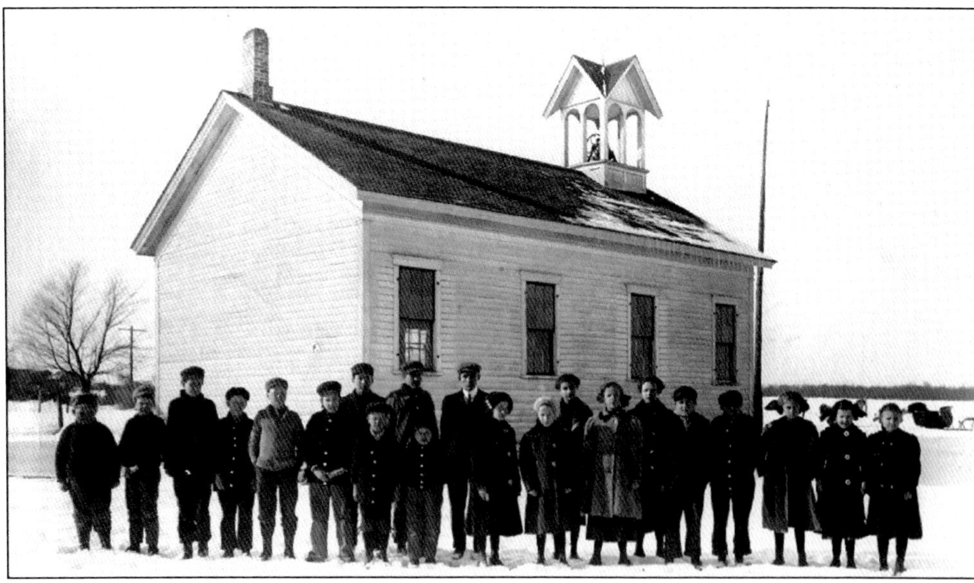

**BRUSHVILLE SCHOOL, 1914.** Shown here, from left to right, are Edward Kissinger, Edward Howard, Elmer Walter, Bill Ziegenhagen, Raymond Crawford, Bill Godson, Leonard Sattler, Louis Ziegenhagen, Oswald Handrick, Harold Strehlow, Don Heaney, Laura Ziegenhagen, Floria Godson, Cicely Blaisdell, Dorothy Byrholdt, Irene Howard, Alfred Handrick, Alvin Ziegenhagen, Ruth Blaisdell, Iva Howard, and Elsie Gaetsch.

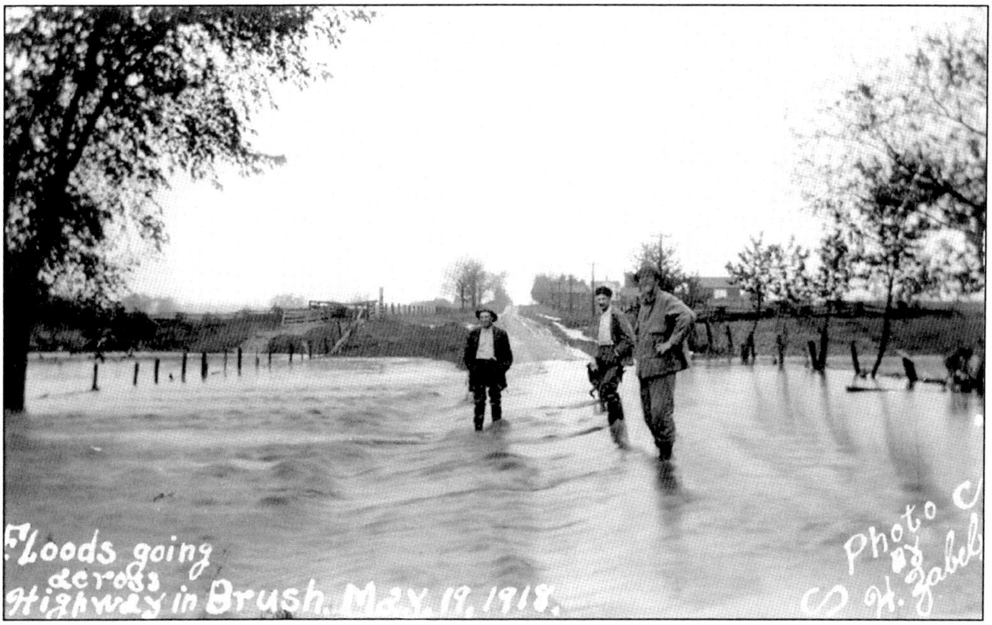


**FLOOD IN BRUSHVILLE, 1918.** In this photograph, taken west of the Stagecoach Inn, the creek that runs north–south overflows across Highway M in Brushville. Frank Blaisdell is pictured in the center, with his dog barely visible behind him.

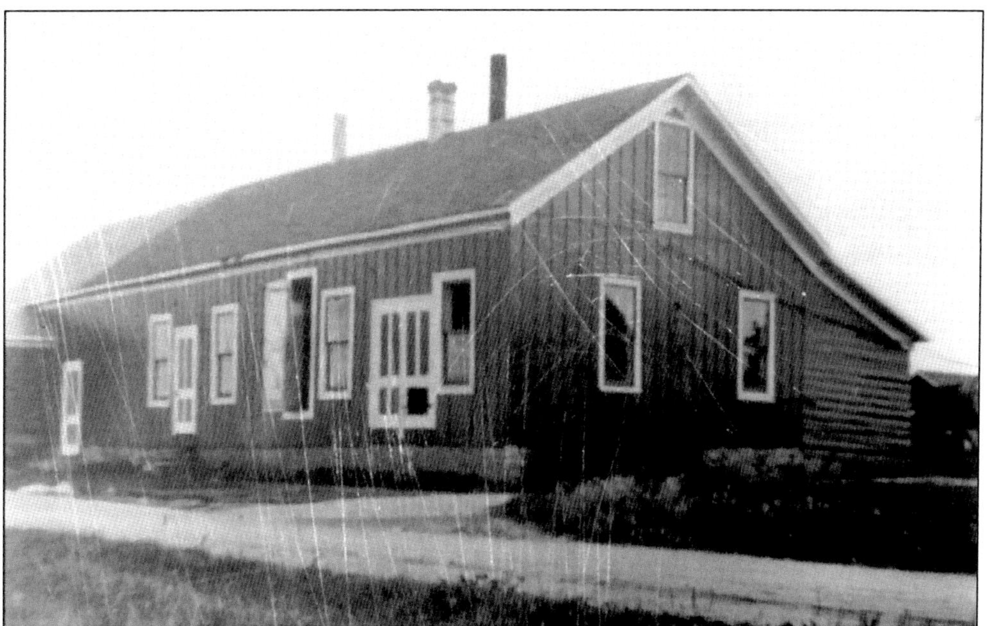

**BRUSHVILLE CHEESE FACTORY.** This scratched photograph shows the Brushville Cheese Factory around 1949.

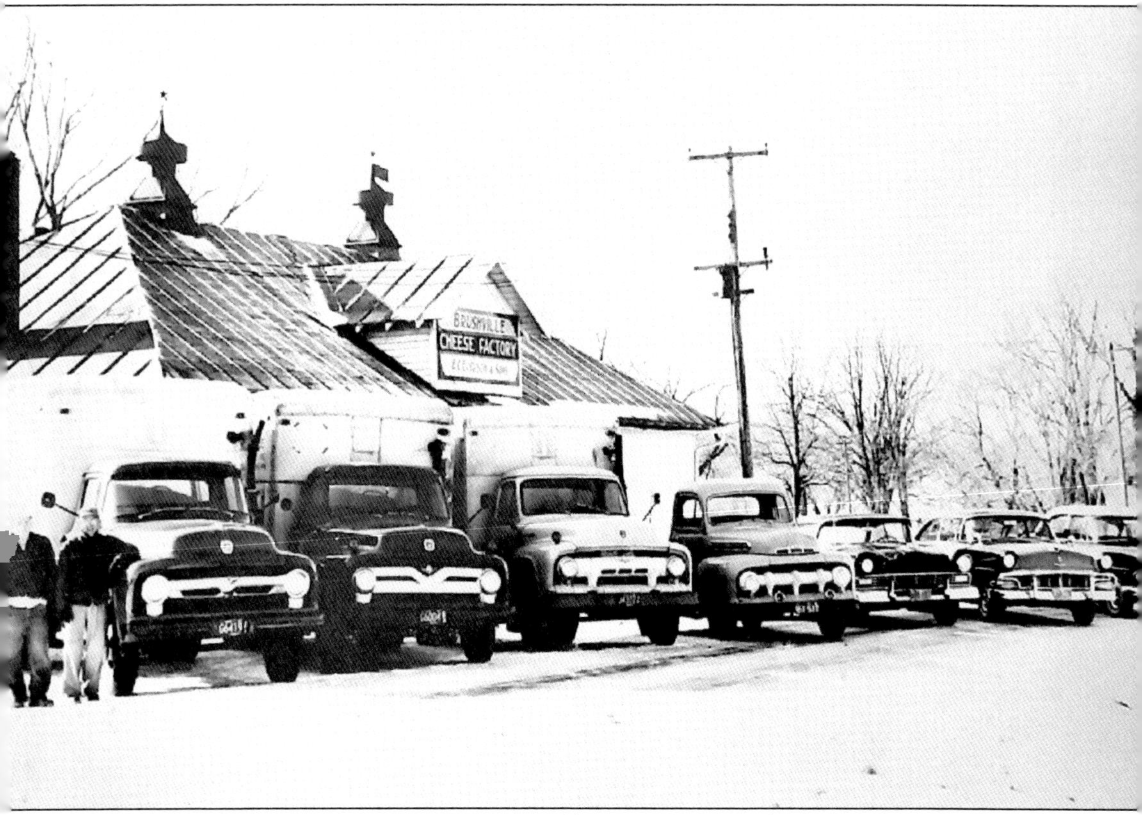


**EVERSON AND SONS, 1957.** Jim Everson and his son, also named Jim, show off the line of Fords they owned as work trucks and personal cars. Lloyd Everson, the other son, was absent when this view was taken. The cheese factory occupies the background.

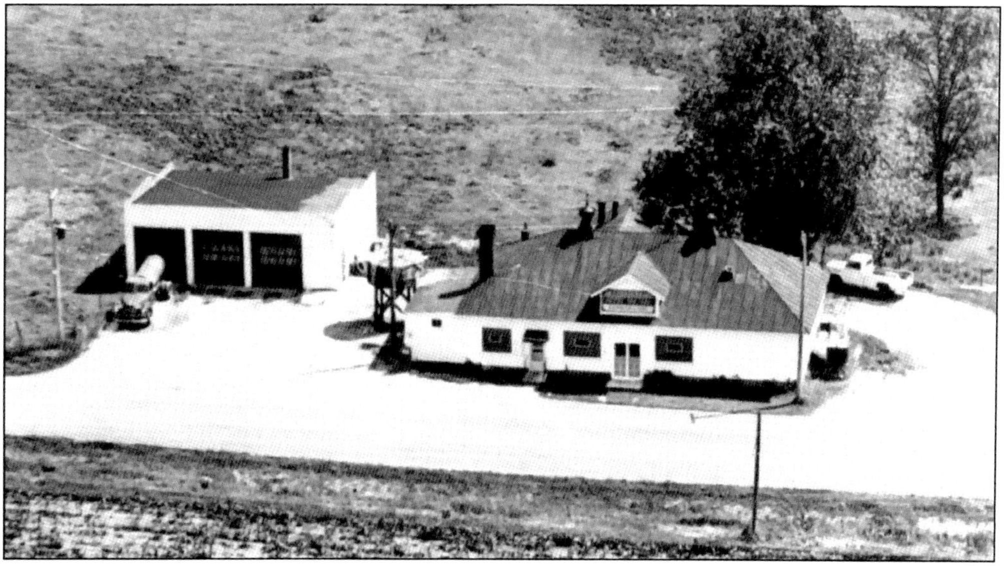

**BRUSHVILLE CHEESE FACTORY.** The cheese factory is seen from above in this 1960 aerial view. The Eversons owned and operated the factory from 1947 to 1987. The building still stands, although vacant.

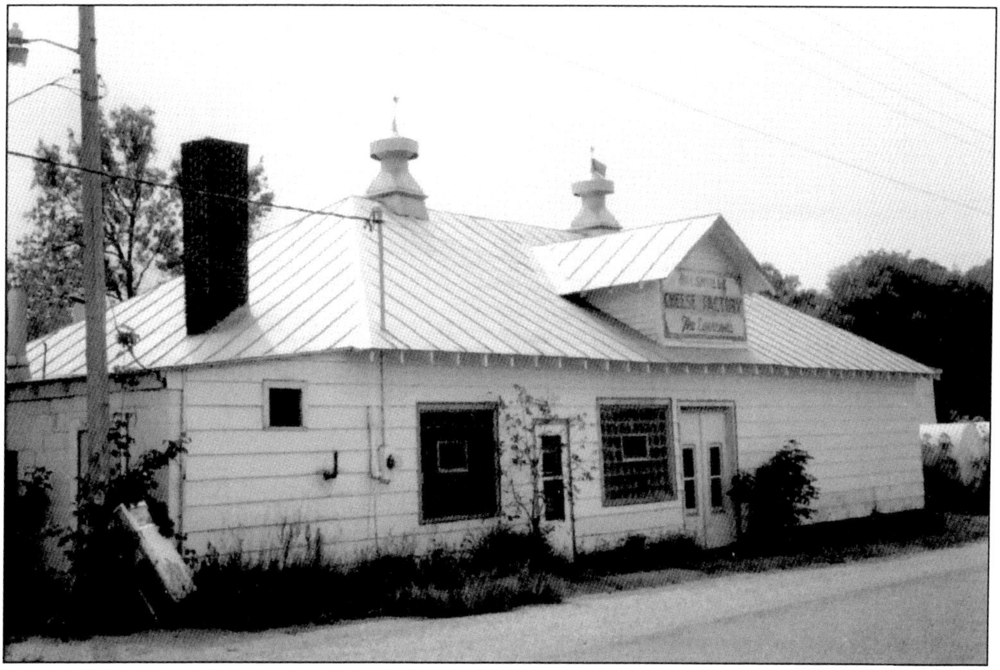


**EVERSON AND SONS CLOSED.** This view shows the Everson and Sons Cheese Factory a few years after its 1987 closing.

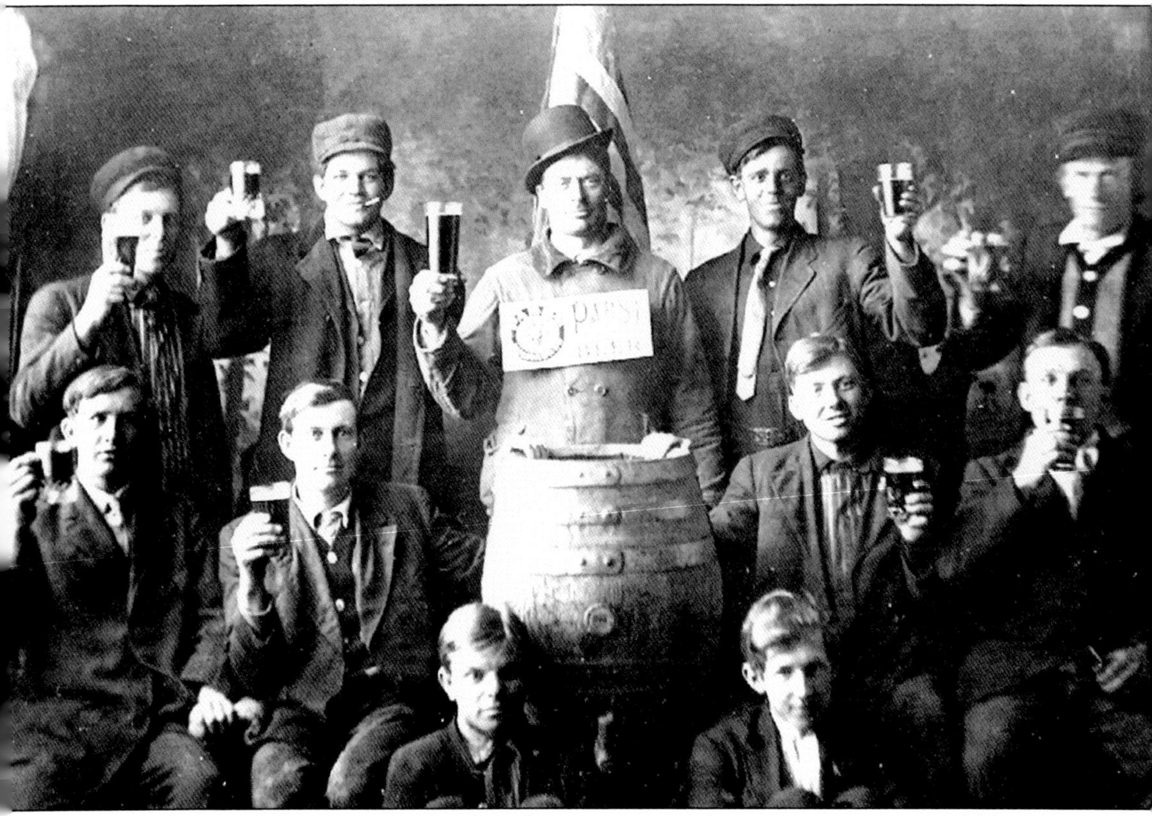


**TOASTERS.** While the reason for this photograph is unclear, the motivation could have been the repeal of Prohibition. Pictured here, from left to right, are the following: (first row) Walter Wendt and Allie Howard; (second row) Louie Stumpner, Lewis Walter, Fred Wendt, and Otto Deppe; (third row) Louie Wendt, Alvin Hendrich, Bert Cornell (with the Pabst sign), Henry or Oscar Nelson, and George Hanson.

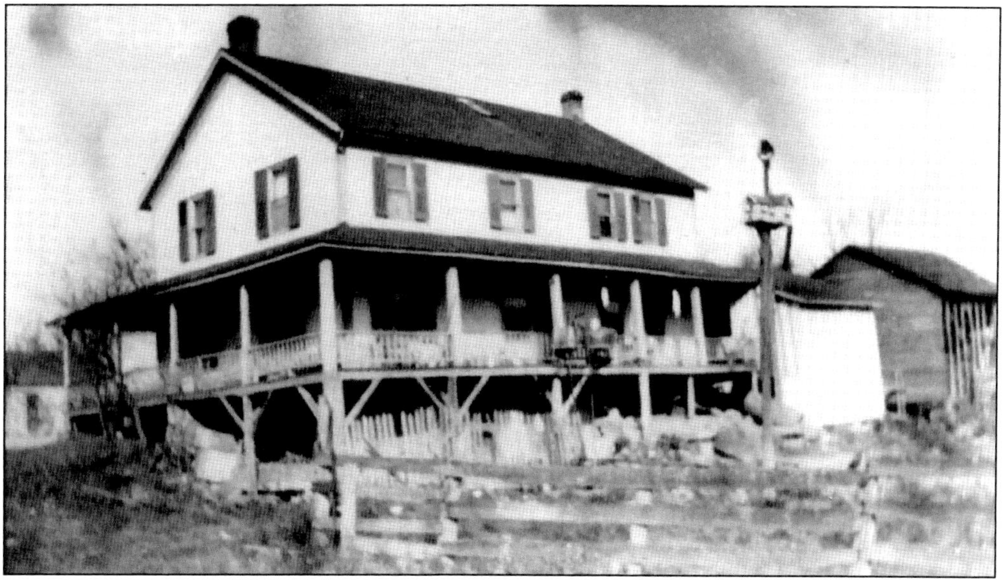

**STAGECOACH INN OF BRUSHVILLE.** This view was taken from the back side of the building. The inn, with its wraparound porch, was a popular place for travelers to stop for the night. The building still exists, but the porches have been removed. The backyard sloped toward Spring Creek, running behind the inn.

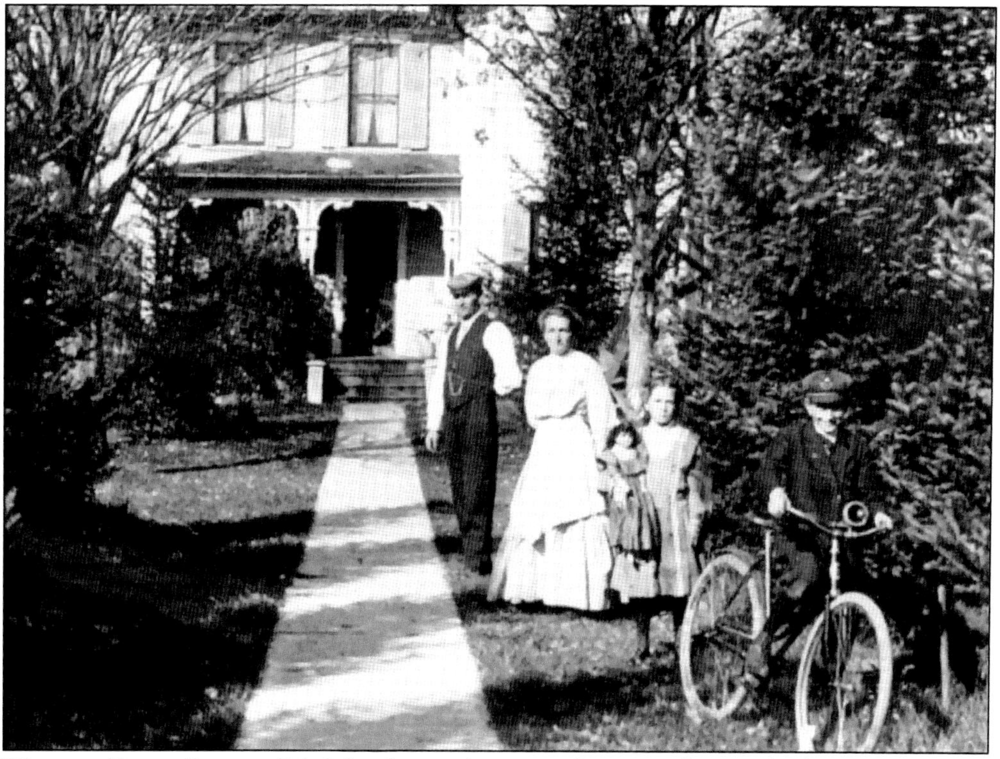

**WILLIAM ZABEL FAMILY.** Zabel family members pose for a snapshot in the front yard of their farmhouse, located just west of Spring Creek, which ran their sawmill. Helmut is the boy and Della the girl in this photograph.

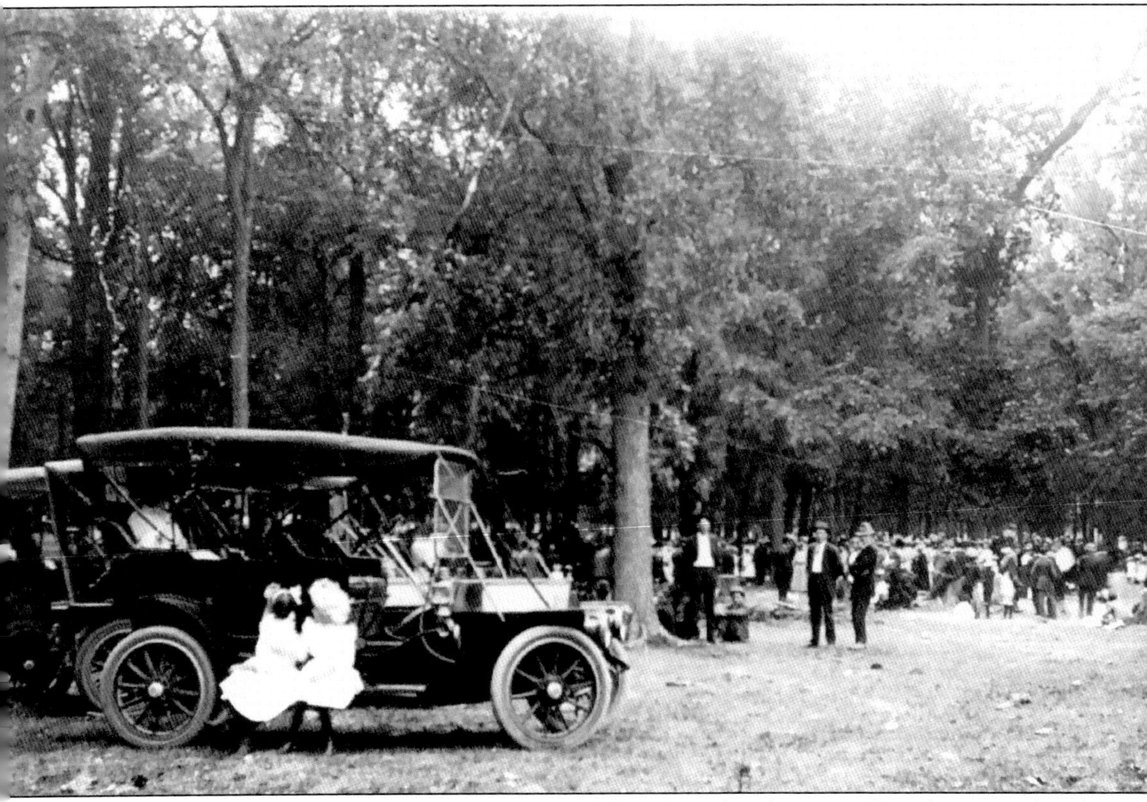

**PICNIC IN SATTLER'S WOODS.** Neighbors and friends gather for a Sunday afternoon church picnic in Sattler's Woods. This 1920s view shows the mode of transportation for the day, as some of the women sit in automobiles to avoid the sunlight. Curiously, it was popular for women to remain in the  during such affairs. Maybe they had young children to care for.

**MAKING BUTTER IN BRUSHVILLE.** Butter was one of the products made in the Brushville Cheese Factory. Here, Cephas J. Walters, the owner of the factory at the time, cuts butter into blocks to be boxed in paper containers for market.

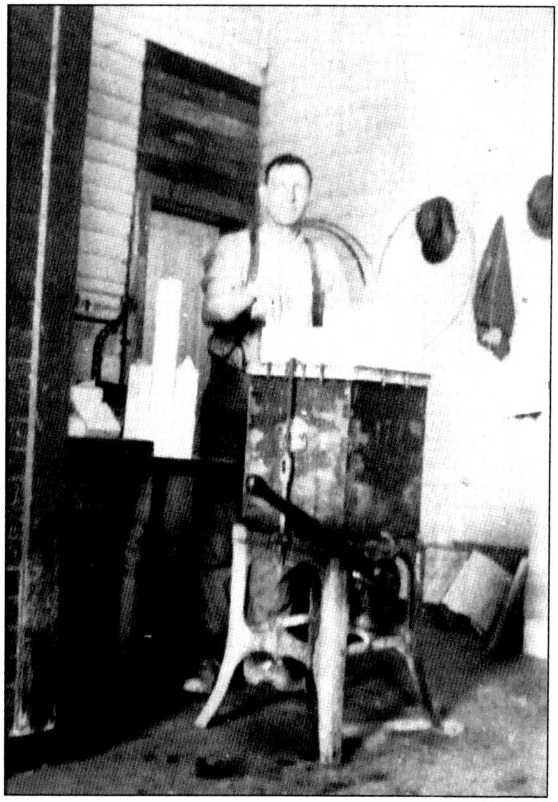

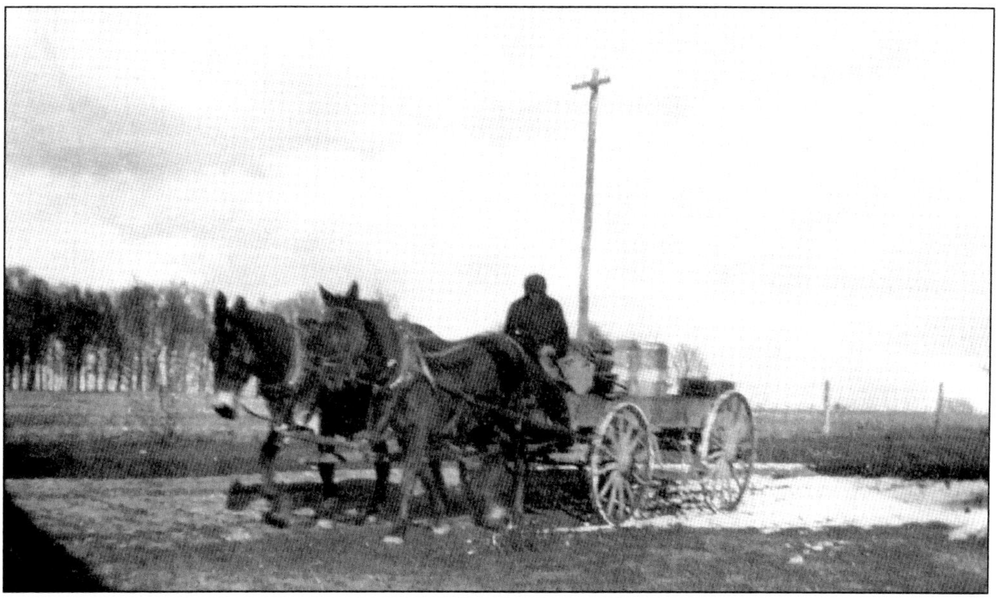

**HAULING MILK TO BRUSHVILLE DAIRY.** Milk is hauled via horse-drawn wagon to the Brushville Cheese Factory in this undated photograph. The man on the wagon may be Cephas J. "Uncle Ceph" Walters, who ran the dairy. He started making butter in Brushville in 1884. Having worked for 37 years, he retired in 1920. Walters died on January 16, 1947, at the age of 89 and is buried in the Eureka Cemetery.

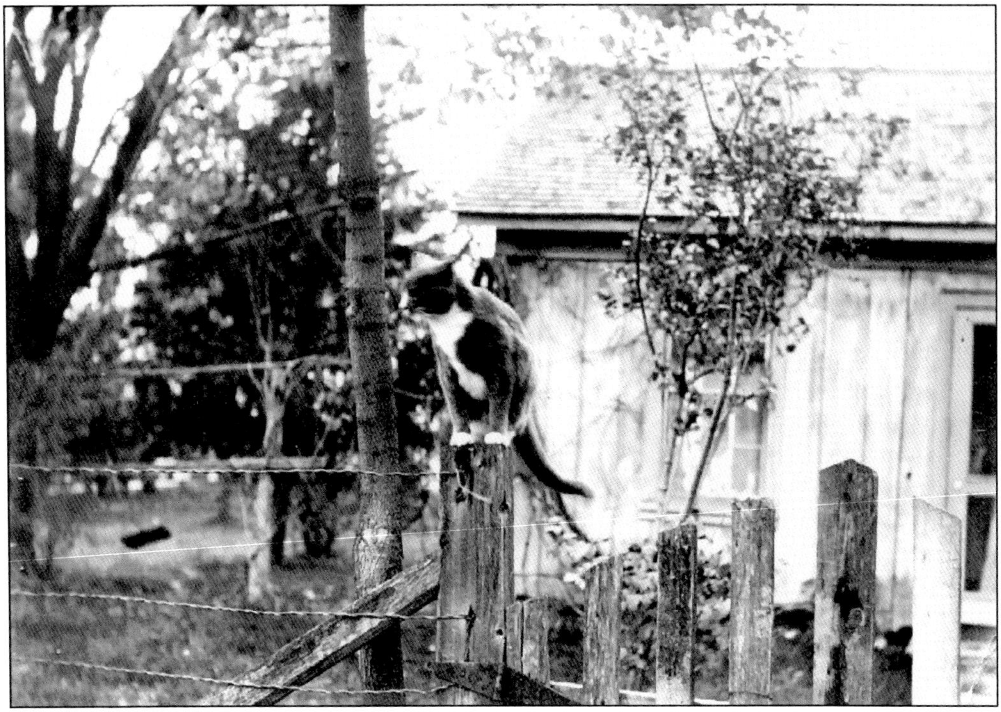

**Cat on the Fence Post.** A cat waits for Uncle Ceph to drive by with his horse-drawn milk wagon. When the wagon neared, he would jump into the wagon and ride along.

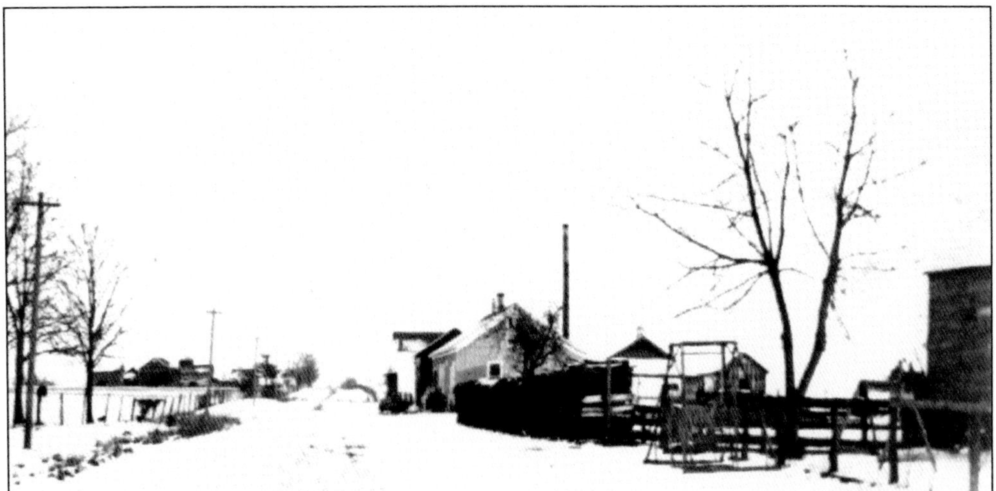

**Brushville, As Seen from West.** In what seems to be an image from any early American small town, this view of Brushville was taken in front of the Stagecoach Inn looking east. To the far right is the cheese factory. Ed Velte ran his store in the white building behind the factory.

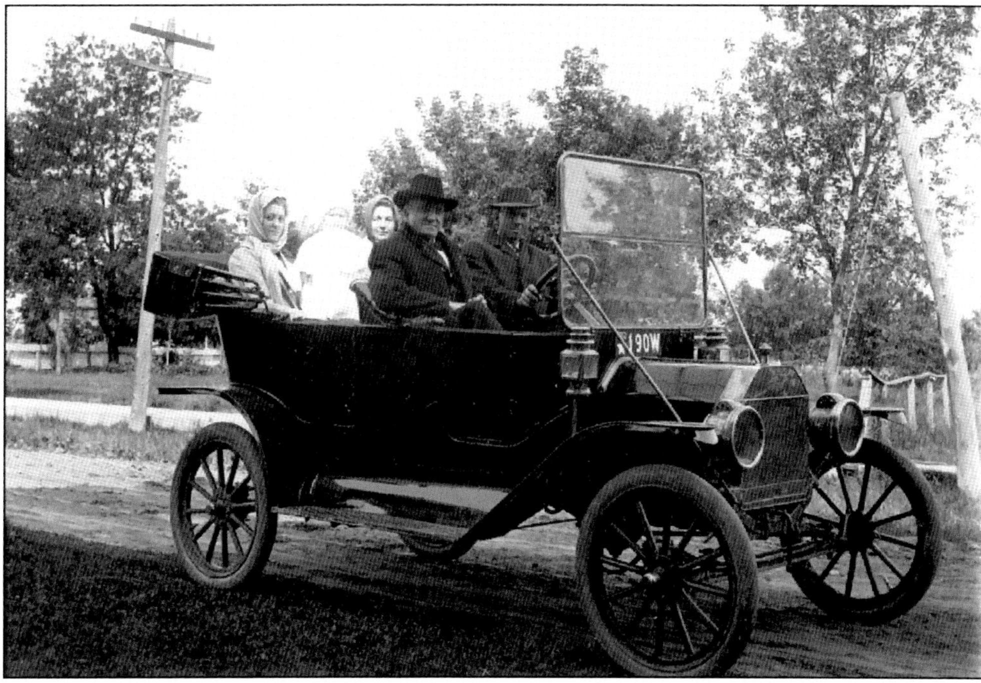


**ED VELTE'S NEW AUTOMOBILE.** Taking his new automobile out for a ride, Ed Velte steers the wheel while Richard Wendt sits in the front passenger seat. Augusta "Gustie" Wendt is in the back seat with her daughter Anna and the Velte baby Carol.

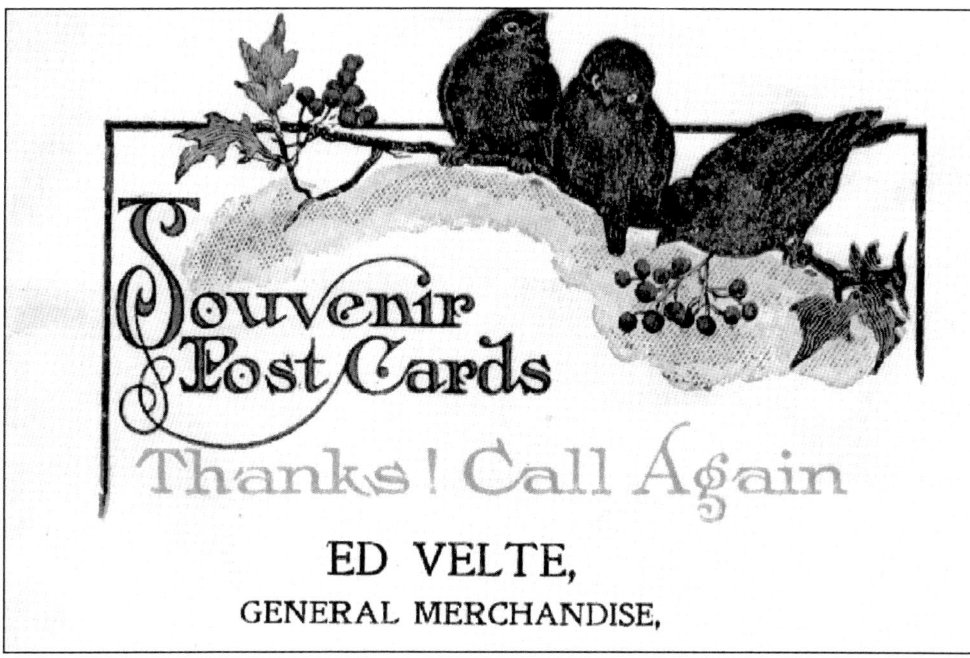


**VELTE SOUVENIR CARD.** One of the few mementos of the Velte Store is this envelop, used as a souvenir card. The store fell down after being abandoned for many years. Velte sold crackers, and if the buyer did not have enough money to buy the whole cracker, he would break off the part not purchased. Everyone called him "Crackers" because of this.

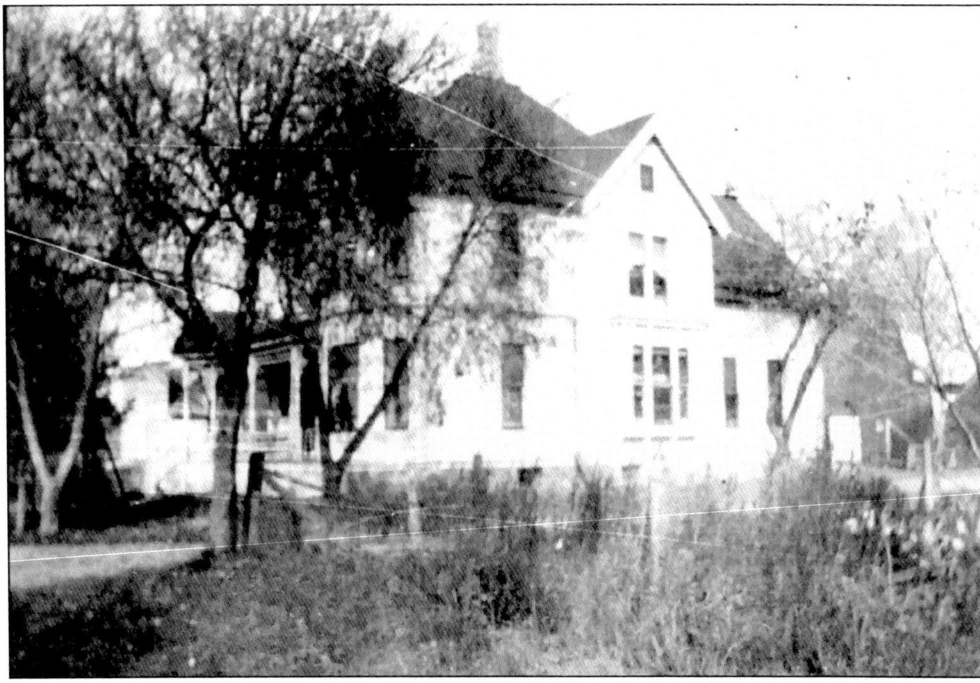

**RICHARD WENDT HOUSE AND FARM.** Just south of the Stagecoach Inn, on the other side of Spring Creek, is the Richard Wendt house and farm. The building still stands today. The Wendt families had settled several places in the area, this being one of them. Several of the Wendt descendants remain in Brushville.

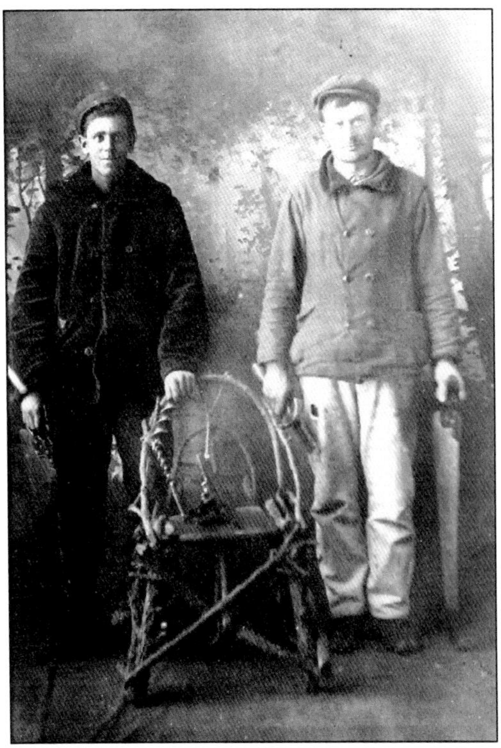

**CHAIR MAKERS.** The man on the left, who is either Henry or Oscar Nelson, also appears in the "Toasters" photograph on page 86. The man on the right is Bert Cornell, a popular fiddle player in the early days. He worked in the Brushville Sawmill for 20¢ a day, six days a week, and evidently made chairs on the side. Cornell is buried in the Brushville Cemetery.

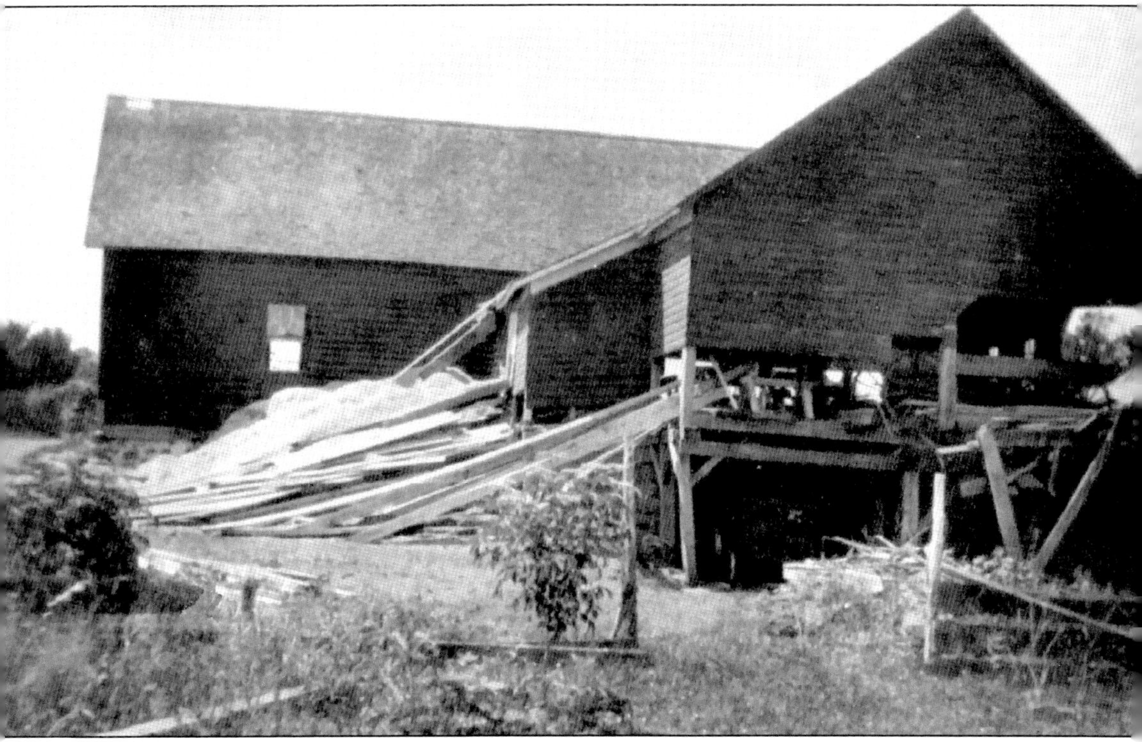

**BRUSHVILLE SAWMILL.** This mill was located next to Spring Creek, southwest of the Stagecoach Inn. The road to the Wendt farm and the Blaisdell farm separated the mill from the inn. The sawmill office, at one time, was office for the justice of the peace. The first sawmill was built by Justin Noble and Charles Stowen in 1857, although others say that Eliphalet Brush started the mill. The first mill had several owners, but with Cady Wilson, the mill caught fire and was leveled. Another mill was built, and Wilson ran it for 13 more years. The next owners were Reed and Dan Clark, and business was very good. After the mill closed in 1887, some of the custom work was still being done there. Soon after, however, the equipment was moved to Antigo and the mill was left in despair. Eventually, it fell down, and today, nothing remains.

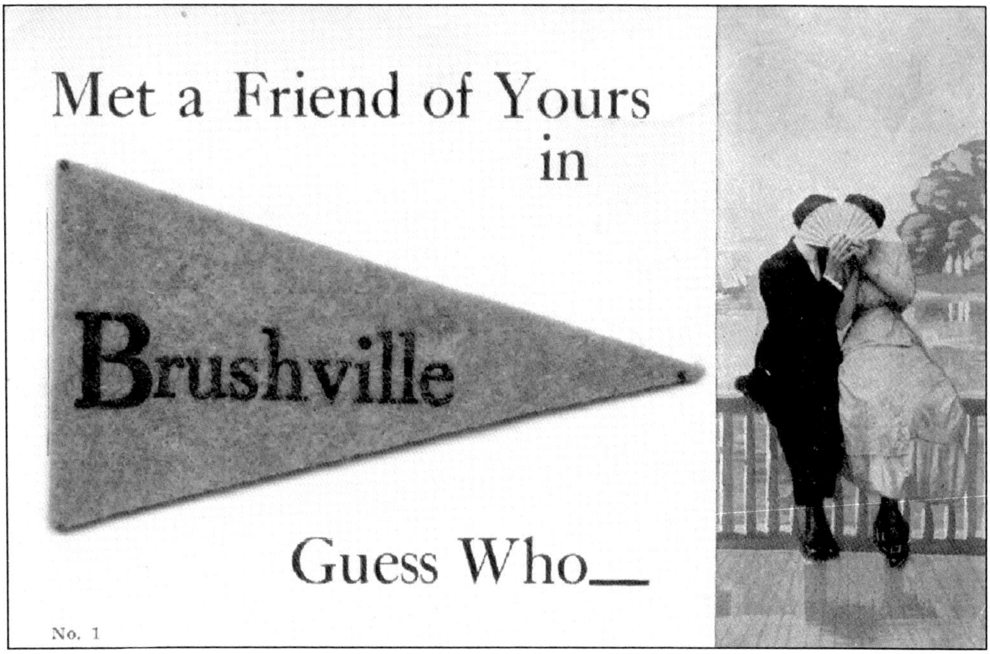


**BRUSHVILLE POSTCARD.** This postcard from Brushville includes a felt pendant.

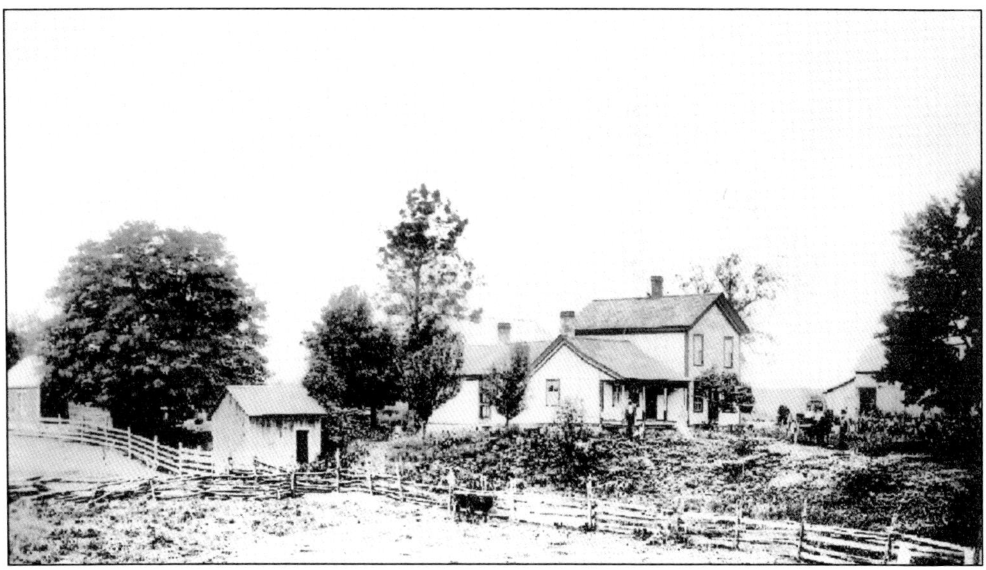

**BLAISDELL FARM.** The Blaisdell farm was owned by Franklin Blaisdell, mentioned earlier in the book. The family came to the area in 1859 and was one of the first to settle in Brushville. The farmhouse burned down in 1901 and was rebuilt in the same year. This is the original homestead. Blaisdell, along with Ewing and Hawley, was from the state of Vermont.

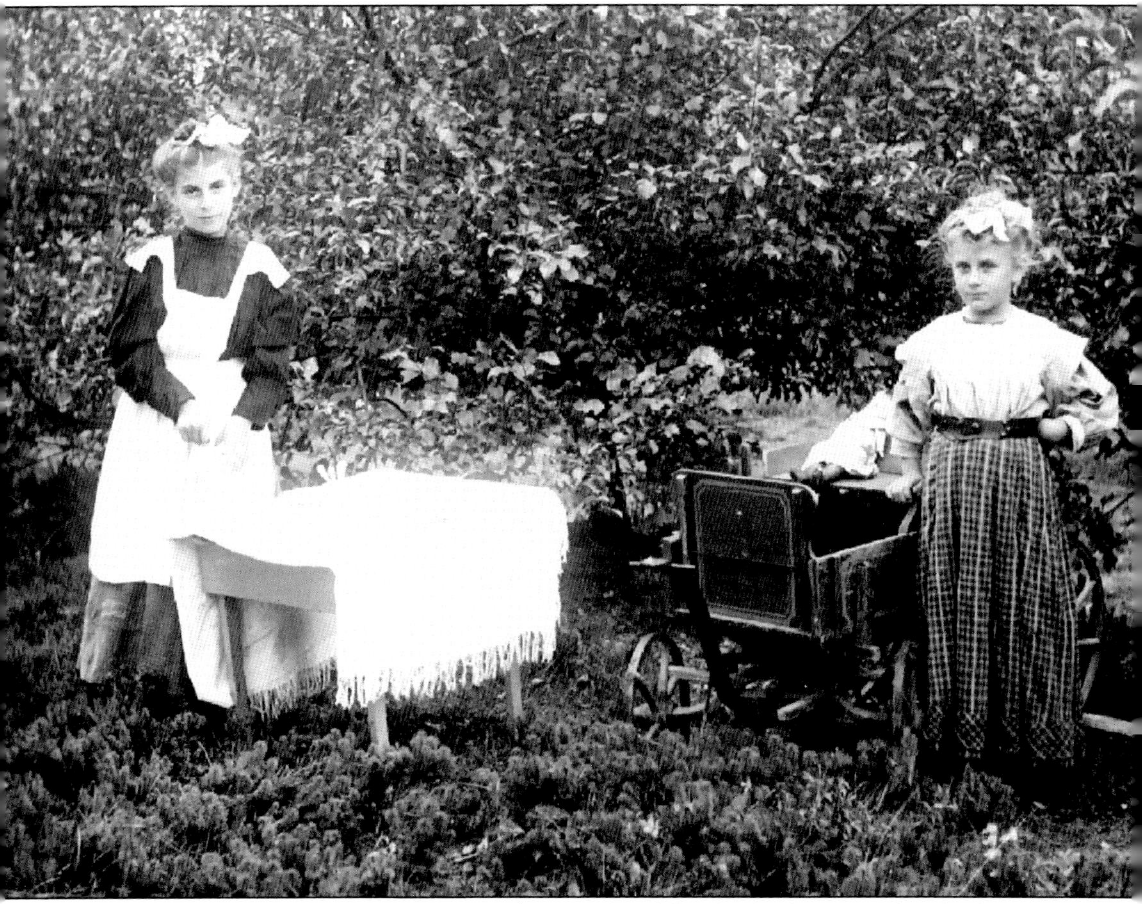

**CICELY AND RUTH BLAISDELL AT PLAY.** The two Blaisdell girls play house in their backyard. Their house was just south of Brushville on the road that cut between the Stagecoach Inn and the sawmill. Cicely pretends to pour water into a glass, while Ruth tends to the carriage.

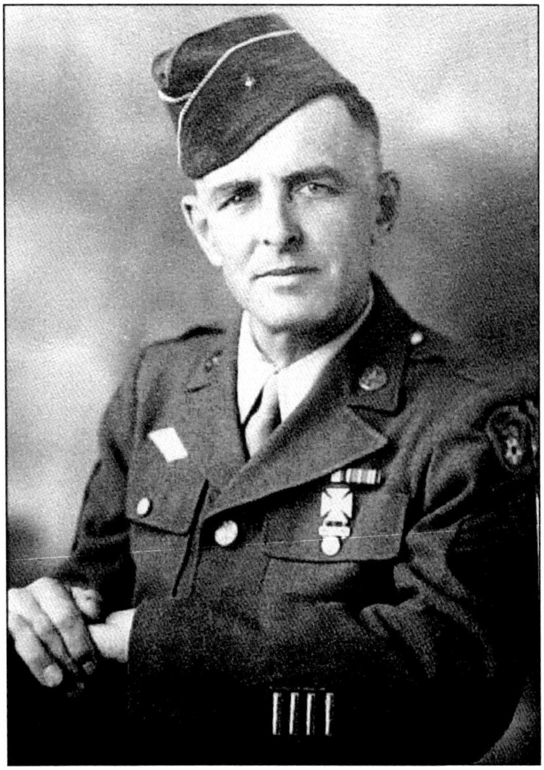

**ALVIN ZIEGENHAGEN.** Enlisting in World War II at the ripe age of 45 years old, Alvin Ziegenhagen served in a tank division. An architect by trade, he enjoyed drawing many of the area's structures. He was very generous in giving these drawings away to friends and neighbors. Ziegenhagen's artistic renderings appear on the following pages.

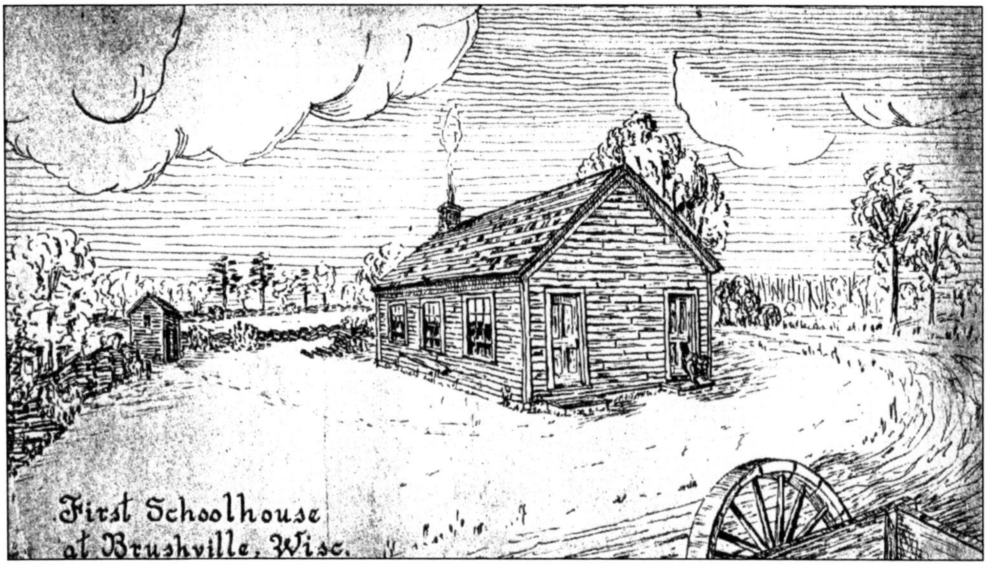


**FIRST SCHOOLHOUSE OF BRUSHVILLE.** As one can expect in an early American settlement, the buildings were log structures. This schoolhouse was not any different. Ziegenhagen depicts the schoolhouse in the drawing as it looked in its earliest days. The schoolhouse was located just northwest of the Ziegenhagen farm, and the two were later divided by Highway 49. This site, south of the cemetery, is farmland now. The new schoolhouse, built in 1875, took the place of the old log cabin schoolhouse. The new school was constructed across the road, to the south. For a while, the old school was used as a church until being torn down.

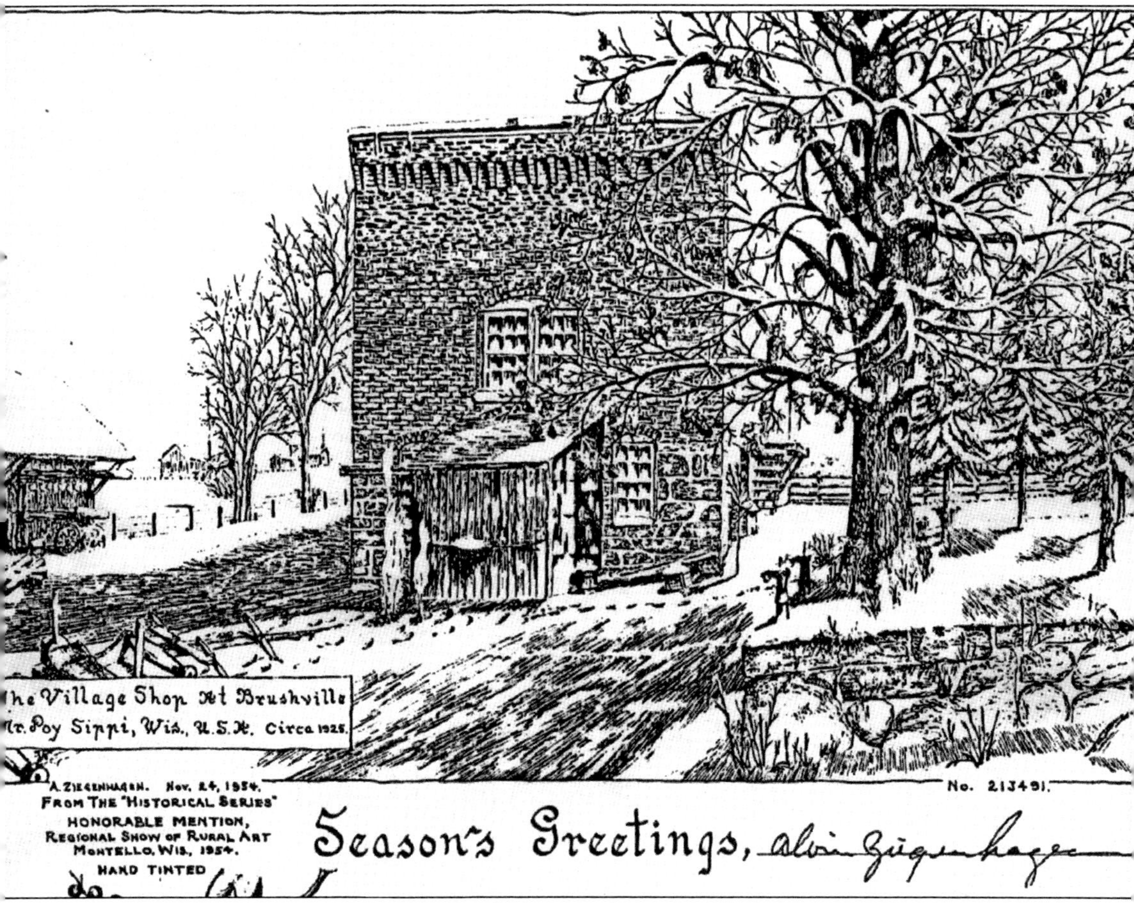


**BLACKSMITH SHOP IN BRUSHVILLE.** In this 1954 Christmas card by Alvin Ziegenhagen, the blacksmith shop of Brushville is illustrated as a two-story building. With the source of income being derived from farming, the blacksmith shop was the farmer's friend and the center of the community. This structure had a dance hall on the second floor in its early days and a gift shop inside. The blacksmith shop was on the Richard Wendt property near the Wendt house.

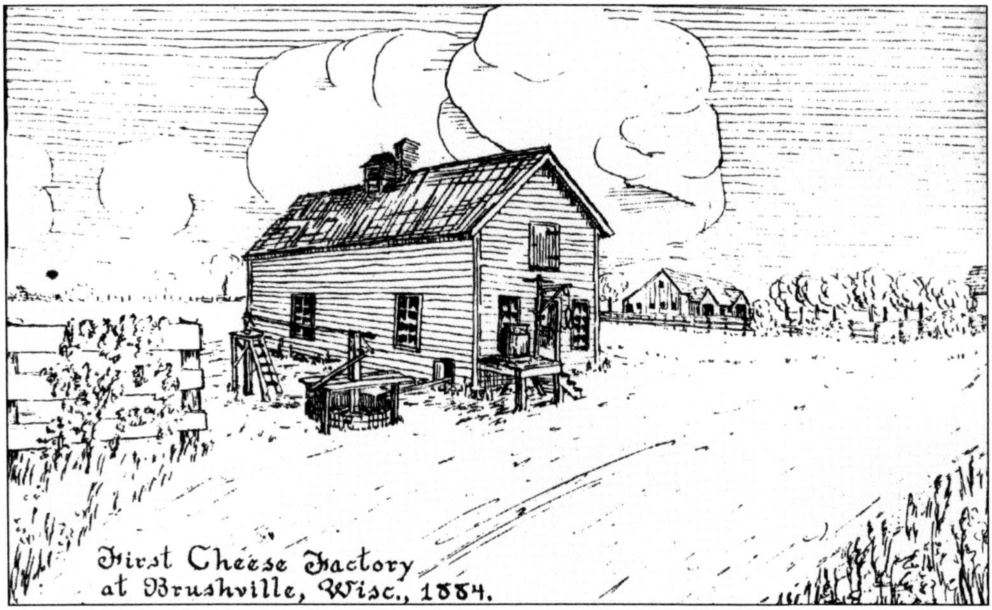


**First Cheese Factory of Brushville.** This Ziegenhagen drawing depicts the first cheese factory of Brushville in an 1884 setting. The cheese factory was located about a mile west of the Ziegenhagen farm.

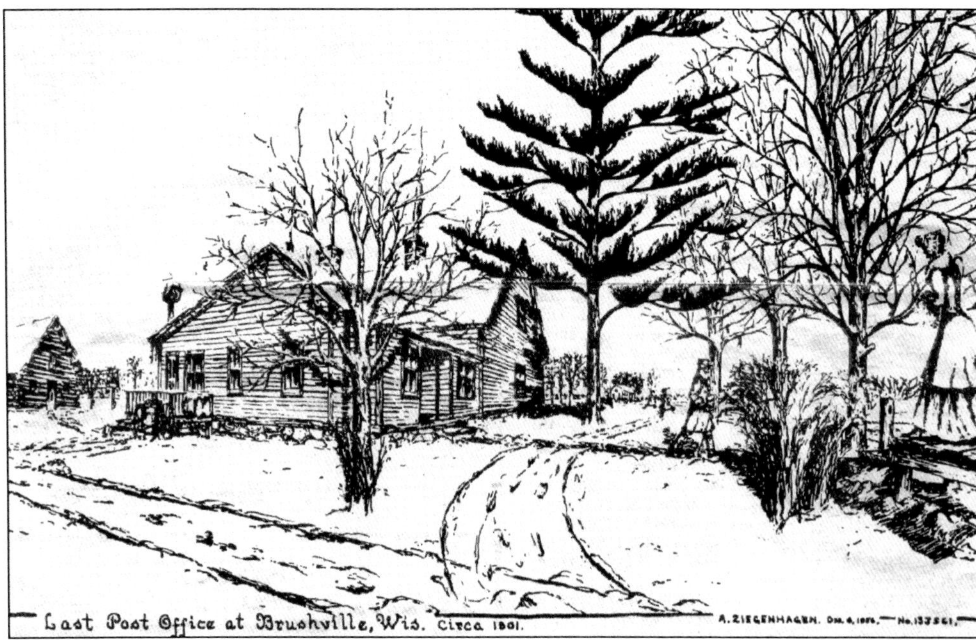


**Last Post Office of Brushville.** Another Ziegenhagen drawing shows the post office of Brushville in 1901. The last postmaster was William Godson, a native of England. After a fall reduced his ability to do farmwork, he took on the postmaster job. A portion of his home, the porch, was adapted for the post office. The last mail delivered to this building was on July 28, 1902. Godson is remembered as willingly handing out the mail to anyone who came to his door at any time of day or night.

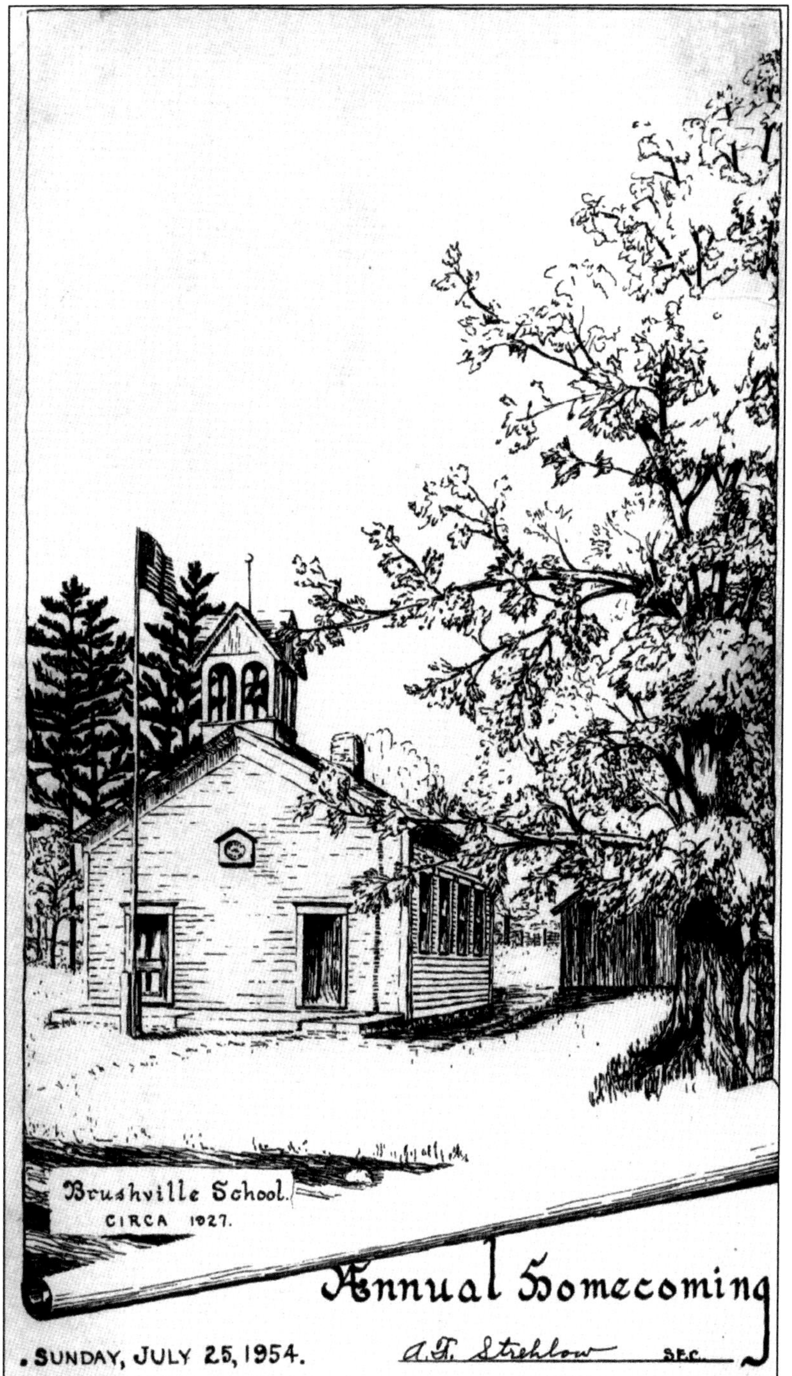


**BRUSHVILLE SCHOOL.** Ziegenhagen created many drawings of the popular buildings for events such as this Homecoming in 1954. The drawing depicts the Brushville School in a 1927 setting.

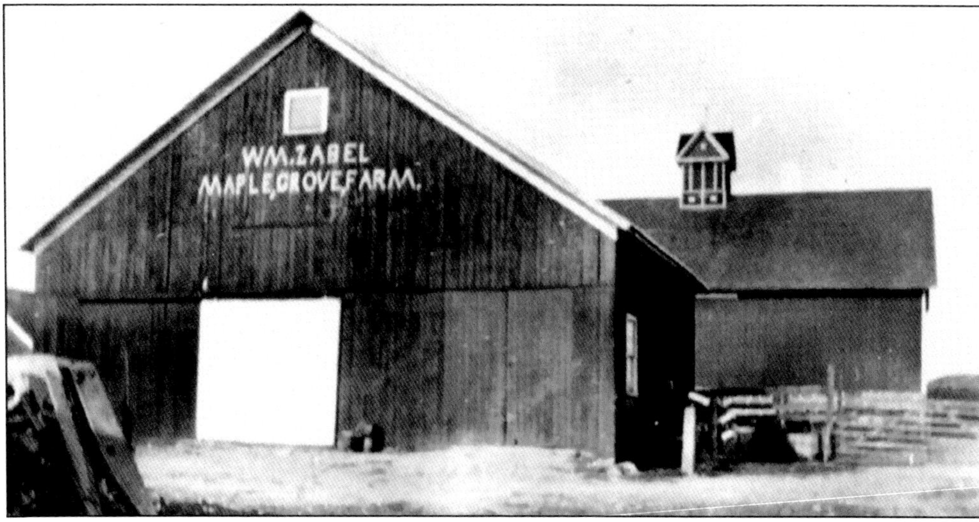


**William Zabel Maple Grove Farm.** This view is similar to the farming community that surrounds the area. While this is the Zabel farm from years ago, it looks like many of the farms still in business today in the Brushville area.

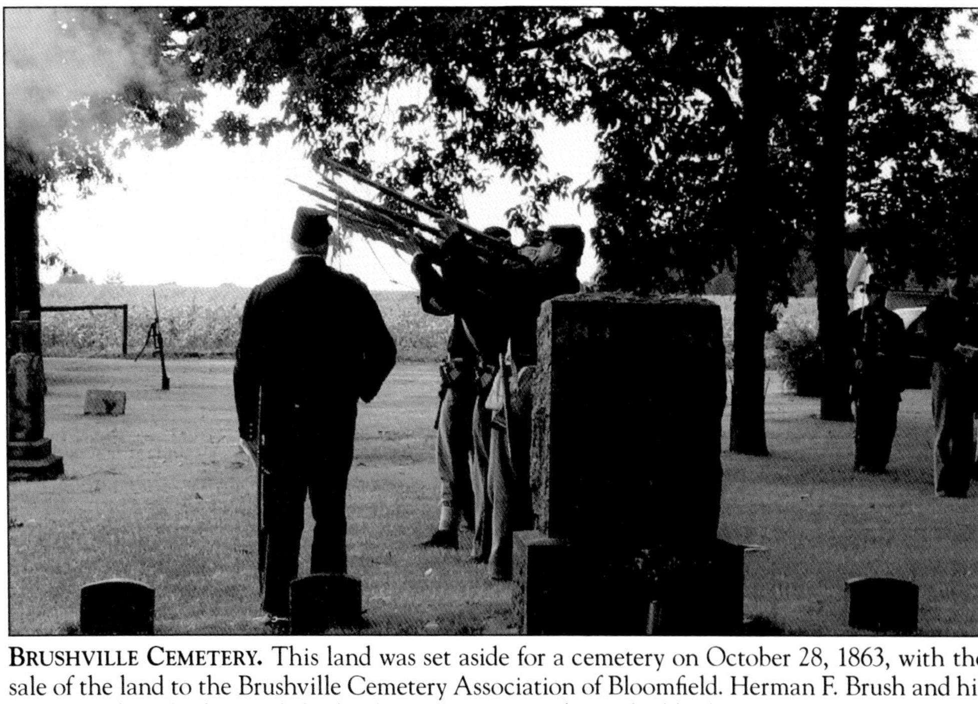

**Brushville Cemetery.** This land was set aside for a cemetery on October 28, 1863, with the sale of the land to the Brushville Cemetery Association of Bloomfield. Herman F. Brush and his wife, Caroline, had owned the land since 1853. Members of Old Abe Camp No. 8 of Central Wisconsin, Sons of Union Veterans of the Civil War, attend the dedication of the new headstone marker for Franklin Blaisdell as part of Poy Sippi's 150th celebration. Shown are Alan Petit, camp senior vice commander; Randy Novak, past Wisconsin department commander (as the closest man in the camp guard); Kim Heltemes, Wisconsin department junior vice commander (standing guard on the far left); and Brian Peters, camp commander and past Wisconsin department junior vice commander, who led the ceremony (far right).

# *Seven*

# TUSTIN

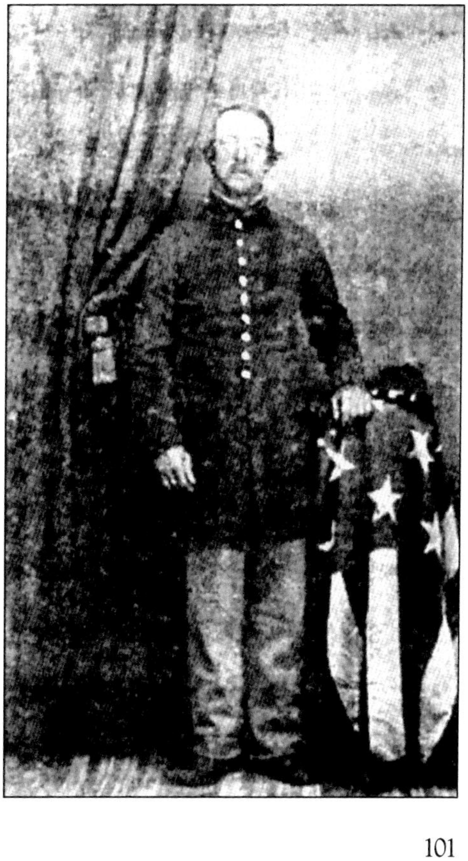

**CHARLES FREER.** Charles Freer is the man responsible for the start of Tustin. He bought a half-section (160 acres) of land from the federal government and settled there in 1856. Here, he is shown in his Civil War uniform, as he served in the 13th Wisconsin Infantry, Company E. Drafted as a private on December 31, 1864, he was mustered out on July 13, 1865. He went back to farming after his return from the war. Freer died in 1906 and is buried in the Brushville Cemetery.

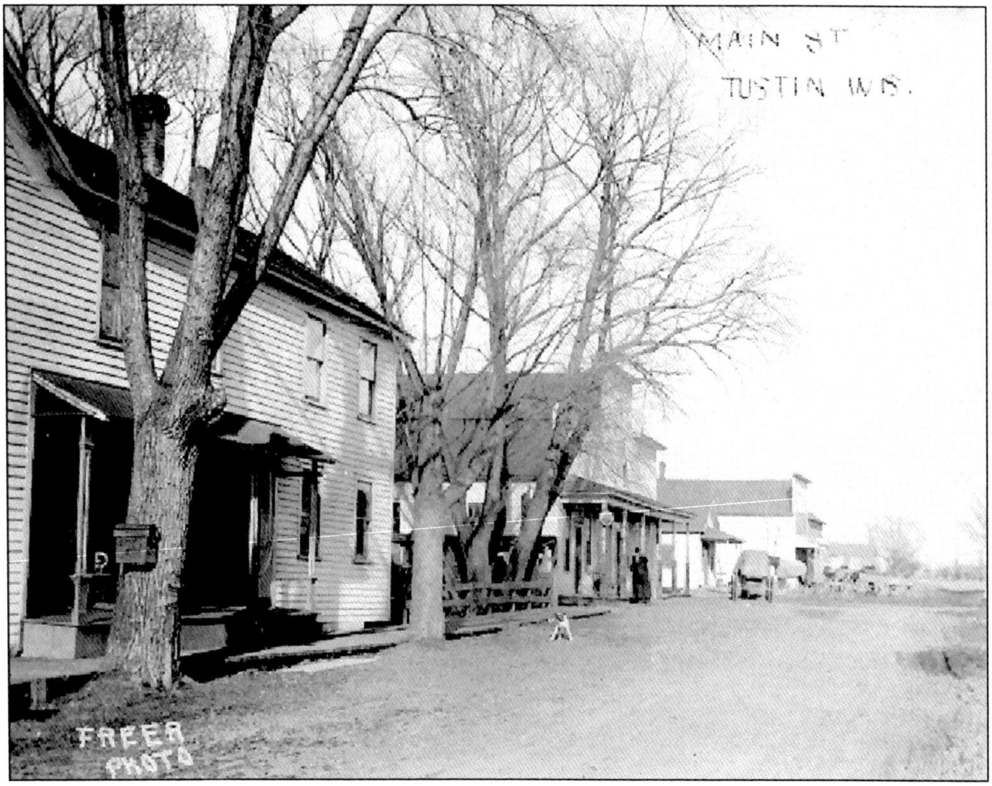


**MAIN STREET OF TUSTIN.** In this early-20th-century view of Tustin, the Boyson Store appears in the center and the Gottlieb Velte Saloon in the background. Boyson had married Velte's sister but remained competitive for business.

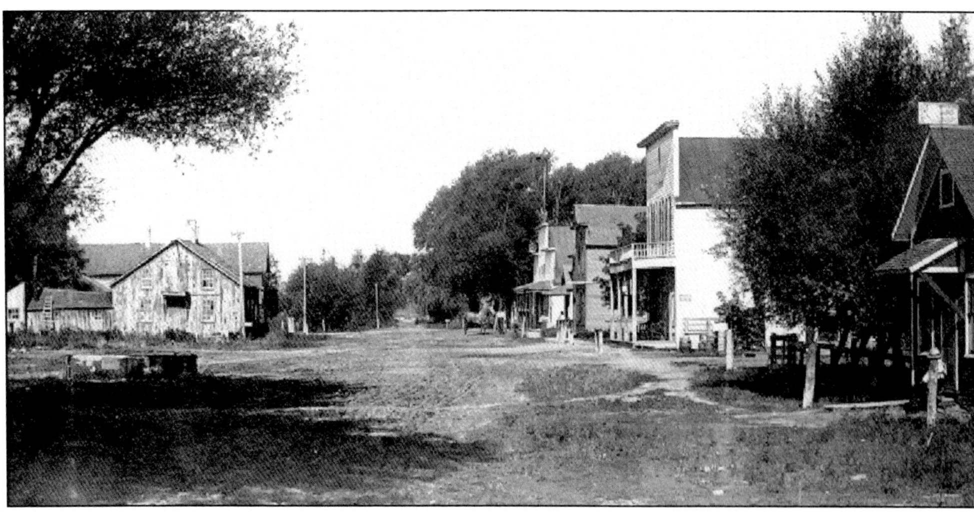

**EARLY TUSTIN.** This photograph is also featured in Charles H. Velte's book *The History of Lake Poygan*. The water fountain on the left was drilled by Charles Freer in 1856. The building on the left is the LaBorde Boat Company. The building in the right background is the John Boyson Store. The Krueger's owned the middle store, and Velte owned the nearer white building. The fountain area was made of concrete in 1912, so the photograph dates to after that time.

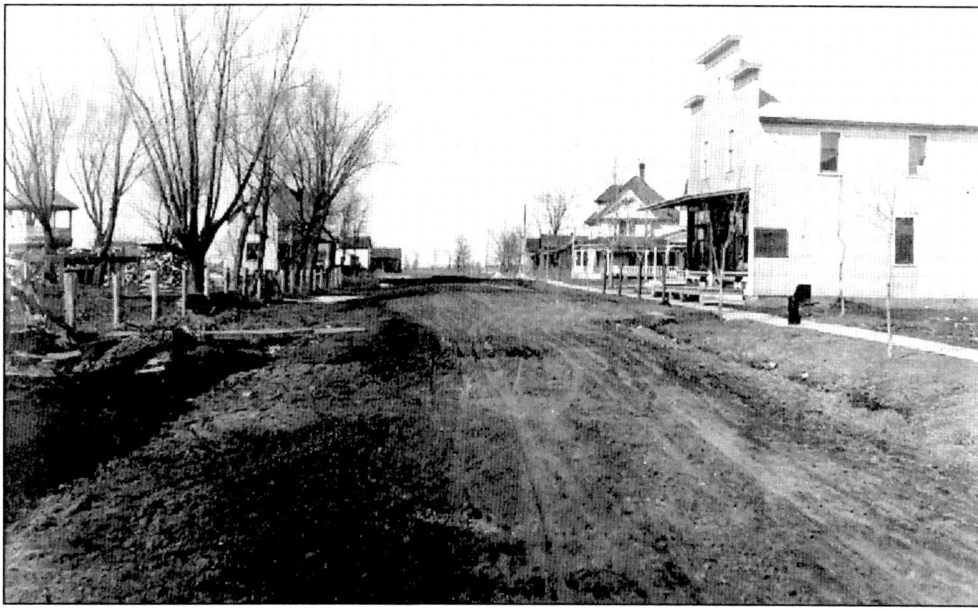

**Tustin.** The building on the right is the Boyson Store. Across the street is a raised gazebo.

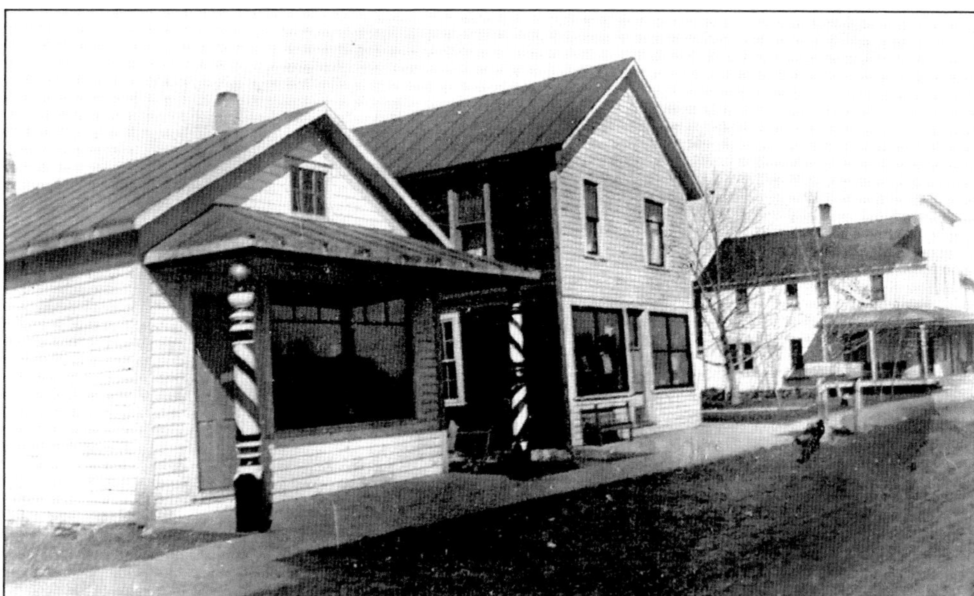

**Barbershop in Tustin.** Many older residents still remember the barbershop. To its right is the furniture store and funeral home building, with John Boyson as undertaker. The hotel fills out the right background.

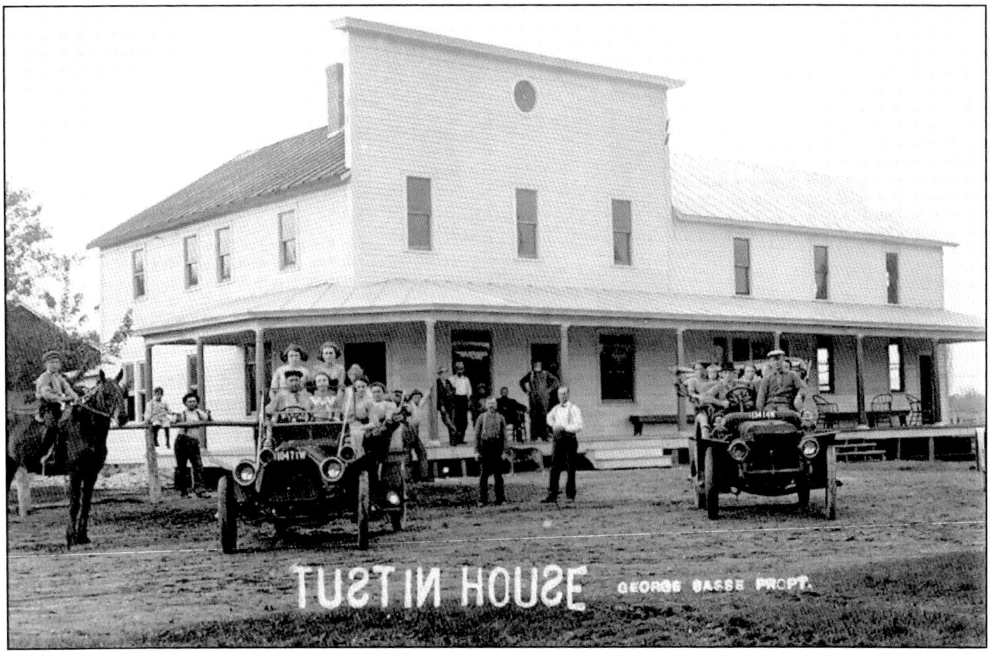


**TUSTIN HOTEL.** John Boyson was the manager of the hotel in Tustin for a time. Again, the people were proud to show off their "novel" cars.

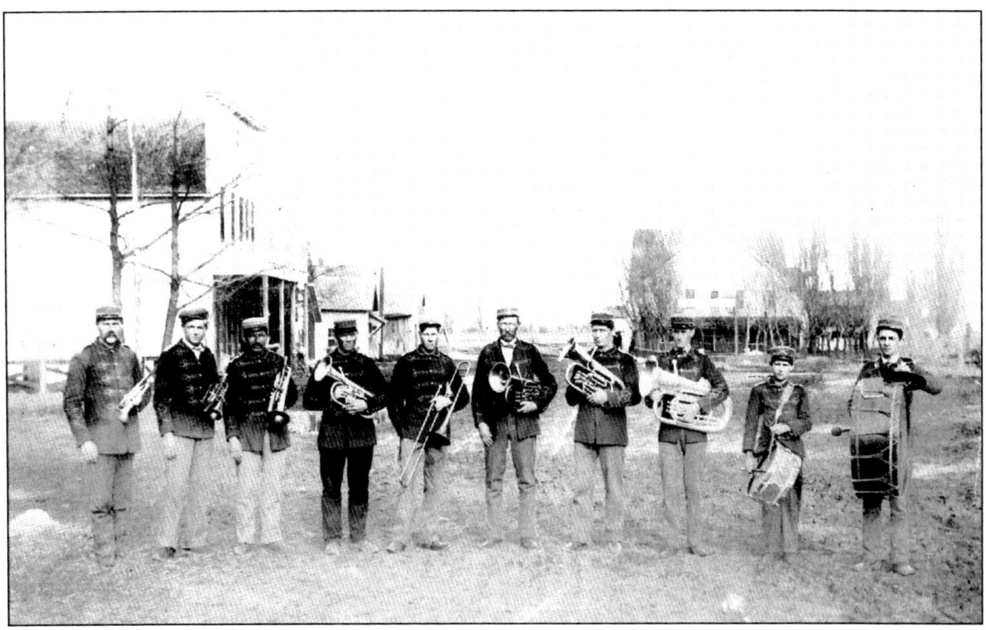

**TUSTIN BAND.** This c. 1898 photograph shows the Tustin Band on Main Street with the hotel in the left background. Originally called the Lake House, the hotel was started by Mrs. Drumm. Band members, from left to right, are Mr. Krueger, Frank Yehrke, Carl Nehring, Henry Steinberg, Jed Brewster, Fred Ringling, Fred Grim, Paul LeFevre, John Boyson Jr., and Charles Velte. Fred Ringling was a cousin to the famed Ringling Brothers, and Charles Velte was the author of *The History of Lake Poygan*.

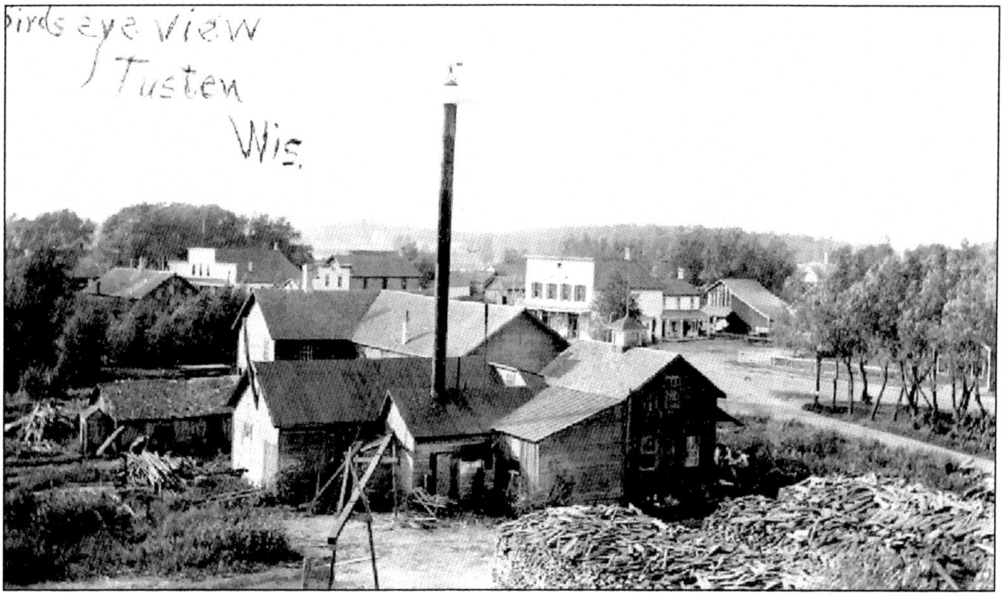


**BIRD'S-EYE VIEW OF TUSTIN.** With the Wolf River and the Lake Poygan waterways, the logging industry was booming in the Tustin area. Great stands of pine and hardwood nearby were making it easier to get the timber to the mills. Using men called "river rats," the loggers managed to feed the mills. In the left background is the Boyson Store. The middle store was owned by The Krueger's, while the large white building in the foreground was Velte's Store.

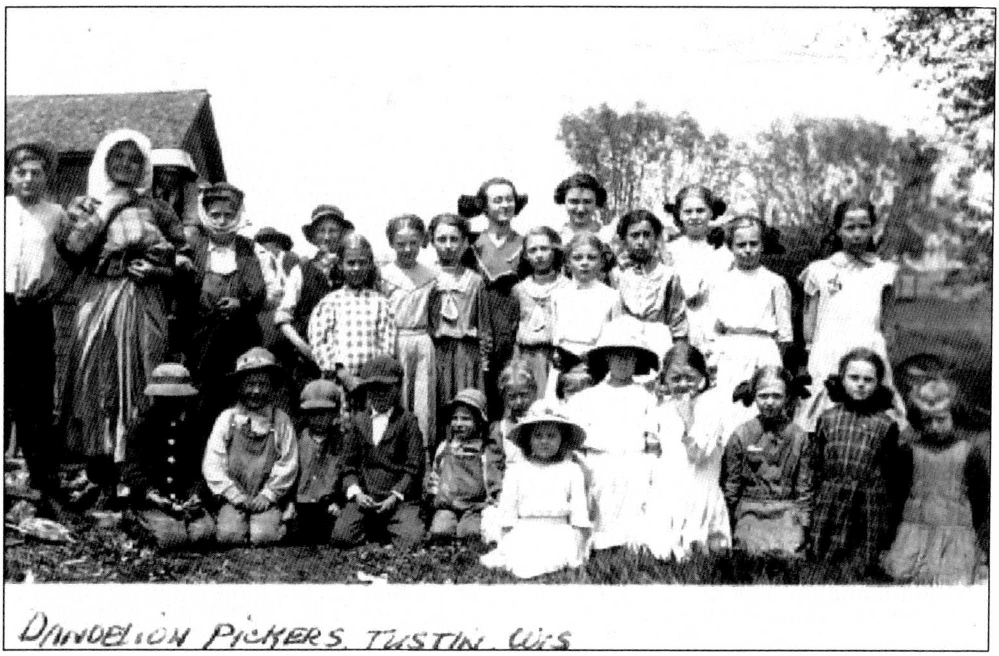


**TUSTIN DANDELION PICKERS.** In order to clean up the yard or gain ingredients for winemaking, people are gathering to pick dandelions. The woman second from the left might well be Grant Boyson dressing as a gag for the photographer.

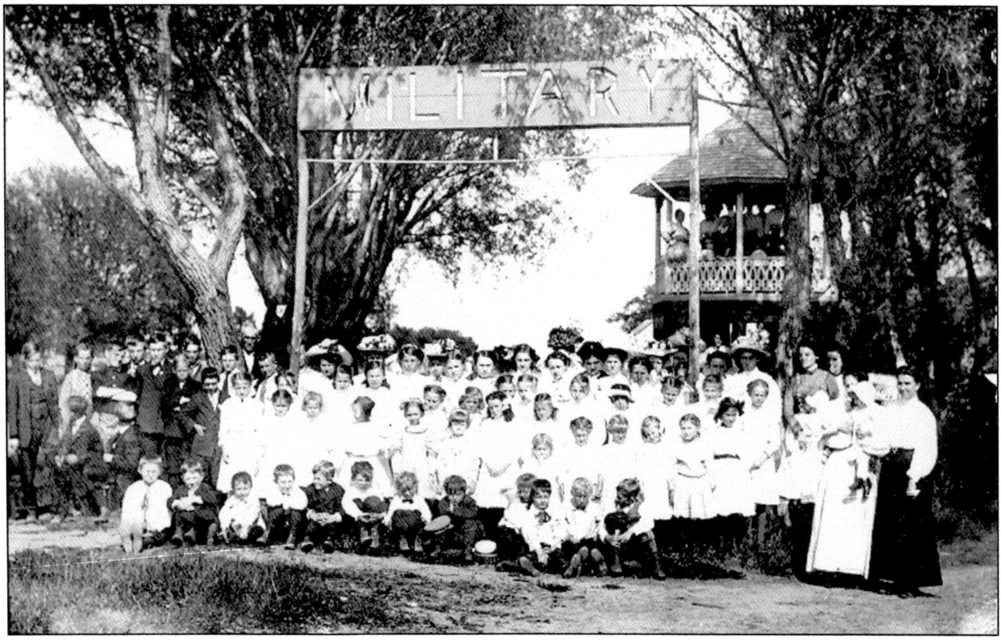


**MILITARY PARK.** The occasion for this photograph may have been the end of the school year or a confirmation. Notice the raised gazebo behind the trees. It has recently been torn down.

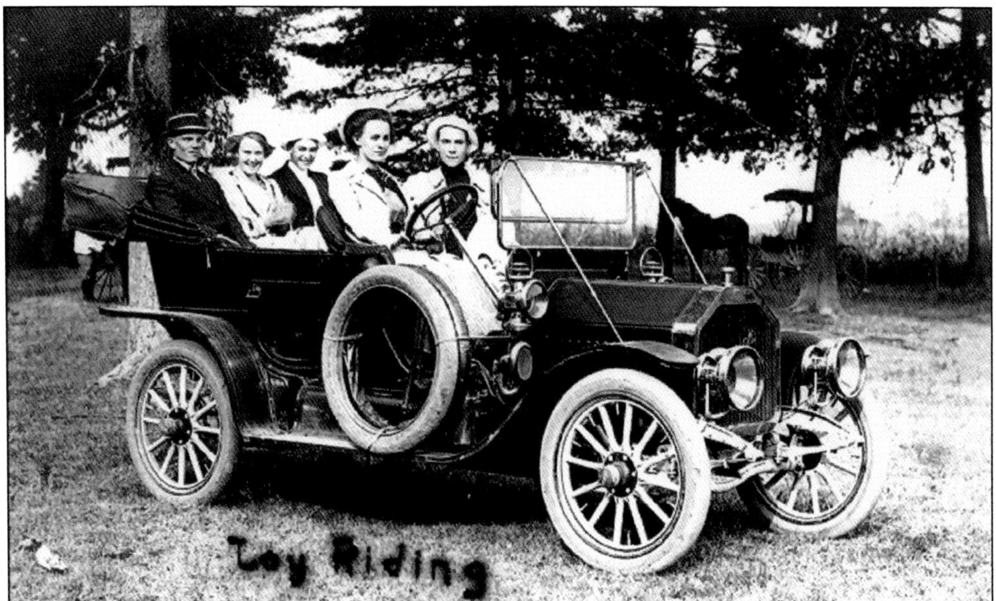


**JOY RIDING.** This photograph shows the transition from the surrey, as seen behind the Buick, to the modern form of transportation, the automobile. Lillian Boyson sits in the driver's seat, and one of the LeFevre girls is in the back seat.

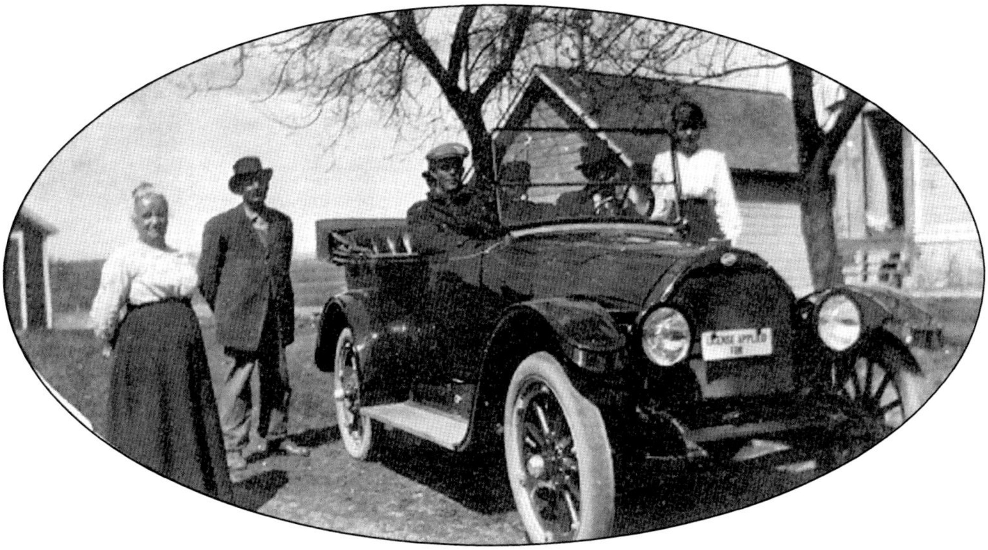

**NEW CAR.** Many families of the time had their photograph taken with the new car. Notice the "license applied for" plate on the radiator shroud.

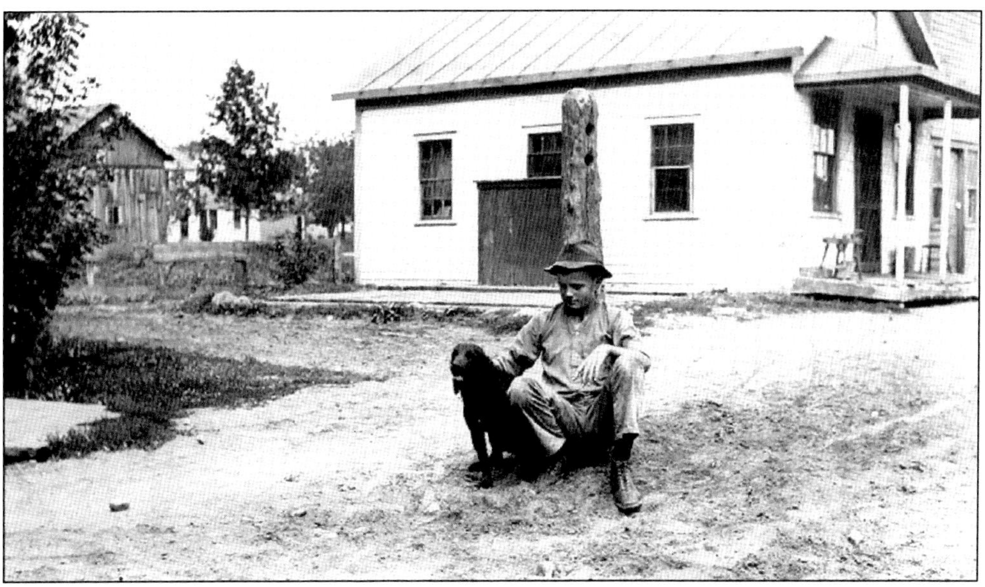

**A BOY AND HIS DOG.** John Boyson's son Grant is pictured with his dog about 1909.

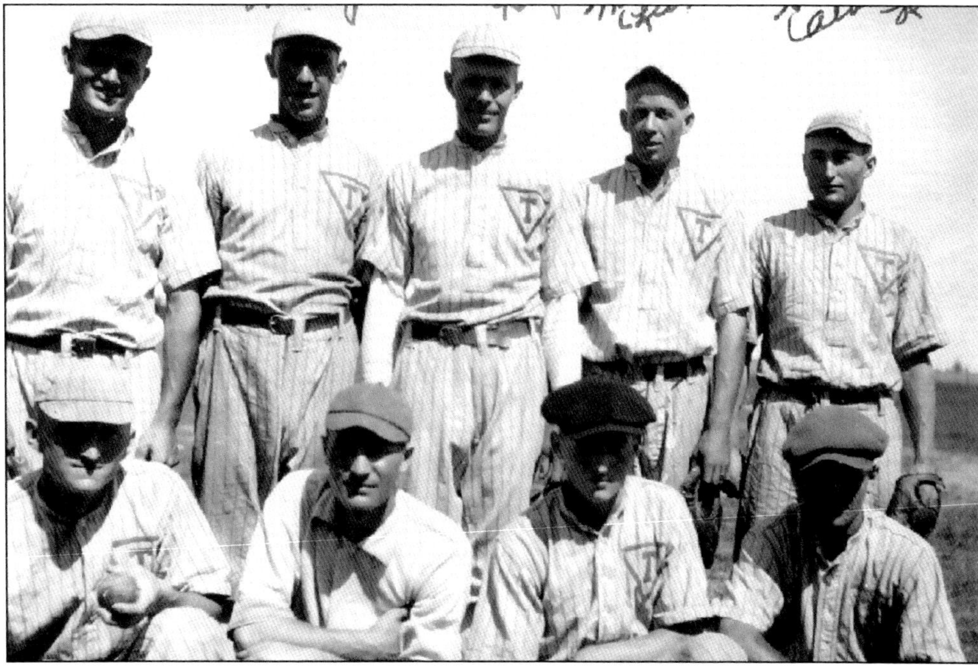

**TUSTIN TEAM.** Some members of the Tustin team also played on the Poy Sippi team. What happened when they faced each other?

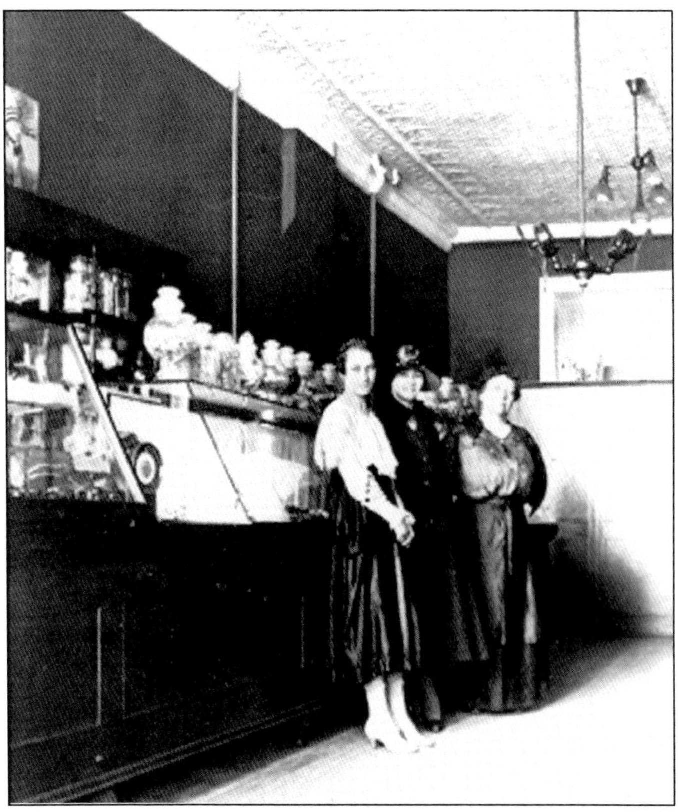

**INSIDE BOYSON STORE.** This may be the only surviving shot of the Boyson Store interior. Mrs. LaBorde (center) and Mrs. Oaks (right) stand with an unidentified woman.

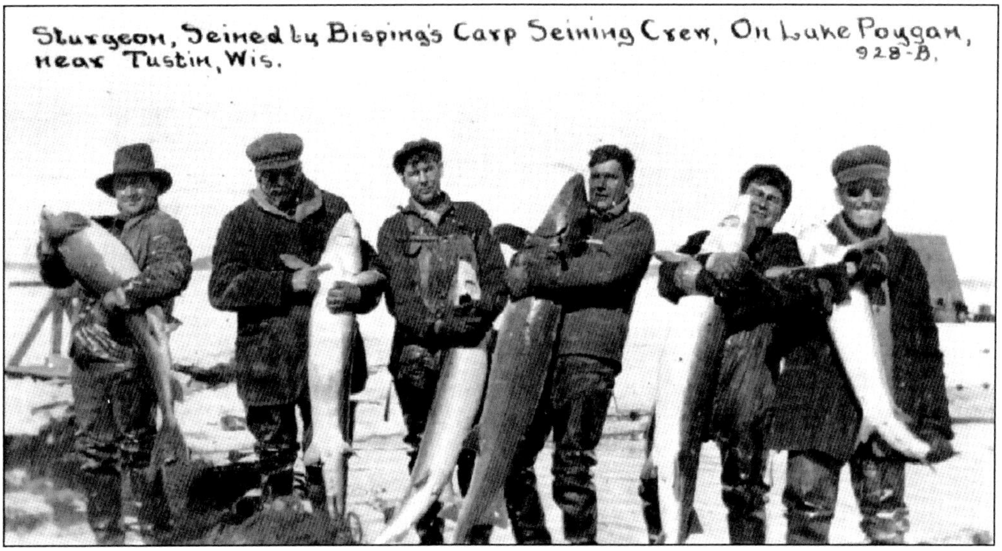


**STURGEON FROM LAKE POYGAN.** These men, working for the Bisping's Carp Company, show off some of the sturgeon seined while trying to get carp. Fishing in Lake Poygan brings a lot of tourists to the area, but the season for sturgeon is now quite limited. The limit regulations were different in the earlier days.

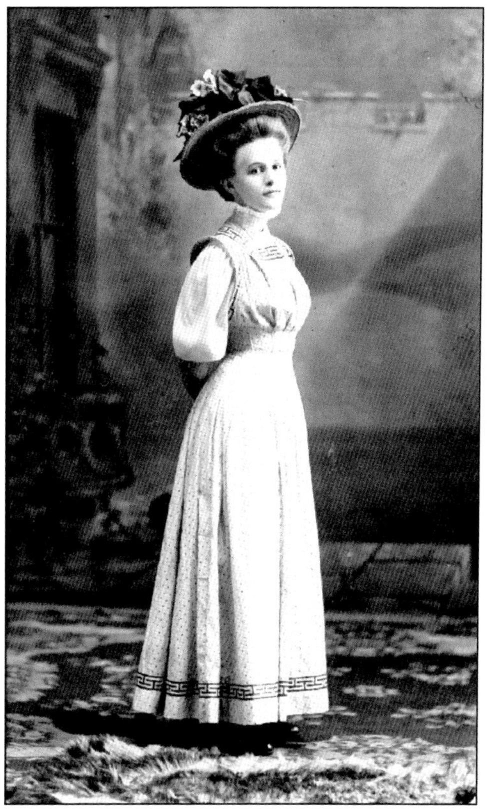

**LILLIAN BOYSON.** The daughter of John Boyson stands ramrod straight for her photograph at about 18 years old.

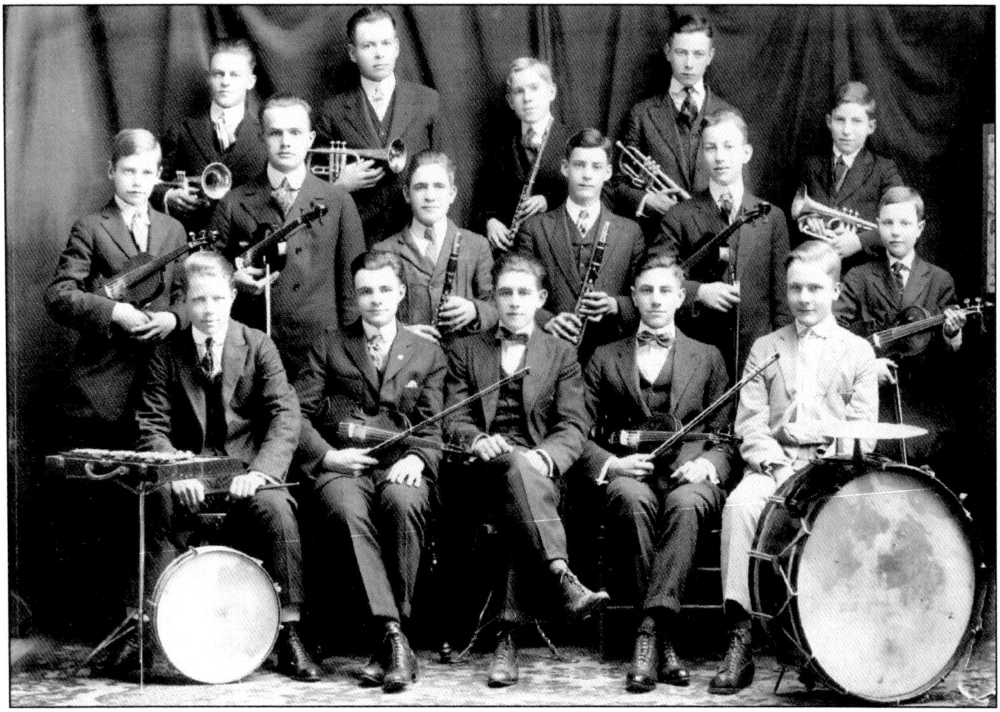

**Grant Boyson in Oshkosk Orchestra.** This 1916 photograph shows Grant Boyson (second row, second from left) while he was a member of the Oshkosh Orchestra. Grant was a violin player with the orchestra, as well as with several bands that played in the Poy Sippi and Tustin areas.

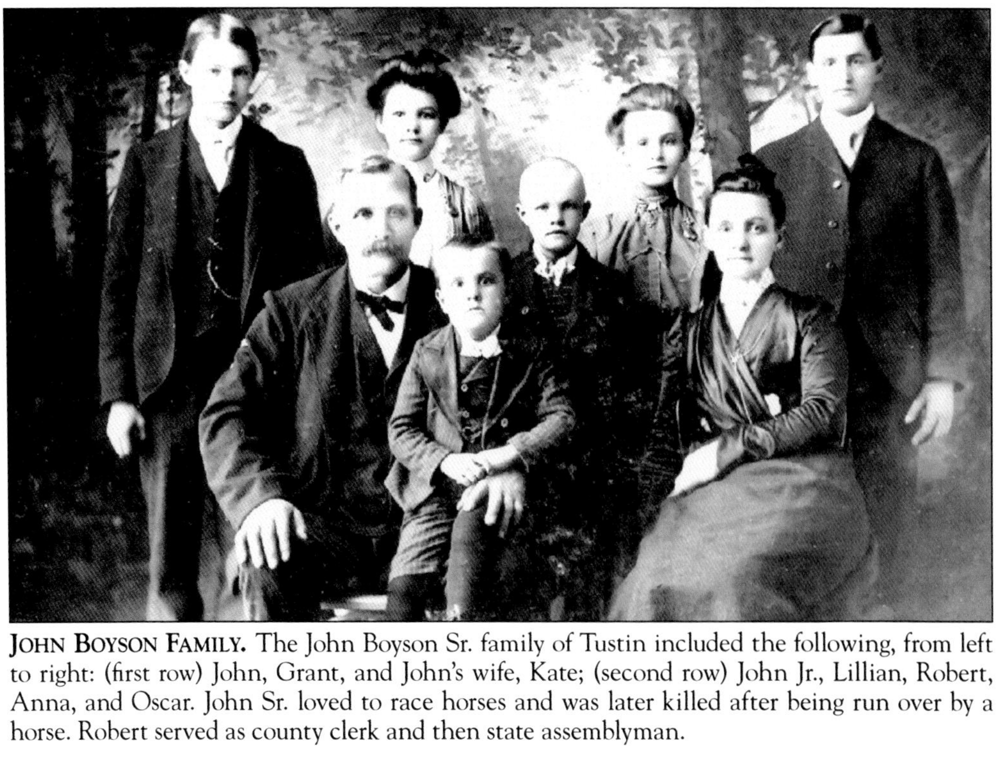

**John Boyson Family.** The John Boyson Sr. family of Tustin included the following, from left to right: (first row) John, Grant, and John's wife, Kate; (second row) John Jr., Lillian, Robert, Anna, and Oscar. John Sr. loved to race horses and was later killed after being run over by a horse. Robert served as county clerk and then state assemblyman.

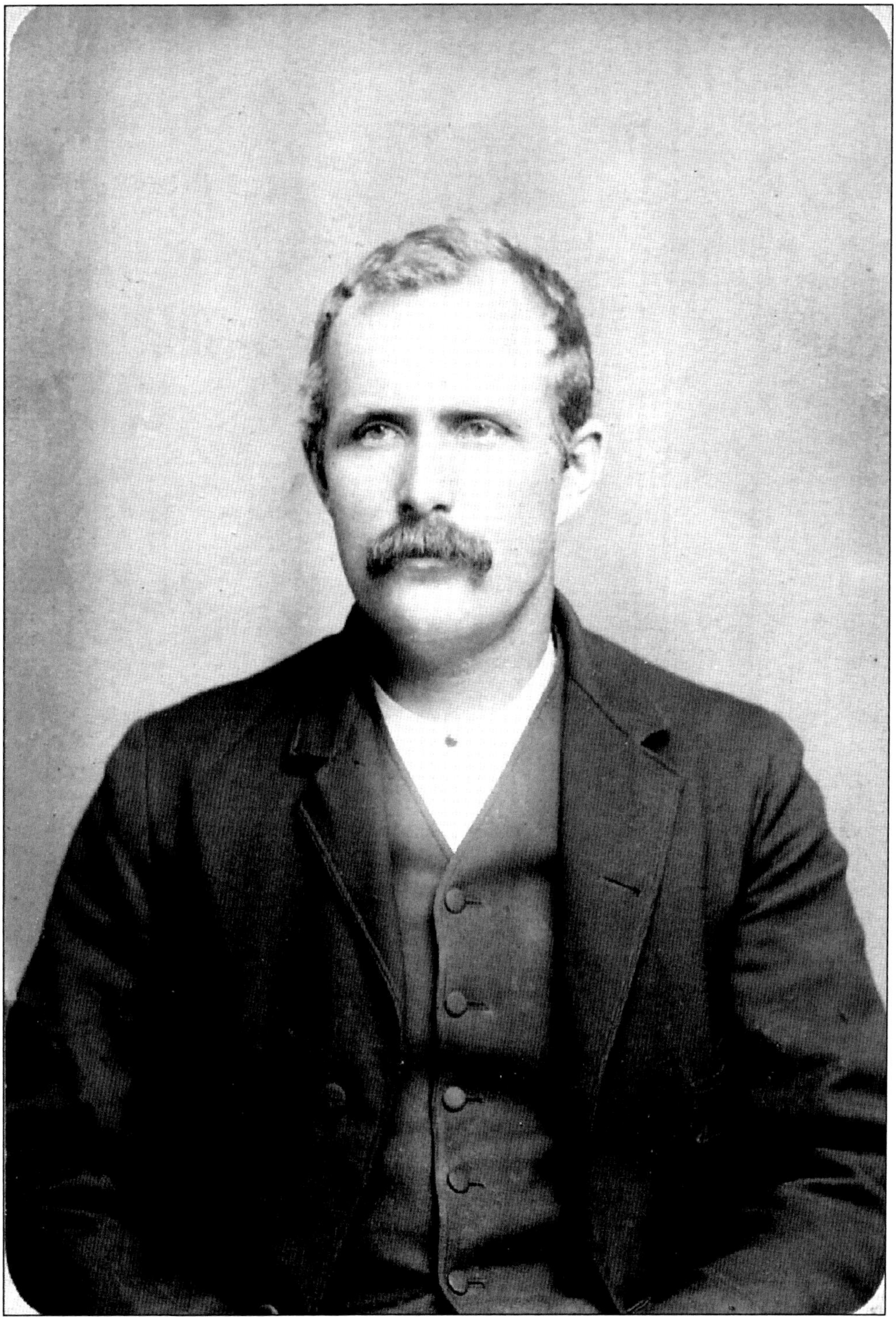

**John Boyson Sr.** The family photograph predates this one. John's father was Charles Boyson, who was a seafarer before settling down in the Tustin area. John owned a store on Tustin's Main Street, different from the one owned by his son John Jr.

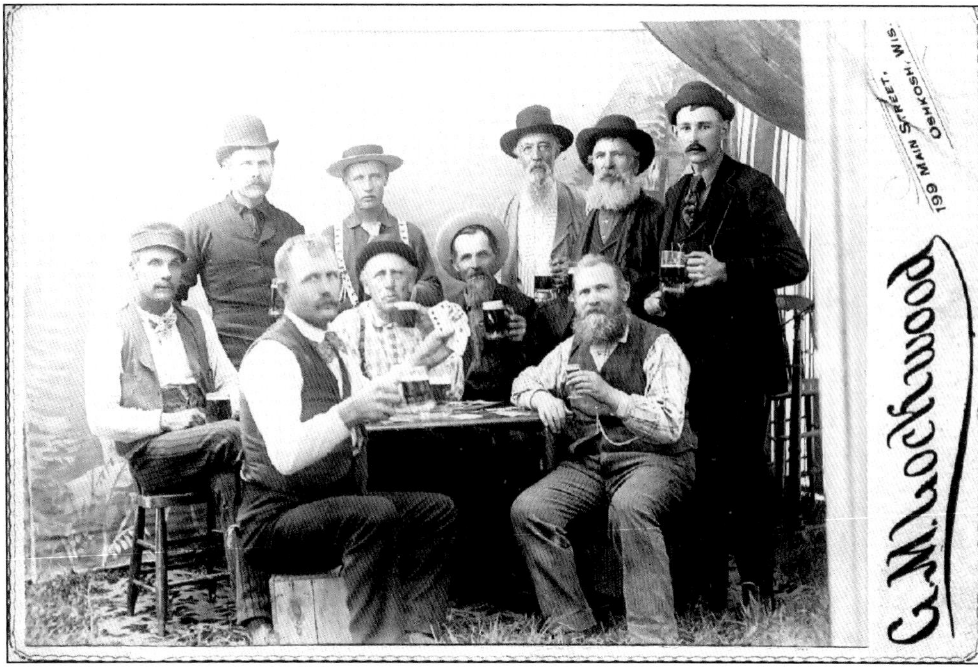


**JOHN BOYSON AND CRONIES.** John Boyson relaxes with some of his friends. He is the man nearest the camera; the others are unidentified.

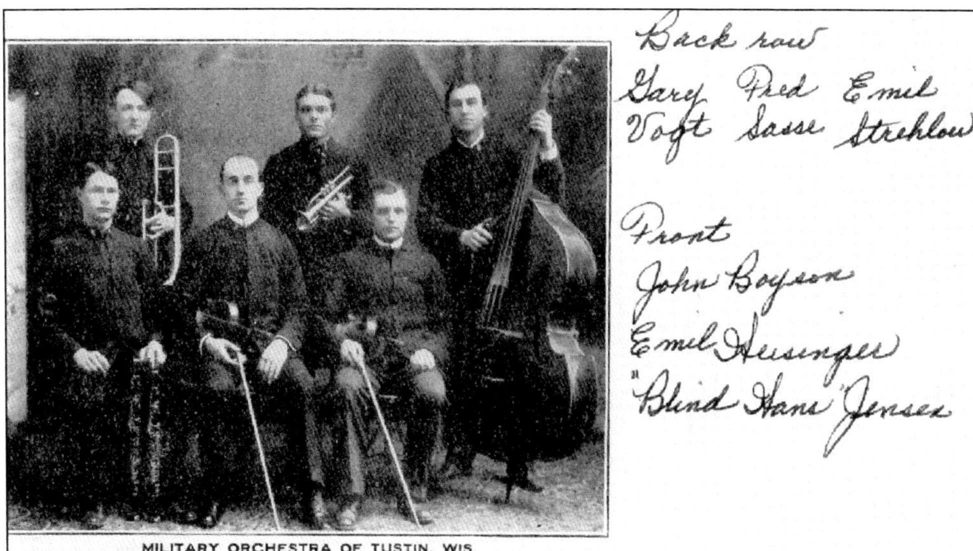


**JOHN BOYSON JR.** Appearing in the Tustin Military Band, John Boyson Jr. is the man on the left of the first row.

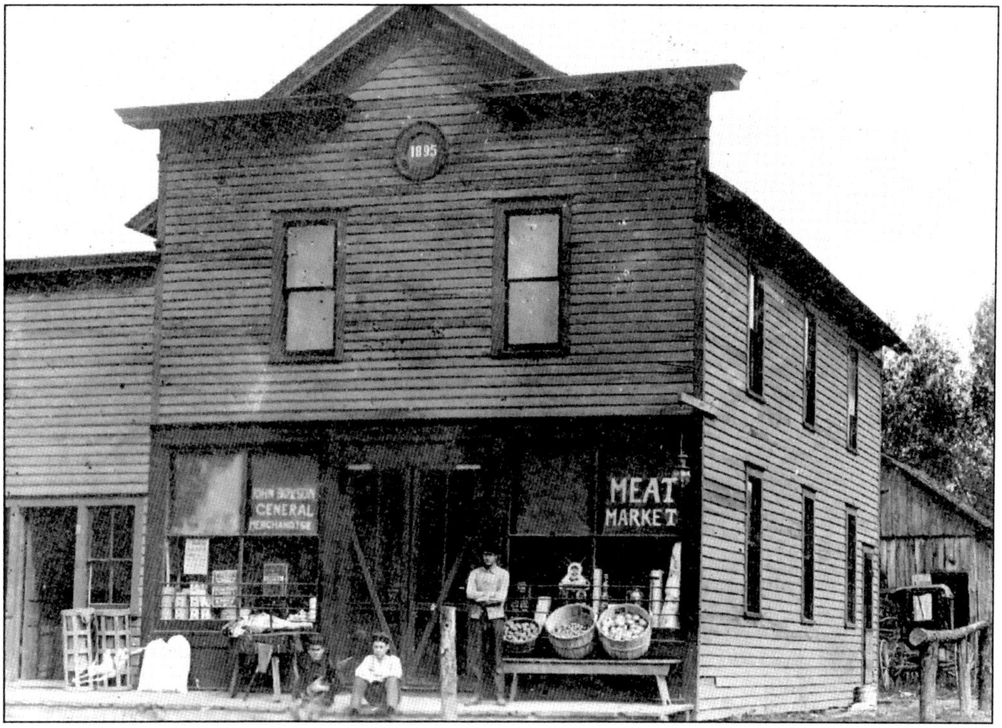


**CITY MARKET STORE OF TUSTIN.** John Boyson Jr. owned this meat market and general store in Tustin. Sitting on the boardwalk is his brother Oscar, in the white shirt.

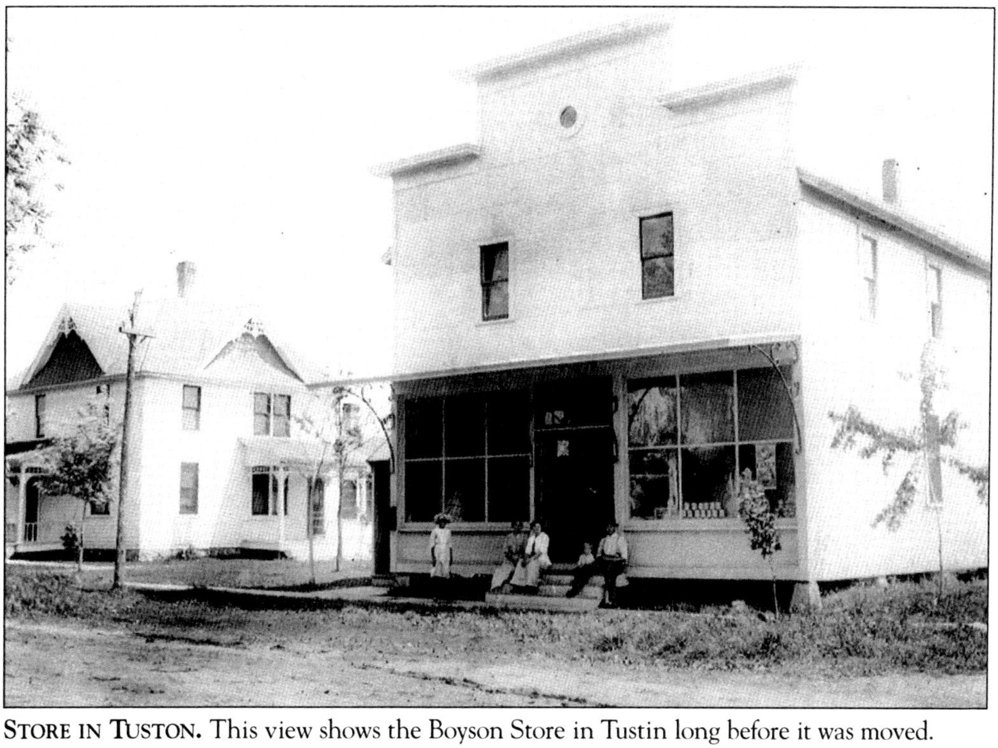

**STORE IN TUSTON.** This view shows the Boyson Store in Tustin long before it was moved.

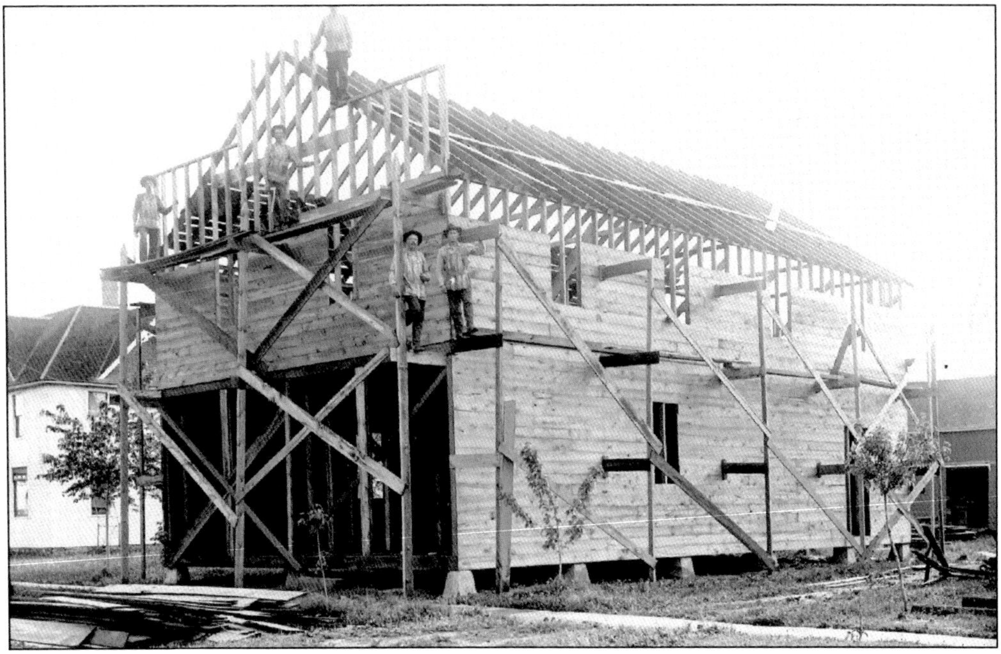

**BOYSON STORE IS BUILT.** Notice the neat scaffold arrangement as the men build upward. The foundation is of concrete pillars, typical of the time. This style of foundation made it easier to raise and move the building, as shown in the photographs on pages 115 and 116.

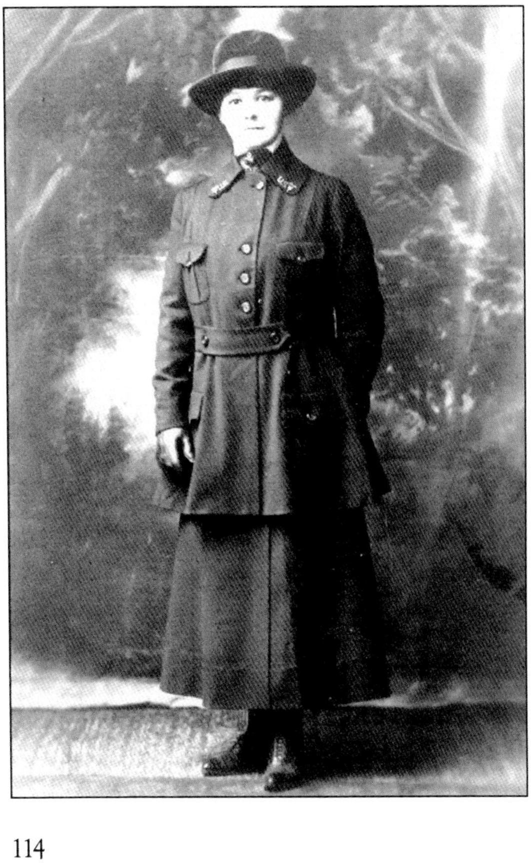

**ANNA BOYSON.** Anna married Art Hildebrand, who died six months later of a ruptured appendix. Not wishing to see others die so young, she made up her mind to become a nurse. She graduated from the Illinois Training School for Nurses at Cook County Hospital. Then, for two years, she worked as an anesthetist and as an assistant for Dr. C. J. Combs in surgery work. She served in the army cantonment and reported to Camp Bowie at Fort Worth, Texas. One of the first called for duty during World War I, she served in France while her brother Grant was on the front lines there—although the two never got to see each other. After the war, she married a Dr. Smith and lived in Amherst, Wisconsin. For a short time, she taught at the Tustin School.

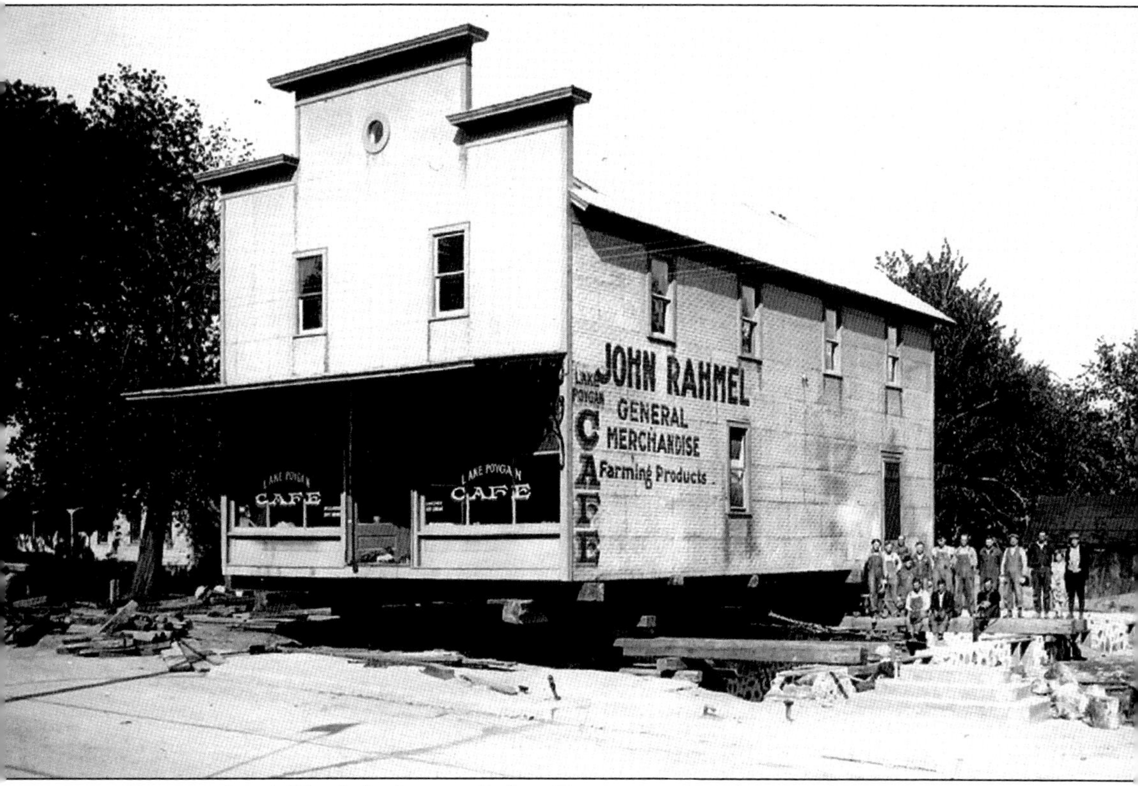


**LAKE POYGAN CAFÉ.** The Lake Poygan Café in Tustin is ready to be moved to Poy Sippi. Notice the crew posing for the camera. The building had served as the Boyson Store and had been passed on to Grant Boyson. The upper floor was used for dances and parties. While John Boyson owned the store, it sold general merchandise.

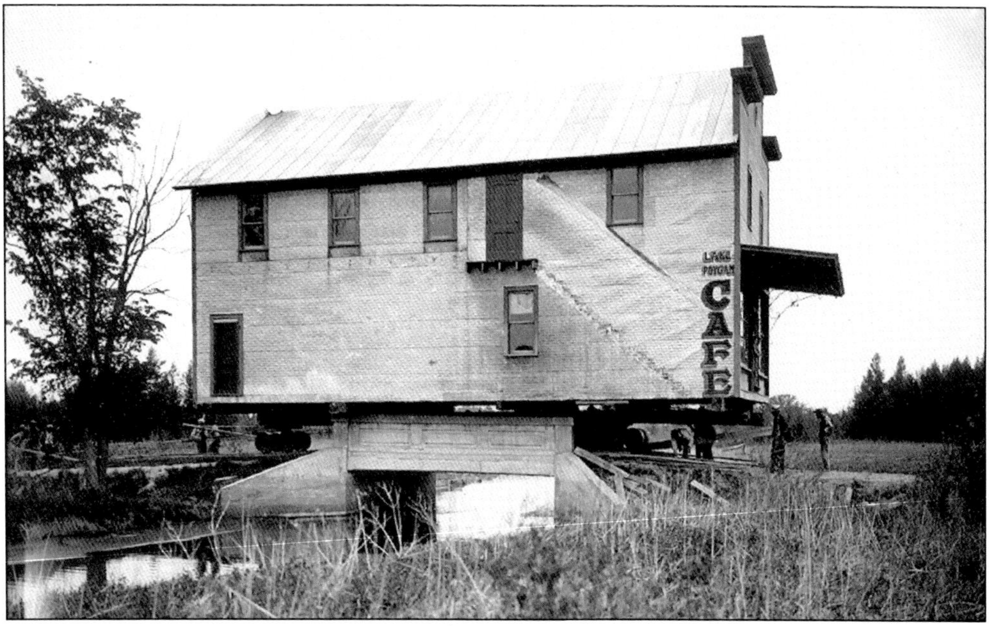


**Café on the Move.** As the café was moved to Poy Sippi, several small bridges were encountered. In this image, the men move planks to stay ahead of its progress.

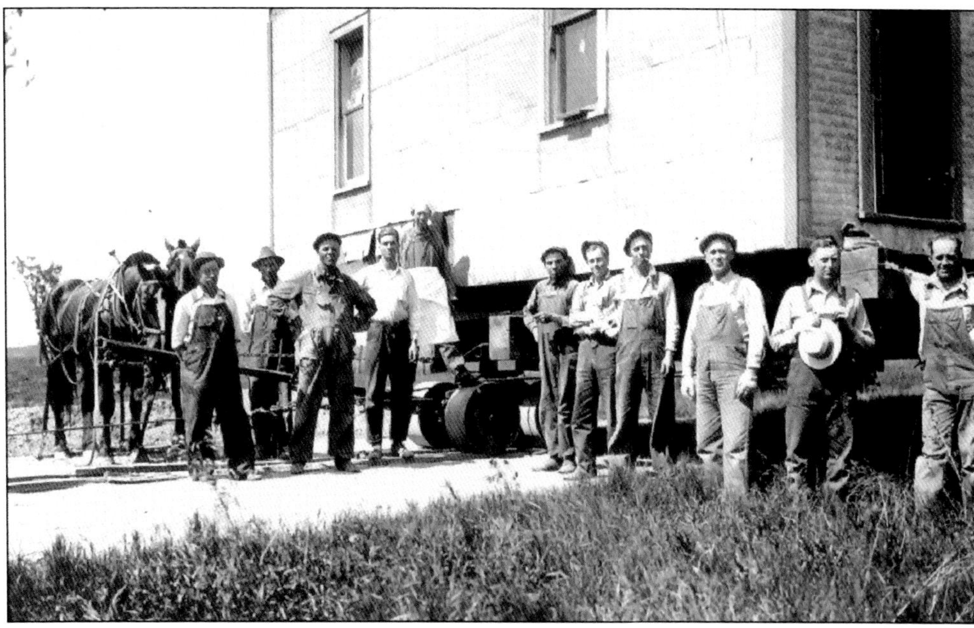

**Movers of Lake Poygan Café to Poy Sippi.** Grant Boyson inherited the store in Tustin from John Boyson, his father. After the general store in Poy Sippi burned down, Grant decided to move the store from Tustin to his burned-out lot in Poy Sippi. The men used dollies and teams of horses to complete the move. Planks were laid down for the dolly wheels to ride on a smooth surface. One of the men, Paul Swanke, supposedly never got off of his knees due to moving planks for five miles. Pictured here, from left to right, are unidentified, Harold Beck, unidentified, Ralph Jorgensen, the cook, Paul Swanke, Irvin "H. I." Davis, Royal Wais, Charlie Madison, Earl Cartwright, and Marvin Madison.

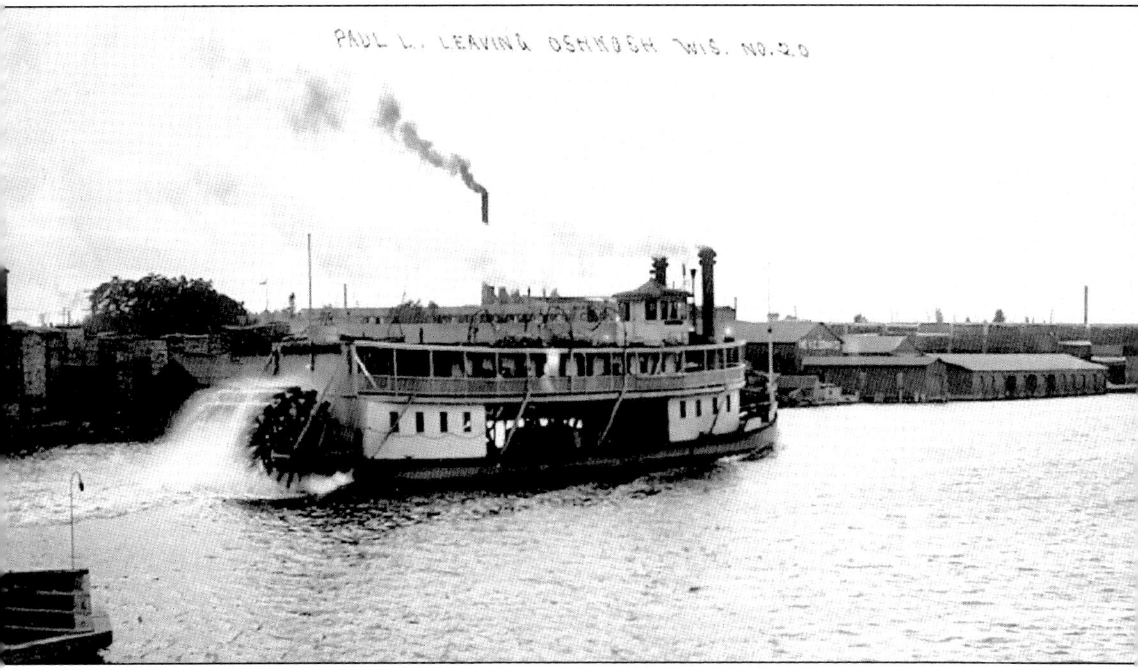


**PAUL L. LEAVING OSHKOSH.** The *Paul L.* was one of the most well-known steamboats running on the waterways of Lake Poygan and the Fox River to Oshkosh. Named after the owner and operator, Paul LeFevre, the steamboat carried supplies and passengers alike. Many Tustin and Poy Sippi people relied on the *Paul L.* and other such ships as a means of transportation instead of the surrey and horse.

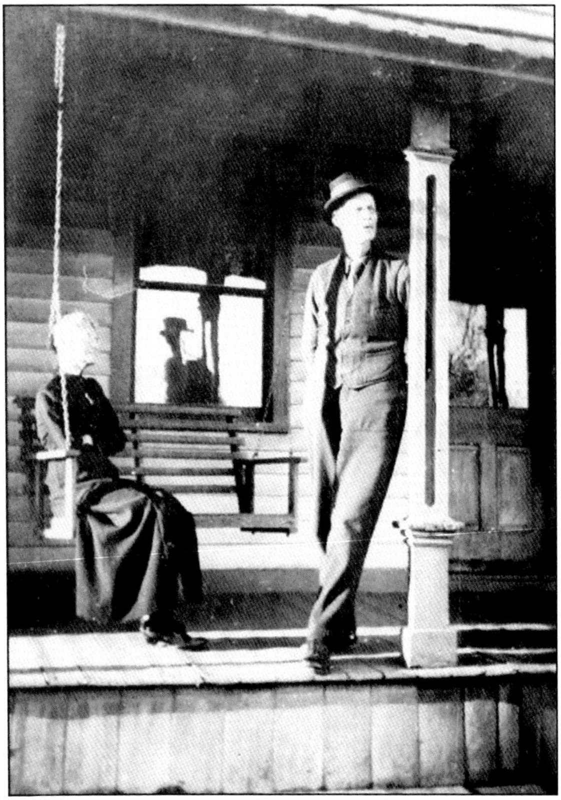

**LEFEVRE PARENTS.** This photograph shows the parents of Paul and Arden LeFevre. The LeFevres were noted as steamboat owners and operators on the waters between Oshkosh and Tustin. The steamboat was the easiest way to get to the bigger cities for shopping and travel. Paul worked on the *John Lynch* boat as a boy. The *John Lynch* burned "at sea," and the fire could be seen for miles. John Boyson was a part owner of that boat.

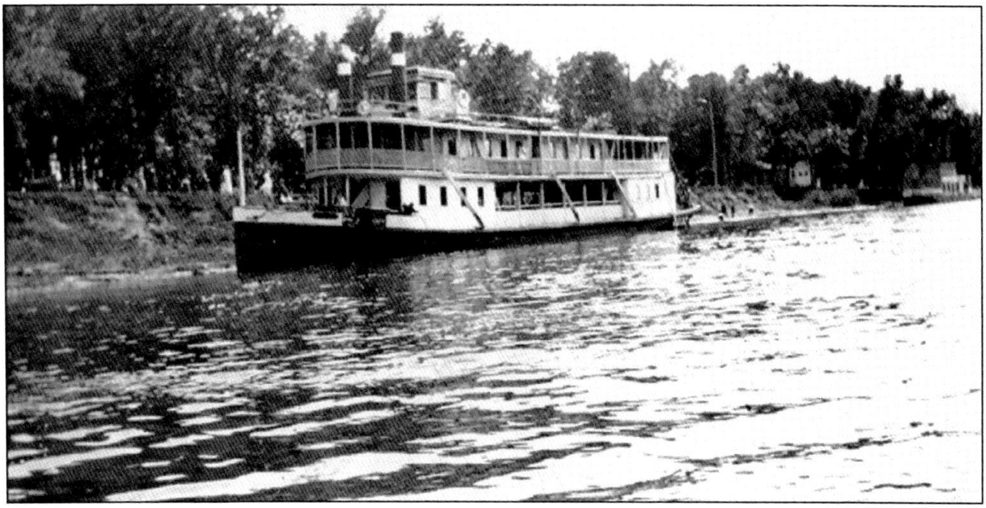

**PAUL L.** The *Paul L.* appears to be docked, as the wheel is not turning. Paul LeFevre put the boat into service in 1907 after running the vessel *LeFevre*, which had been sold and moved to Sandusky, Ohio. He was the captain on the *Paul L.* for 13 years until his partner, Charles R. Clark, died in 1920. LeFevre was then the tugboat captain for the Kimberly-Clark company, towing coal from Green Bay to Appleton, Wisconsin. In 1922, he commanded the *Valley Queen*, a Mississippi-style boat. The *Valley Queen* was the last of its kind to cruise the area lakes. LeFevre had also commanded boats on the Great Lakes.

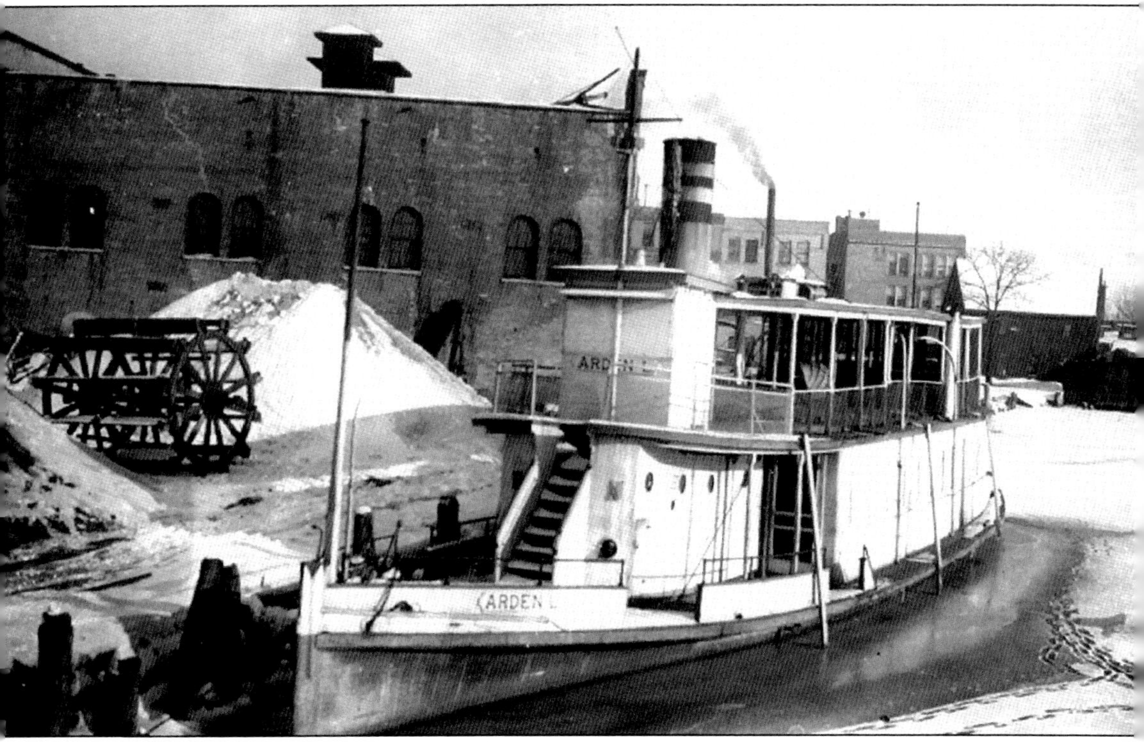


**ARDEN L.** The *Arden L.* was the sister ship to the *Paul L.* This boat, owned by Paul's brother Arden LeFevre, was a single-stack steamboat, while the *Paul L.* was a twin-stack stern-wheel boat. Not many photographs of the *Arden L.* have been published in other area historical books.

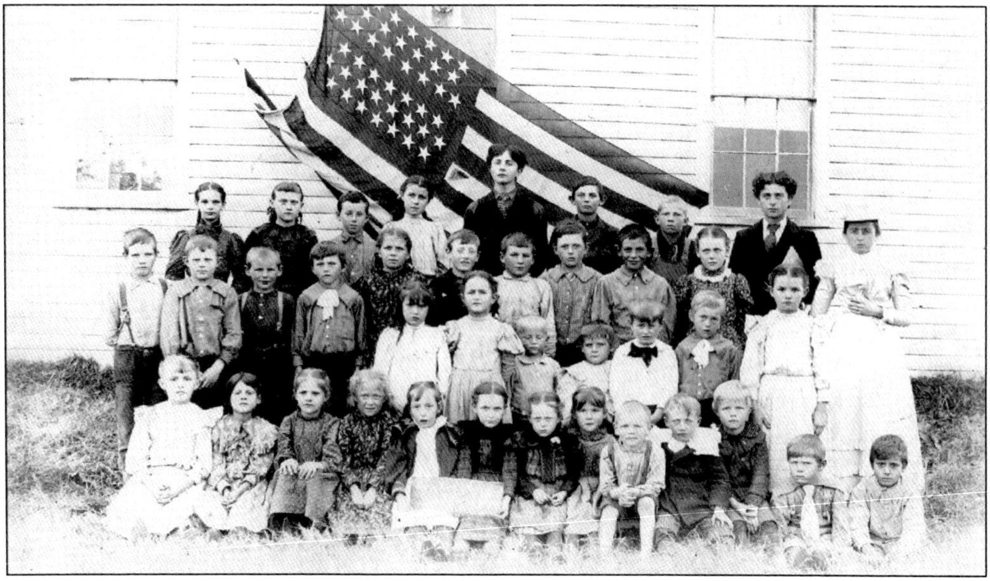

**TUSTIN SCHOOL, 1898.** Notice the flag in this photograph from 1898. Pictured here, from left to right, are the following: (first row) Lillian Boyson, Blanche Brewster, unidentified, Annie Pufahl, ? Irig, Nellie Lovejoys, Libbie Schindelholz, Hazel LaBorde, two unidentified students, Robert Boyson, unidentified, and Bernie LaBorde; (second row) unidentified, Lillie Burger, Frank Pufahl, three unidentified students, Anna Boyson, and the teacher's sister; (third row) unidentified, ? Stienberg, ? Yesse, unidentified, Clara Pufahl, Eddie Gabel, Herman Yesse, Oscar Schindelholz, Walter Velte, and Ella Schindelholz; (fourth row) Ida Mielke, Laura Moak, ? Luce, Alice LaBorde, Charles Velte, Eddie Velte, Frankie Pufahl, and the teacher.

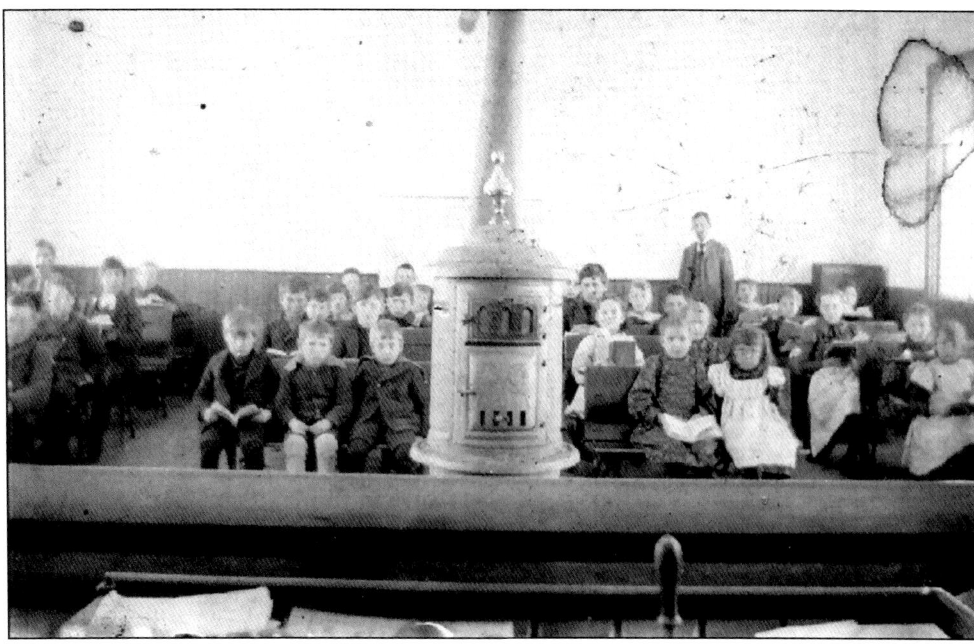

**TUSTIN SCHOOL INTERIOR.** This may be the only photograph of the inside of the Tustin School. It is undated but could be from the early 20th century. Note the old wood stove and the handle for the school ringer.

# *Eight*

# AURORAVILLE

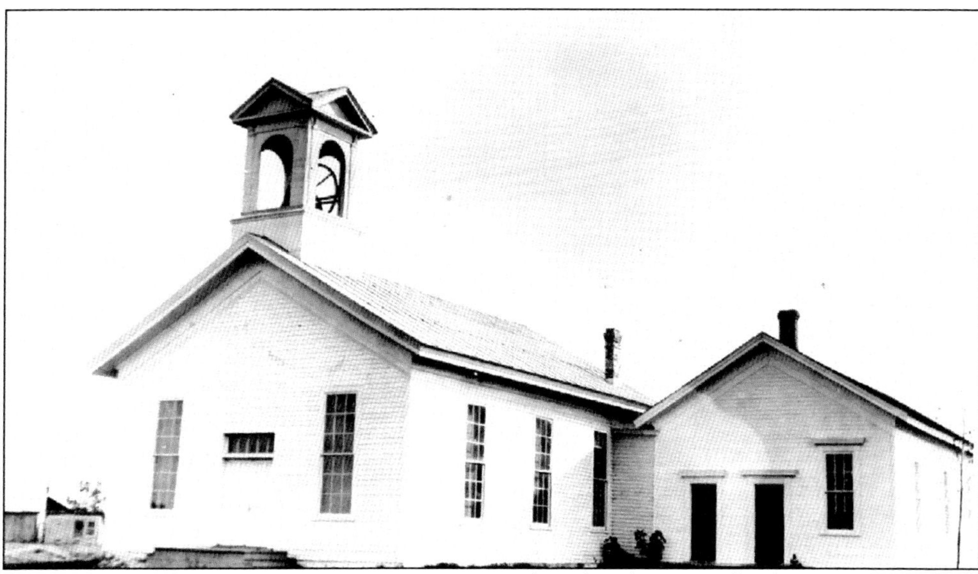

CONGREGATIONAL CHURCH OF AURORAVILLE. This church, originally the United Brethren Church built by a Mr. Merrill, was later taken over by the Congregational church. The small building to the right was used by the Good Templars. Many families were members of the Good Templars in an effort to bring about a better place to live. The church had also previously been used as the Grange Hall.

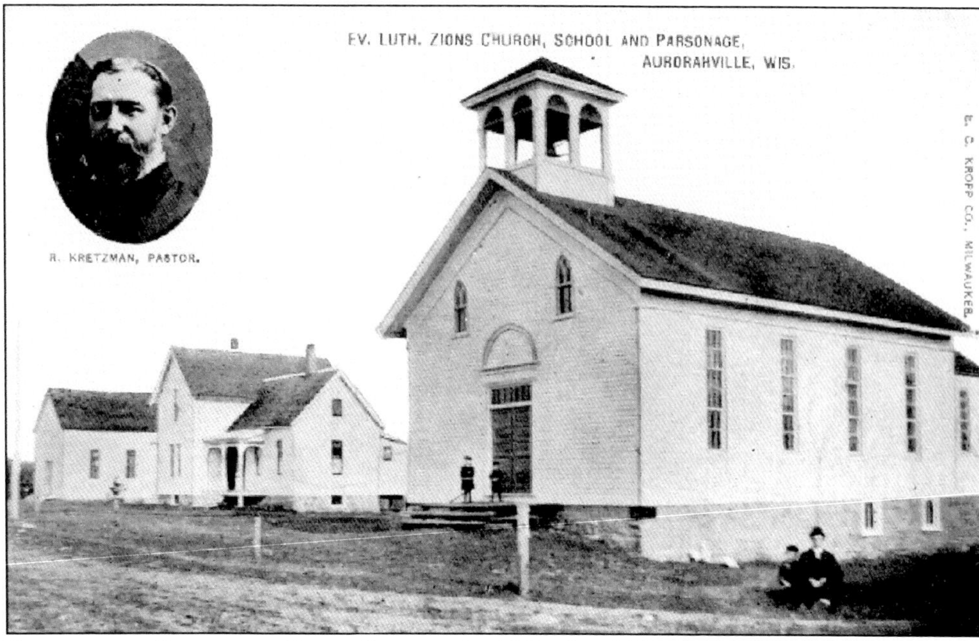


**EVANGELICAL LUTHERAN ZIONS CHURCH.** In 1908, the old Methodist building was moved to the hill on the north side of town, where it became the Evangelical Lutheran Zions Church. The church now serves the Immanuel Lutheran congregation.

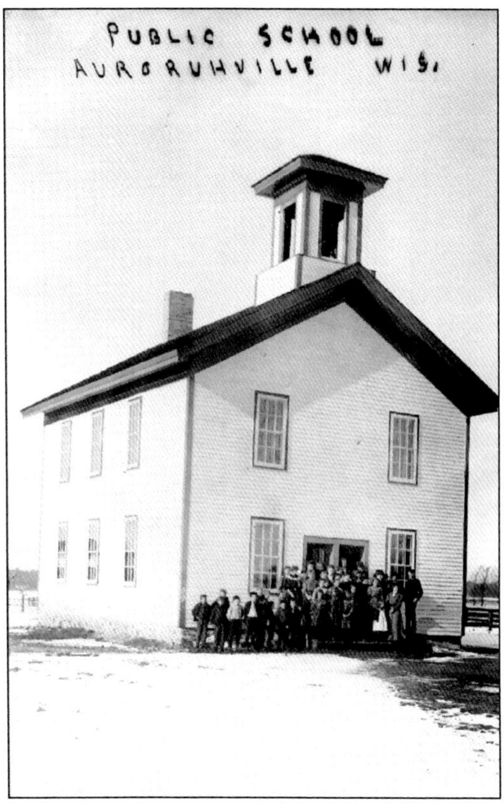


**AURORAVILLE PUBLIC SCHOOL.** Children pose for a school photograph.

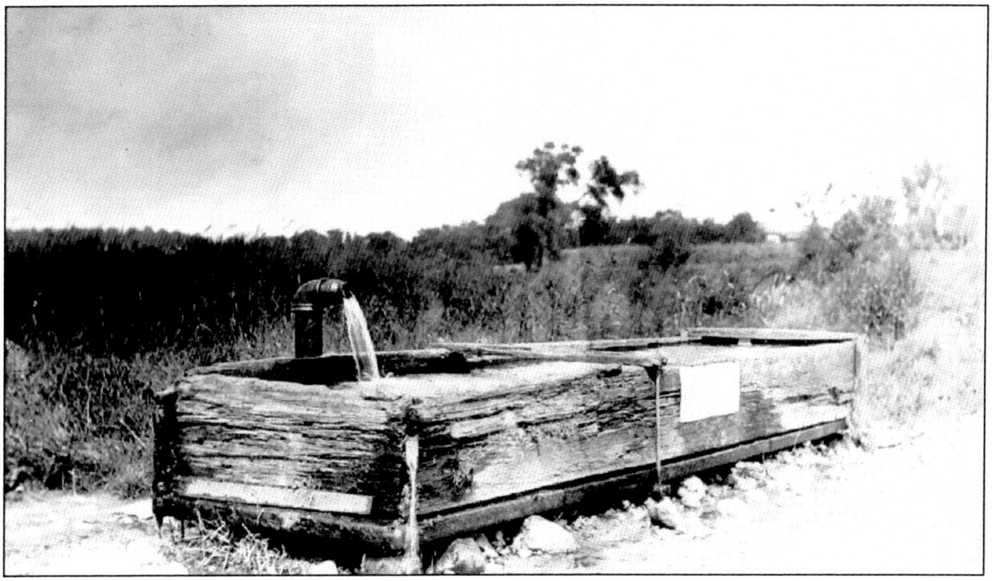

**OLD FOUNTAIN.** The Old Fountain, as it was called, was located in the center of town. Used by everyone since it was near the roadside, this artesian well was popular.

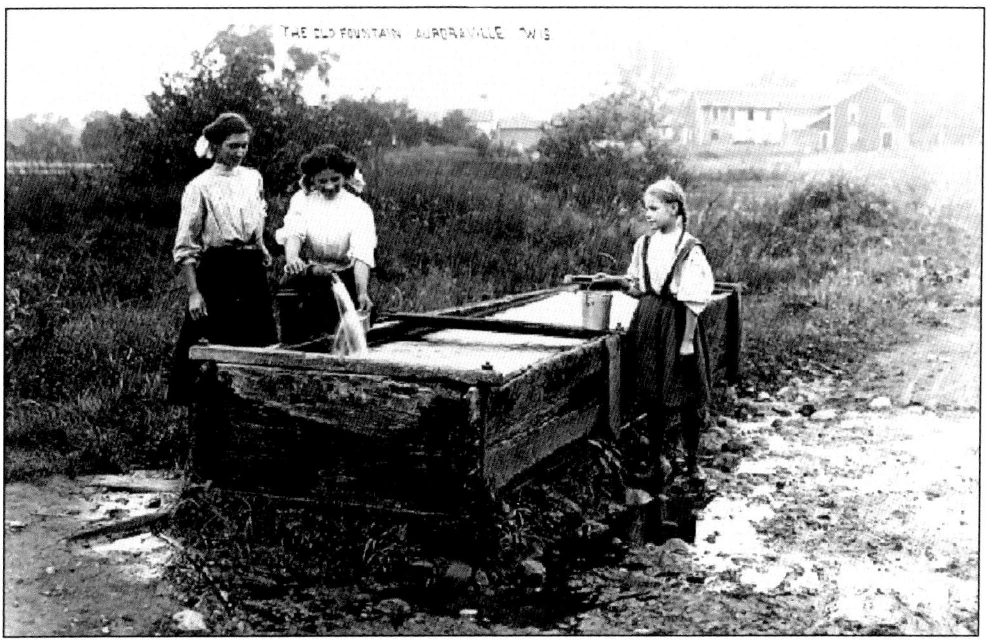


**FOUNTAIN IN AURORAVILLE.** The fountain next to the mill pond was an artesian well. Here, it is shown with a wooden structure to hold water. It was used as a watering hole for horses as well as a spot for people to get their drinking and cooking water. In 1927, the cheese factory had burned down and one of the vats was moved to this location to hold water. The fountain was redone with a granite stone surround in 1936 by the Work Projects Administration.

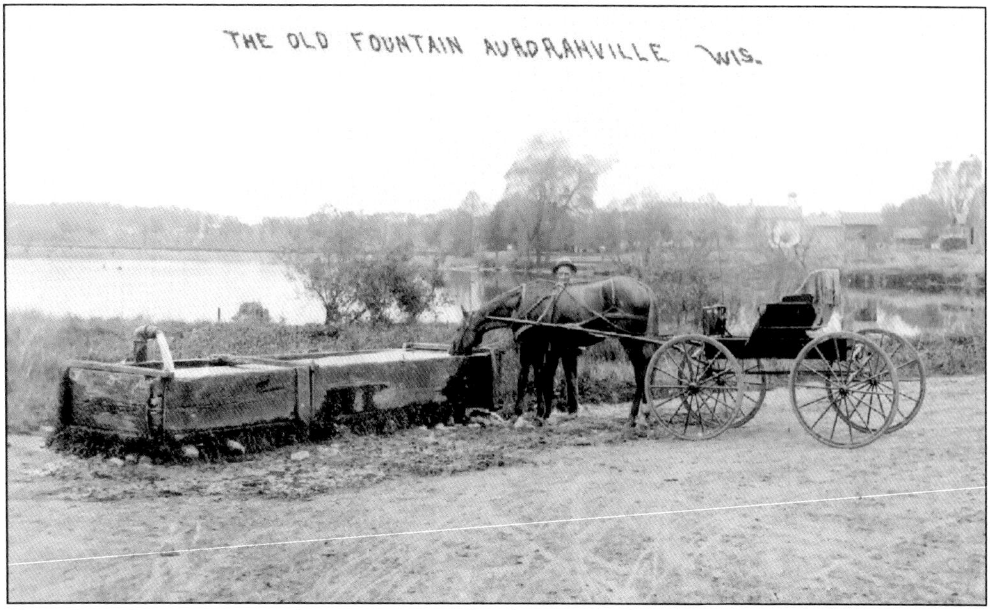


**THE OLD FOUNTAIN.** In this 1909 view, the fountain is being used as a watering hole for horses. This image shows the riggings of the surrey better than most. In the background, the cheese factory and the mill pond are visible. Note the amount of tracks in the dirt leading to the fountain.

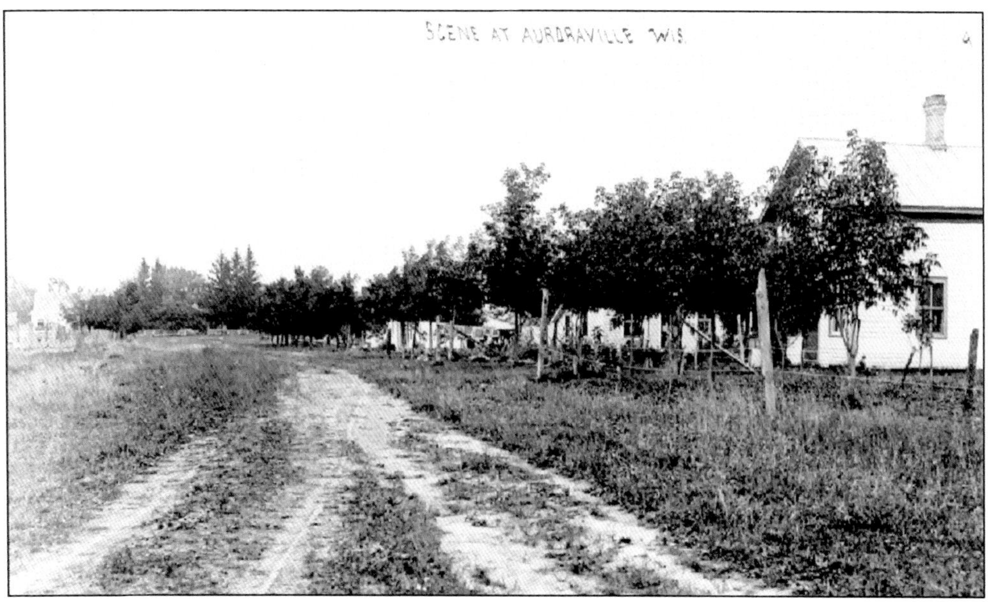


**BACK STREET OF AURORAVILLE.** This scene remains quite similar today. The back side of town has not seen much development in some time.

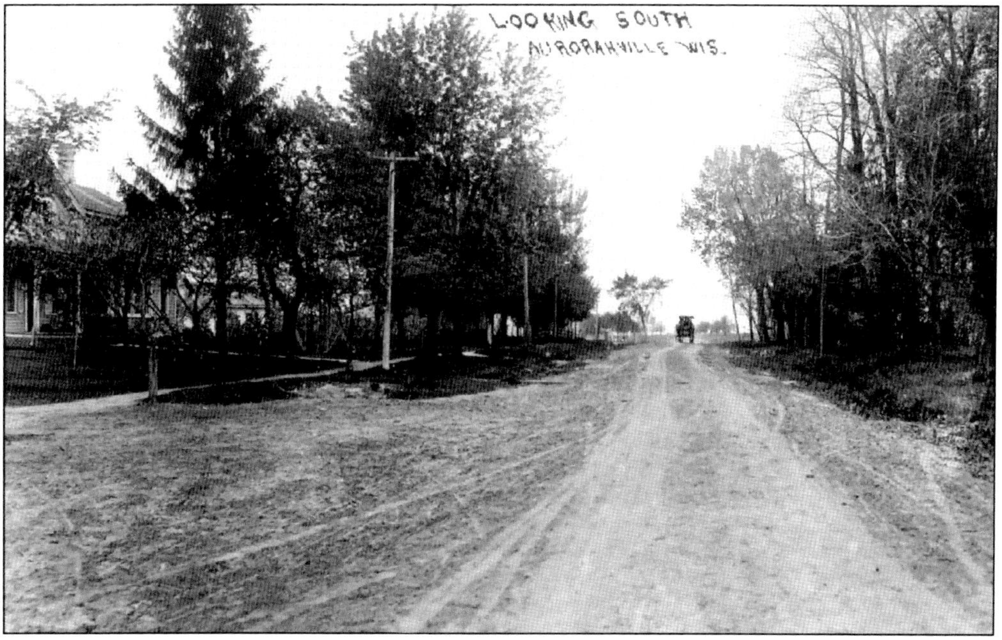


**LOOKING SOUTH OF AURORAVILLE.** A lone wagon travels toward the photographer along the wide road that leads to either Berlin or Redgranite.

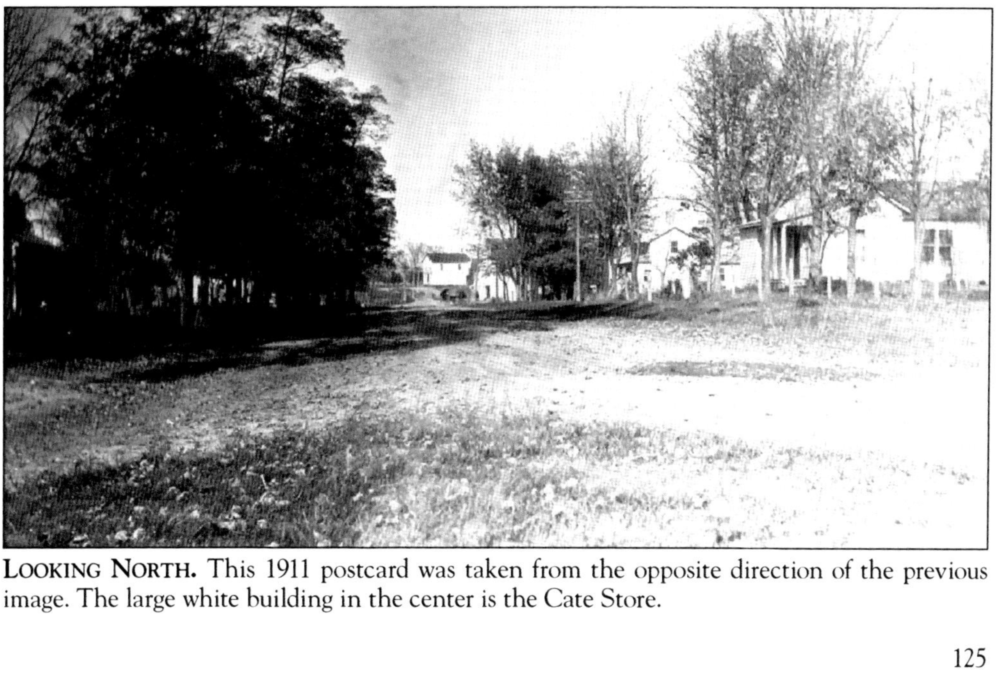

**LOOKING NORTH.** This 1911 postcard was taken from the opposite direction of the previous image. The large white building in the center is the Cate Store.

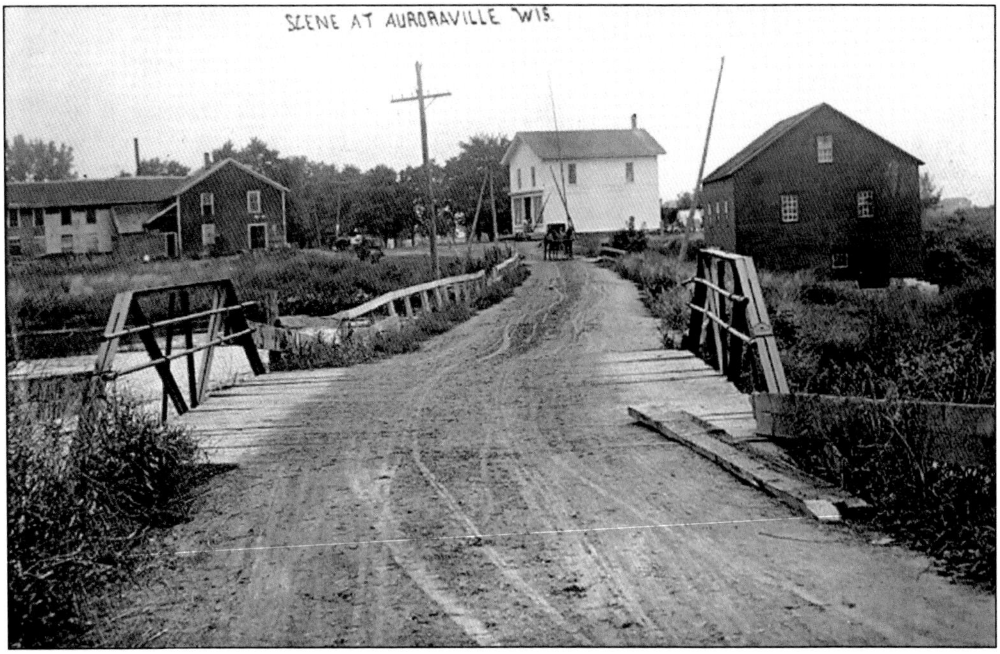


**SCENE AT AURORAVILLE.** The bridge over the Willow Creek is seen from the south. The span is nothing more than a plank bridge with a dirt covering. The buildings, from left to right, are the cheese factory, the Cate Store, and the mill.

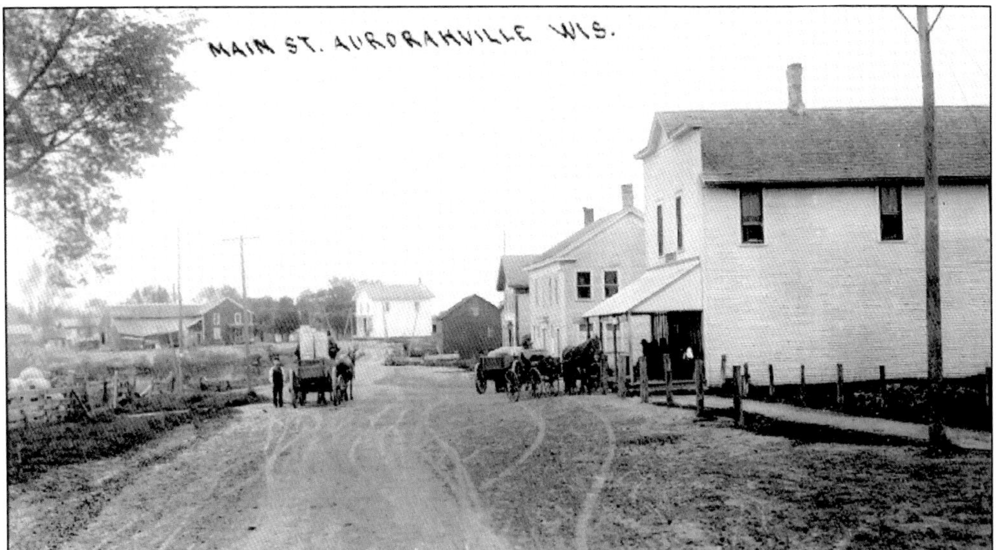


**MAIN STREET, AURORAVILLE.** This early-20th-century view of Auroraville, looks north. From left to right, the buildings are the cheese factory, the Cate Store, the mill, Strang's Store, Mathew's Hotel, and the Mikesell Store. The cheese factory burned down in 1927. The Cate Store was traded off for a farm after 10 years. The mill operated under many owners throughout the years. Strang's Store was started, in 1859, by Amaziah Strang and his son-in-law Harvey H. Wells as a dry goods and general merchandise store. It also held the post office for a short period of time. Mathew's Hotel was noted as being well kept. Also at one time housing the post office, the Mikesell Store was owned by Will Mikesell.

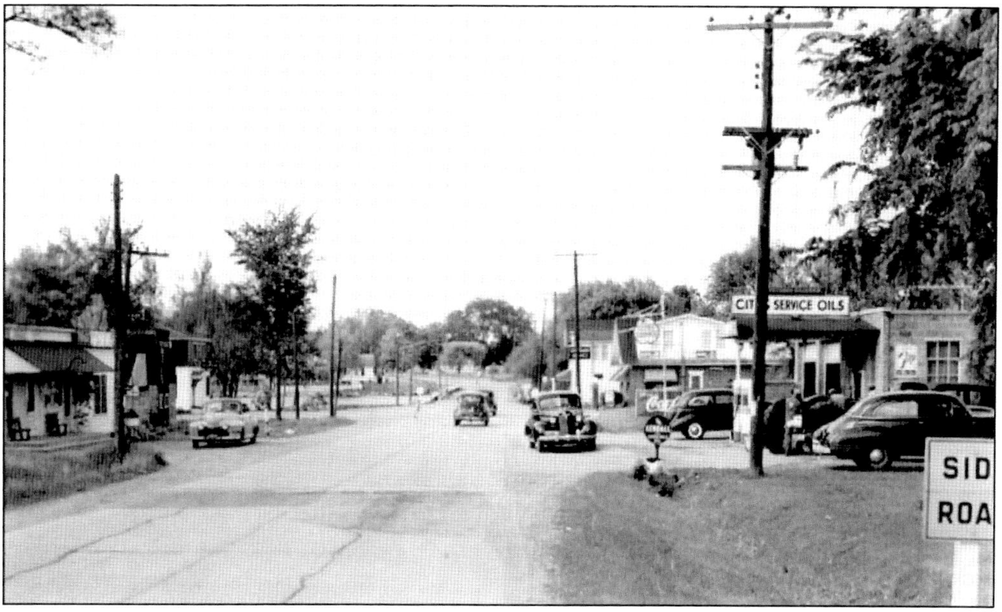


**MAIN STREET, 1950.** It is a busy time in the small town of Auroraville in this northward view.

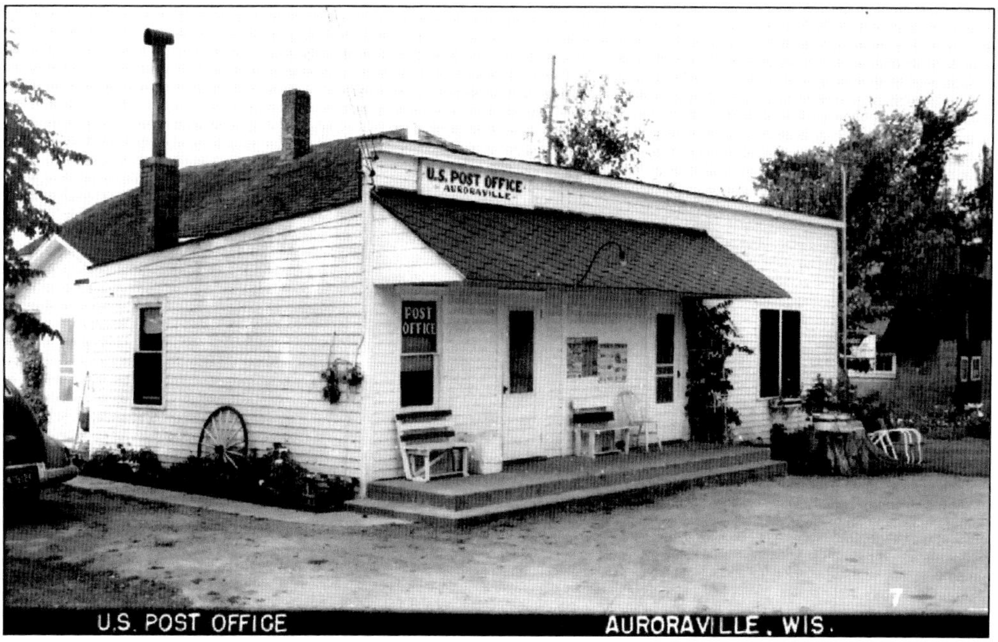


**AURORAVILLE POST OFFICE.** Before this *c.* 1950 image was taken, the post office had been housed in several other buildings. For some unknown reason, when the post office started in town, an "h" was placed in the name to read "Aurorahville." It was not until March 1, 1941, that the name was changed back to its original Auroraville.

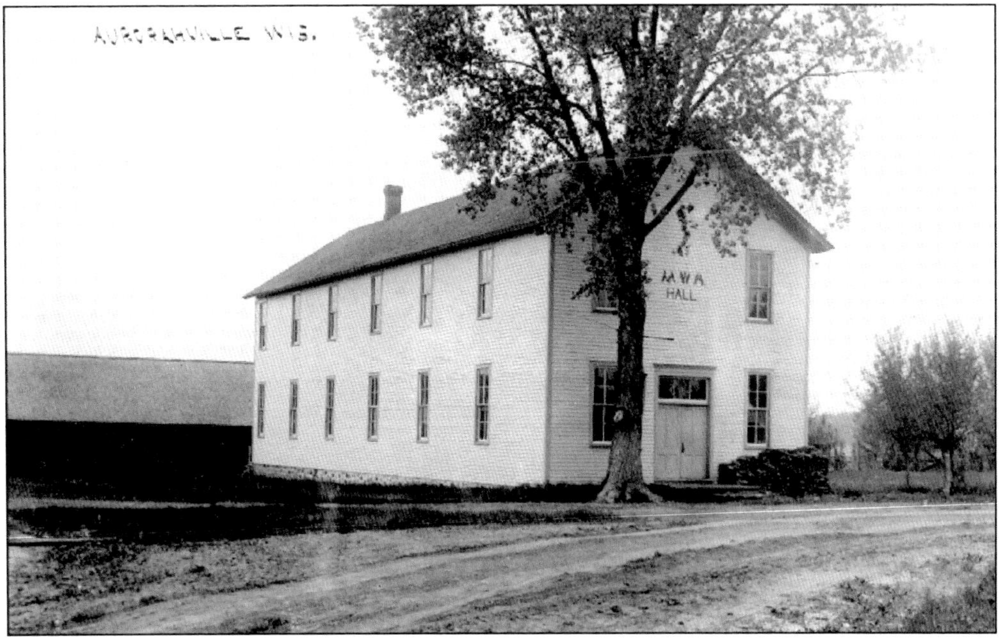


**WOODMAN HALL BUILDING.** The Woodman Hall building in Auroraville was used for social activities for the Methodist church and the Good Templars. The Grange later held meetings there. The building still stands and is used for storage.

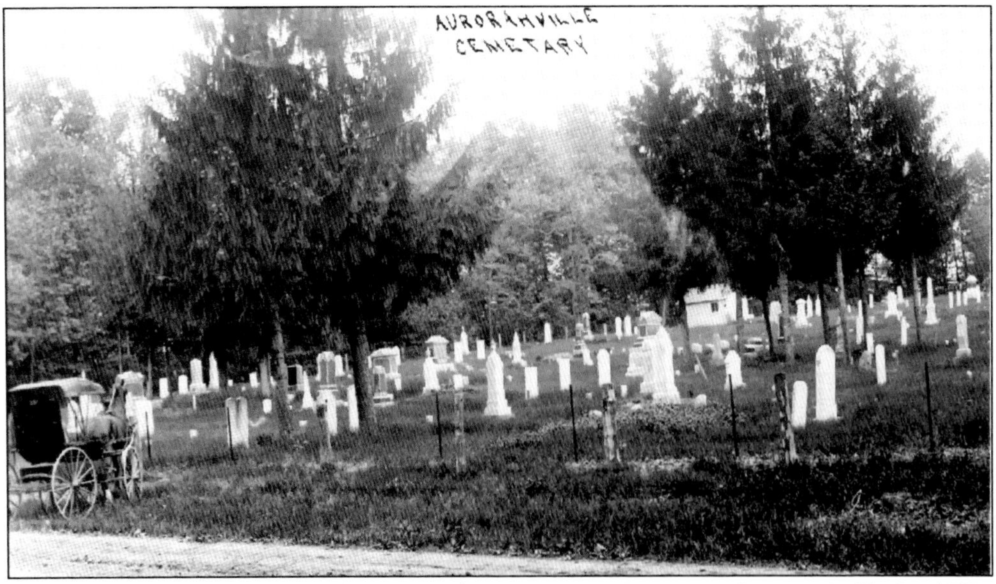

**AURORAVILLE CEMETERY.** Now known as the Pine Grove Cemetery, this spot holds Civil War veterans, many who were fundamental in settling the area. This *c.* 1920 postcard shows some of the early headstones. Recently, a new marker for Charles Spencer was installed. A dedication was held by the Sons of Union Veterans of the Civil War, Old Abe Camp No. 8. Spencer, who served in the 18th Wisconsin Infantry, Company H, was a noted carpenter and cabinetmaker.